2005

FROM EMPIRE TO COMMUNITY

OTHER BOOKS BY AMITAI ETZIONI

My Brother's Keeper:
A Memoir and a Message (2003)

The Monochrome Society (2001)

The Limits of Privacy (1999)

The New Golden Rule:
Community and Morality in a Democratic Society (1996)

The Spirit of Community:
The Reinvention of American Society (1993)

The Moral Dimension:
Toward a New Economics (1988)

Capital Corruption:
The New Attack on American Democracy (1984)

An Immodest Agenda:
Rebuilding America Before
the Twenty-first Century (1983)

Genetic Fix:
The Next Technological Revolution (1973)

The Active Society:
A Theory of Societal and Political Processes (1968)

FROM EMPIRE TO COMMUNITY

A New Approach to International Relations

Amitai Etzioni

FROM EMPIRE TO COMMUNITY
copyright © Amitai Etzioni, 2004

First published by PALGRAVE MACMILLAN™
175 Fifth Avenue, New York, N.Y. 10010 and
Houndmills, Basingstoke, Hampshire, England RG21 6XS.
Companies and representatives throughout the world.

PALGRAVE MACMILLAN is the global academic imprint of the Palgrave Macmillan division of St. Martin's Press, LLC and of Palgrave Macmillan Ltd. Macmillan® is a registered trademark in the United States, United Kingdom and other countries. Palgrave is a registered trademark in the European Union and other countries.

ISBN 1-4039-6535-8

Library of Congress Cataloging-in-Publication Data
Etzioni, Amitai.
   From empire to community : a new approach to international relations / Amitai Etzioni.
      p.   cm.
   Includes bibliographical references and index.
   ISBN 1-4039-6535-8 (hardcover)
   1. United States—Foreign relations.   2. United States—Military policy.
3. Security, International.   4. International cooperation.   5. Terrorism—Prevention.   I. Title.

JS1480.E89   2004
327.73—dc22
                                                        2003064013

Design by Letra Libre, Inc.

First edition: May 2004

10 9 8 7 6 5 4 3 2 1

Printed in the United States of America.

The most important change that people can make is to change their way of looking at the world. We can change studies, jobs, neighbourhoods, even counties and continents, and still remain much as we always were. But change our fundamental angle of vision and everything changes—our priorities, our values, our judgments, our pursuits. Again and again, in the history of religion, this total upheaval in the imagination has marked the beginning of a new life . . . a turning of the heart, a "metanoia," by which men see with new eyes and understand with new minds and turn their energies to new ways of living.

—Barbara Ward, 1971

CONTENTS

PREFACE

AFTER MANY DECADES DURING WHICH IT HAD BEEN AGREED THAT A world government was a pipe dream, envisioned only by dewy-eyed idealists, we are discovering that swelling transnational problems cannot be handled by nation-states nor by international organizations alone. These problems beseech us to create an additional layer of governance whose jurisdiction will equal the scope of the unmistakably global problems that challenge us.

The global government that is currently being formed is a far cry from the democratic regime that idealists have hoped for. It was born out of blood, the blood of the victims of terrorists, the terrorists themselves, and others who are often referred to merely as "collateral damage." It is called an empire, a form of government in which a few powerful countries foist their policies on numerous others. The new empire is led by the United States and its allies, but its reach extends to the four corners of the Earth and spans the seven seas. It has an armed presence in 170 out of some 200 nations, and most nations collaborate with its antiterrorism campaign for one reason or another. It is form of world government—although hardly the one most people have expected.

Where do we go from here? I argue in the following pages that nations historically cobbled together by the use of force (Germany, Italy, the United Kingdom, the United States) have nevertheless over time developed democratic regimes and a fair measure of community. The same might be achieved on the global level. What role will the United Nations, which itself must be made much more representative of the people of the world, play in the evolving new world order? Are regional bodies such as the European Union helping or hindering the rise of a true world government? What ought to be the role of supranational institutions such as the International Criminal Court (ICC) and the World Trade Organization (WTO)? How much of what must be done can be carried out by the global civil society? Can the global civil society provide for a new global order without any features of a world government?

I take as my working hypothesis that the development of a world government, however narrow its initial scope and mandate, is and will continue to be reminiscent of the rise of nation-states. In both cases, safety has been the primary goal. The first wing of the evolving new form of government is in effect a global police department limited largely, so far, to fighting terrorism. The second wing, rapidly expanding, is also concerned with safety: This wing is seeking to curb nuclear weapons. Nuclear weapons in the hands of rouge states that may use them, or from which terrorists may acquire them, are much more dangerous than terrorists limited to using box cutters, machine guns, and car bombs. (Ergo, the "Pakistan's" of the world are much more dangerous than the al Qaeda franchises.) Others wings, which are in much earlier stages of development, concern fighting pandemics (such as SARS) and providing humanitarian interventions to prevent genocide. Those that deal with issues not directly related to safety, such as the environment or the reallocation of wealth, are particularly lacking. I ask under what conditions they may be more richly endowed.

All of the matters so far listed occupy the second half of this book. I deliberately devote the first half to issues less often explored by those who approach international relations largely as matters of military assets and economic prowess while slighting normative issues. In doing so, I attempt to answer the following questions: Which moral norms should guide foreign policies and international relations in the near future? Can the world community be centered around Western values such as liberty and human rights—or does the East, even more varied than the West, also have much to offer? And, how might these various values be synthesized to make a limited but compelling set of norms around which we can all come together, rather than ushering in a "clash of civilizations"? Can we address the spiritual hunger that inflicts many parts of the world (including the affluent ones) and prevent billions of people from turning to various self-destructive forms of religious and secular fundamentalism?

Many specific points and a fair number of policy suggestions are included in the pages of this book. Ultimately, though, they all address one question: What will make for a safer, healthier, freer, and a more caring world, one in which all people will have a rich basic minimum so that they can live with dignity? Can we progress without some sort of global government? And—if one is needed—how might it be best formed?

INTRODUCTION

THE OLD TESTAMENT TELLS OF SAMSON, WHO CAME UPON A YOUNG lion and tore it apart with his bare hands. When he saw the carcass a few days later, bees had settled in and were busy producing honey. Samson observed "From might came sweet."[1] This book is an account of how the American semi-empire can be converted into a legitimate new global architecture, one that the world badly requires. The recent American global projection of power can serve a role in building a new world order; in somewhat similar ways, the exercise of force was used in many nation-building endeavors. The application of might was often followed by institutional and social changes—including democratization and community building—that rendered the new regime increasingly legitimate as well as expanded the missions to which it did attend.

To put it more bluntly: Whether one is highly critical of the American global projection of power or celebrates that the United States has accepted that it is destined to bring order and liberty to the world, for now, it is a fact of life that affects the lives of people everywhere. Call the American empire lite, virtual, neo, or even liberal; it is omnipresent.[2] True, by the end of 2003, the empire—evidence to follow will show—was already starting to metamorphose into a different formation. The questions hence are: Where do we go from here? And how can we make our world sweeter?

This book moves on two levels: One concerns short-term developments, asking what lessons emanate from the different ways in which the United States confronted the terrorist threats after September 11, 2001 and Saddam Hussein's Iraq in 2003. The lessons are not just for American policy makers, but for allies, critics, and adversaries alike. In the immediate future—despite the debacle in Iraq—we still must learn how to cope with weapons of mass destruction (WMD) in the hands of failing states and of terrorists. The second level deals with longer-run developments that call for responses to a much longer list of transnational problems, from international Mafias to environmental degradation, from cybercrime to traffic in sex slaves, developments that the nations of the world are unable to address on their own.

The book lays out a pathway between the might-makes-right course, a Jacksonian version of neo-conservative international relations, and the consensus-makes-might hyper-liberal course, which presumes that a new order can and should be based on international laws and institutions and multilateral commitments. Resentment of the American course is reaching unprecedented levels, as are the costs of sustaining the U.S.-imposed regime. It is rejected by the overwhelming majority of both those directly affected and members of other nations. The American public itself is both bitterly divided about the course followed and unlikely to be willing to shoulder the costs of such a resented global presence in the longer run.[3] This time, the rice paddies are spread worldwide. At the same time, the hyper-liberal approach—which favors negotiations, economic aid, debt forgiveness, and free medications as means to "drain the swamp of terrorism" and prefers building international institutions to imposing regime change—is profoundly inadequate. This approach fails to recognize that, in a brutal world, application of force is sometimes justified, and not only in humanitarian interventions. It does not address the question of whether large-scale terrorism and the proliferation of nuclear weapons demand a whole new approach to the ways that world affairs are managed, one that focuses on public safety. Instead, many liberals seek to rely on the Wilsonian fantasy of democratizing the world to make it peaceful, a very attractive idea but also a dangerously deluding and distracting idea, which, we shall see, cannot be relied on to uphold even a minimal level of global law and order in the foreseeable future. Providing security, though, is the most basic need to which the evolving global order must attend, as it was and is for the nation-state.

Neither the might-makes-right nor the consensus-makes-might approach speaks effectively to the question of how we are to deal with the rising tide of numerous other transnational problems. Any new global design must be able to withstand the test not only of whether it enhances safety, but also of whether it is able to address these additional needs. Clearly, a third way is called for.

It is tempting to suggest that we should take some from column A (hard power) and some from column B (soft power) and thus obtain a well-balanced meal of legitimate power. The focus of the discussion here is more on how we can get from A to B, or, how we can build a world order that relies less on force and more on other means.

KEY QUESTIONS FOR THE THIRD WAY

To map a third way in the international realm, I ask the following questions.

- Which normative principles, what values, are to guide the paving of the new road? Merely Western values—democracy, individual rights, and free markets? Are there no values that the rest of the world, often simply referred to as the East, can bring to the table? And if the answer to the last question is a resounding affirmative, then how are the two sets of principles being combined? And what implications do they have for international relations and specific foreign policies?
- Values often precede the development of institutions, and building those institutions is very taxing. Is it, then, truly necessary to form a new global architecture? Is it true that what I call the Old System (nation-states and intergovernmental organizations) is ever less able to cope with swelling transnational problems than it had been? If the answer to this question is in the affirmative, then what transnational and supranational institutions are called for to add layers of governance to the Old System?

   I take it for granted that not all global problems can be addressed at the same time, given the limitations of resources, knowledge, and will. (Not much of an assumption.) Hence, we must address the question of prioritization. Is it best to promote human rights before democratic polities are developed? Economic development before either? Or do recent changes in the global condition demand a still different approach?

- What can we learn from the American global projection of power since 2001, especially in Iraq, as compared to the ongoing war against terrorism?
- Going deeper into the future, to what extent can the rising transnational problems be managed by nongovernmental agents, the rising global civil society, transnational social networks, voluntary associations, and social movements? How much global governance without some form of global government is possible?
- Assuming that the combination of the Old System and nongovernmental institutions cannot suffice, to what extent can we draw on new institutions that are being developed, especially those referred to as supranational?
- Can the various new institutions serve mainly as freestanding agencies, as does the International Criminal Court, or do they ultimately require incorporation into one global architecture? Does regionalism like that of the European Union stand in the way of forming a new global system, or can it serve as a stepping-stone? And ultimately, can there be an effective Global Authority without a global community?

A COMMUNITARIAN PERSPECTIVE

Who is the "we" I am writing for? Born in Europe, raised in Asia, an American citizen, a senior adviser to the Carter White House,[4] I am trying to give voice in this volume to a global perspective, one that is concerned with what might serve people of different parts of the globe rather than how one can lord over another. To the extent that the deliberations here are guided by any overarching public philosophy, it is an international form of communitarianism opposed to both conservative and liberal ways of thinking.

Although the vantage point of this book is not American but communitarian,[5] much of the discussion focuses on the United States because it is currently the only superpower. However, the book outlines the ways that changes in the U.S. course can help it better serve the general interest without denying its own. What I mean by communitarian international relations and foreign policy is a subject that requires all of the pages of this book (and more), but to foreshadow some points:

- A communitarian evaluates both current policies and those measures suggested to replace them by two standards: Are they legitimate and effective in their own right? Do they enhance or undermine community building? Multilateralists and champions of abiding by international laws (even if one seeks recasting or expanding them in the process) often stress the need for institution building. Here a much thicker notion of construction, we shall see, is employed.
- A communitarian policy strives to be not merely legitimate (in line with prevailing values), but it also ensures a convergence of interests for the various actors involved. It assumes that legitimacy is good, but not good enough; a course that also speaks to the interests of all involved (even if not always in the same measure) is preferable. It assumes that unless the constituents of the American semi-empire buy into the evolving new global architecture because it addresses their interests, and not just those of the metropolitan country, the new structure will not be sustainable. Much attention has been paid in the past to the decline and fall of various empires, especially those of Rome and Great Britain. I focus instead on why they lasted as long as they did.
- A communitarian approach to international relations concerns itself with the question of whether a group of *nations* can share a robust common purpose and interest, which inevitably entails making considerable sacrifices for others, such as the way the West Germans did for the East

Germans during the 1990s, without forming a community. American history suggests that a community is essential—the United States, with weak communal bonds on the national level until the 1870s, faced a horrible civil war. A similar question now confronts the European Union. Hence, a communitarian must ask whether, in the longer run, effective global governance is possible without a global community. This leads to the most challenging question of all: How, if at all, might this global community come about?

Catching Up: Establishing Human Primacy

Beyond speaking to the immediate challenges that concern elementary safety needs—massive terrorism, WMD in loose hands—this book examines new approaches to a whole slew of numerous and daunting transnational problems with which the world grapples. It holds that these troubles reflect one profound challenge that people everywhere face: to use yesterday's language, to "get a man on the top," or to gain *human primacy*, a term I shall use throughout this volume to refer to making means serve ends rather than allowing means to pervert our purpose. Often, this issue has been framed in terms of the alienation of modern existence. What is new, I shall show, is that *alienation is turning from being chiefly a domestic malaise into a transnational one*, and it is on this level that alienation will have to be treated.

The defining characteristic of the modern age is the enormous expansion of human capacity, the vast increase in the power of instruments. We can send payloads to the moon; blow whole nations away without setting foot in their territories; infect millions with horrible diseases; build billions of dishwashers, cell phones, and other useful and inane things now considered part of civilization; and be much more efficient, rational, and calculating than people ever were in the use of resources. However, as the prowess of our technological and economic means has multiplied many times over, and has increased by several orders of magnitude time and again, our ability to guide these tools to our purpose has lagged ever further behind. Nuclear energy was supposed to provide low-cost, safe energy—not an unprecedented threat to human survival. Armies—the depository of the means of violence—were to serve their governments, not to topple them or dominate them from behind the scenes. Bioengineering was supposed to help us improve our crops and livestock and eradicate disease and famine, not to open the door to eugenics or designer bugs. Markets were meant to allocate resources efficiently and ensure their rational use, not to undermine humanitarian concerns and social values. Corporations—the main depository of the means of production—were to manufacture goods and services, not to control significant segments of domestic and international politics. Civil servants were supposed to implement public policies, not to deflect them. In sum, all too often the logic of instruments has taken precedence over the rationale of ends.

The hallmark of the modern age, the insurrection of the instruments, has been well captured in powerful images from many cultures and traditions, all of which highlight the same point. For Europeans, it is conveyed by the story of the sorcerer's apprentice; for Americans, by movies about Frankenstein; for Jews, the Golem. All these allegories share one theme: We fashion a helper endlessly more powerful than ourselves, planning to employ him for good purposes. But once the helper learns to stand on his own feet, he follows his stars, often in destructive ways, threatening to trash us in the process. We cannot destroy him (any more than we can eliminate nuclear weapons) nor may we wish to do so (as we are hoping to marshal his powers to our goals). We are left flailing, trying to rein in the might we unleashed to serve us, but so far to no avail.

The result has been widespread alienation, the deep sense that the world around us is governed by forces we neither understand nor control. Hence, we are often disenchanted with politics, the forum through which our collective purposes are supposed to be articulated and advanced by our elected representatives, who are to guide (directly or indirectly) that which needs to be governed. The same sense of ennui marks our economic lives, a Sisyphean quest for ever-higher income and the goods it buys, which we ultimately find are not truly satisfying.[6] Hence the widespread, often unspoken, anxiety or anger of millions who seek various kinds of therapists or cults, or live by one Prozac or another, and the restless quest of the young for mind-altering drugs or "causes." No wonder social scientists find that the majority of people, in scores of countries, are unhappy with the direction in which their nation is headed.[7] And the international system, still riddled with wars, increasingly saddled with problems once considered local or national, is even less responsive to our values than nations are.

To determine what must be done for us to take charge, to ensure that the instruments we forge will serve our goals, to establish what I call human primacy, we had best ask what specifically prevents us from guiding to our purpose these phenomenal new powers, the increased reach of the technological instruments, and the gargantuan economic assets modernity has built. Two factors stand out and serve as the focus of this examination: One concerns the values we share, which define the purposes that our means are to serve. The other concerns our political institutions, which are supposed to ensure that we are in charge.

To turn to normative issues first, our moral growth has been lagging behind that of our tools. A few examples suffice to illustrate the issue. Human cloning is a new scientific enterprise, something new we can do. However, so far, from a moral perspective, we have been unable to come to terms with the question of whether we should embrace, limit, or ban such cloning; whether it serves, averts, or undermines our purpose, indeed our very humanity. Similarly, the Internet carries harmful messages—racist, violent, pornographic, and damaging to children—but so far we have not formed a shared moral sense about whether free speech in cyberspace should trump all other normative considerations. (The answer to this question may seem obvious to many progressive American intellectuals, but it is not for most people and for elected representatives of other nations.) As economies are becoming more competitive and efficient, the question arises—but stands unanswered: What social and personal values ought to remain immune to market considerations?

Not only are we unable to formulate shared understandings of what ought to be done, but whatever shared formulations of the good we once had have come apart at the seams. Modernity was built on a rebellion against the rigid traditional values that religious regimes imposed on people in earlier ages. The twentieth century was deeply marred by secular totalitarian governments that forced their sets of absolute beliefs on their own and other people. Also, in the same age, empires established in earlier centuries, and the values they fostered, were laid to rest by national liberation movements. Many other traditional values, from those that extolled the traditional family to those that commanded respect for authority, from those that celebrated the superiority of white people to those that held men in higher regard than women, were left in the dustbins of history.

In the process, most, if not all, strong, shared formulations of the good became suspect; people were to render their own moral judgments. Moreover, judgment became equated with judgmentalism. Moral codes were often replaced with abject relativism and unbounded multi-culturalism. All of this resulted in a widespread moral vacuum, including in the societies that considered themselves the most advanced, modern, and free. Religious fundamentalism—of the Christian, Hindu, Islamic, and Jewish varieties—is rising in part as an attempt to avoid being sucked into this vacuum and in part as a particularly unwholesome, indeed dangerous, attempt to fill it. The question of the age is not how we can avoid shared formulations of the good, as many liberals advocated in response to the totalitarian horrors of the twentieth century, but whether we can find moral values that can be widely shared without legitimating coercion and oppression.

As the twenty-first century dawned, there were few widely shared strong agreements about any of the issues raised by modernity and its tools. Should the powers-that-be make other countries give up their WMDs, or should they rely on a balance of terror? Which sources of energy should we draw on, and which ones should be curbed, if not banned? Should we free the markets more or further control them? And on and on. In the days when ships were powered by sails, Montesquieu noted that no wind will do for a ship that has no designated port. Without shared values, no one can guide to good purpose the instruments and the institutions which they greatly empower, especially the state and the corporation. Call it the moral lag.

Over the last decades the moral lag has become much more severe, because now often even a nationwide shared formulation of the good no longer suffices. If one nation, even a superpower such as the United States, concluded that human cloning ought to be banned, cloning still would be carried out elsewhere, unless there were a much more widely shared moral understanding. Thus the American people, and those of many other nations, would be forced to absorb the negative effects of such cloning, whether or not they approve of such uses. Similarly, Canada, Britain, and Germany may ban hate speech, but if some other nations tolerate it because they value free speech highly, citizens of all countries can access all the hate speech they want, and then some, on the transnational Internet. The people of one nation or another may conclude that preventing global warming is a matter of much value, but their willingness to introduce various measures limiting the use of instruments—especially cars—would be to no avail if other nations did not share this understanding. Alienation has been globalized and it is on this level where it will have to be treated.

We shall see that full global consensus, which might well be impossible to reach, is not required; but these matters are surely no longer merely the province of domestic deliberations. This growing moral lag on the global level is the focus of Part I.

The focus of Parts II and III is the political lag, the lack of growth in the institutions we use to govern, which is the second reason instruments are undermining human primacy. Thus, even if people—whether members of a local community, nation, or a still-more encompassing union—share a moral understanding, there has been a woefully insufficient increase in the capacity of institutions to implement new directives based on these understandings.

Parliaments, it is common knowledge, have weakened as the powers of the executive branch of government have increased, from matters concerning budget to personnel, from laws and regulations to jail cells. Moreover, the executive branch has been characterized as bureaucratic for good reason; it often reflects the rebellion of the instruments, wherein civil servants pursue their own purposes rather than those set by the people through their elected officials. Worse, in many parts of the world corruption (including illegal campaign donations) allows various special interests to deflect political institutions to serve their needs.[8] Although in democratic governments these institutions are failing to cope with most of the problems, other nations are in a much worse condition. There, governments serve a small elite, the whim (and Swiss bank accounts) of an autocrat, or are paralyzed by sharply conflicted parties. All this is within nation-states whose independence was so cherished during the twentieth century and before, precisely because it was assumed that giving people their own state and ensuring their self-determination would provide them with a government that would lead in ways they sought. Far from it.

On the international level, the political lag is much more severe. This situation mattered less when nations were more able to cope with problems on the domestic front. However, over the last few decades, and increasingly in the future, problems, and the power to deal with them, have been usurped from the nation-state (especially from those nations with less power) and now are found in the never-never land of transnationality. True, protection of life and limb, the prevention of war, has long been in part an international matter. Increasingly, however, other challenges, already listed, must be confronted by international institutions, which are particularly weak, even compared to their often impotent national counterparts.

If the moral and political lag could be greatly narrowed, if not overcome, we would be able to establish human primacy, end alienation, and even direct the Golem rather than be pushed around by it. Hence, this volume focuses on the ways to greatly narrow these lags. In the following pages, I examine first the moral lag and then the political one, on the transnational level. I am concerned with both the normative and the sociological issues that are behind foreign policy and international relations, as these are typically understood, as well as their implications for these policies and relations.

Developing the institutions and communal bonds required for establishing human primacy is a monumental task, to put it mildly. But there is a modicum of good news. To the extent that we can develop transnational shared moral understandings and introduce some new, albeit limited, Global Authorities—for instance, those needed to manage the Internet, such as a more effective Internet Corporation for Assigned Names and Numbers (ICANN), a restructured International Criminal Court, and a more responsive and inclusive World

Trade Organization—we benefit from an important fact: There will be no longer any place to hide, no extraterritorial spaces. Recently, even nations that are still reasonably competent are often prevented from effectively dealing with the issue at hand. For instance, the Philippines had no laws against creating computer viruses; indeed, many considered the creator of the "Love Bug" virus, which infected computers all over the world, a national hero. In the same vein, half a dozen nations provide shelter and aid to terrorists who threaten other nations. Cleaning rivers downstream in the United States is of limited value if those upstream in Mexico continue to dump waste into them. And so on. In contrast, to the extent that worldwide agreements can be fashioned and implemented, whether they concern WMD, pandemics, environmental degradation, trade in ivory, the hunting of whales, landmines, or traffic in sex slaves, one problem that bedevils nations will no longer have to be faced: Those who flout such agreements will have no safe havens in which to hide and from which to strike. Then, human primacy—the government of goals over means—will indeed have a prayer.

PART I

The Emerging Global Normative Synthesis

CHAPTER ONE

BASIC CONTOURS

THE EVIDENCE NEXT PRESENTED SUGGESTS THAT OUT OF discordant, often strident, conflicting voices that emanate from the East and the West a new composition is slowly arising. The blended tune has a limited register, on many issues divergent voices will continue to be heard, and it is sure to be accorded divergent interpretations in various parts of the world and over time. Yet the new tune suffices to provide stronger support for global institution-building than was available in recent decades. The metaphorical "voices" I refer to are expressions of basic normative positions, worldviews, and ideologies. They concern values that define what is considered legitimate,[1] a major foundation of social order, and good government.

My position articulated here greatly diverges from two major themes that underlie much recent foreign policy thinking in the West; both claim to predict the direction in which the world is moving, as well as to prescribe the ways it ought to progress.

One theme holds that the world is proceeding (and needs to be encouraged) to embrace several core values, as well as the institutions that embody them, all of which the West possesses: individual rights, democratic government, and free markets. This position has been advanced by Francis Fukuyama, Michael Mandelbaum, and Fareed Zakaria, among others.[2] It has been embraced by the Bush administration, whose 2002 strategic document states:

> The great struggles of the twentieth century between liberty and totalitarianism ended with a decisive victory for the forces of freedom—and a single

sustainable model for national success: freedom, democracy, and free enterprise. . . . People everywhere want to be able to speak freely; choose who will govern them; worship as they please; educate their children—male and female; own property; and enjoy the benefits of their labor. These values of freedom are right and true for every person, in every society. . . . [3]

Tony Blair, who based his New Labour party on the themes of community and responsibility, departed from these communitarian values when he addressed the global society. He stated: "Ours are not Western values, they are universal values of the human spirit. And anywhere, anytime ordinary people are given the chance to choose, the choice is the same: freedom, not tyranny; democracy, not dictatorship; the rule of law, not the rule of the secret police."[4]

The other theme holds that the world outside the West is largely governed by religious fundamentalism or other alien sets of values, which are incompatible with Western ones, and, hence, these antithetical civilizations are bound to clash. Samuel P. Huntington and Bernard Lewis are proponents of this view.[5] To provide but one quote from Huntington:

At a superficial level much of Western culture has indeed permeated the rest of the world. At a more basic level, however, Western concepts differ fundamentally from those prevalent in other civilizations. Western ideas of individualism, liberalism, constitutionalism, human rights, equality, liberty, the rule of law, democracy, free markets, the separation of church and state, often have little resonance in Islamic, Confucian, Japanese, Hindu, Buddhist or Orthodox cultures.[6]

Both viewpoints imply that non-Western nations have little to contribute to the global development of political and economic institutions or to the values that they embody.[7] Rights, liberty, and capitalism are, after all, Western contributions to the world. (In Thomas L. Friedman's succinct journalistic lingo, the West has the slick, modern Lexus; the East, old and dusty olive trees.[8])

I beg to differ. First, as we shall see, there are significant lessons concerning both the development of domestic polities and economies, as well as international relations and the design of new global architectures, that the world can and should learn from non-Western cultures. This is especially true in matters concerning respect for authority, obligations to the common good, and the nurturing of communal bonds, although only if these values and the relevant institutions are greatly moderated.

Moreover, I will present evidence to suggest that the world actually is moving toward a new synthesis between the West's great respect for individual rights and choices and the East's respect for social obligations (in a variety of ways, of course); between the West's preoccupation with autonomy and the East's preoccupation with social order; between Western legal and political egalitarianism and Eastern authoritarianism; between the West's rejection of grand ideologies, of utopianism, and the East's extensive normative characterization of "dos" and "don'ts"; between Western secularism and moral relativism and visions of the afterlife and transcendental sets of meanings, found in several Eastern belief systems including Hinduism, Confucianism, and select African traditions. The synthesizing process entails modifying the elements that go into it; it is not a mechanical combination of Eastern and Western elements, but rather it is akin to a chemical fusion. For reasons that will become evident, the emerging synthesis might be referred to as "soft communitarianism."

One can, of course, compare various belief systems on many other scales and come out with different results and groupings. To give but one example: If we grouped belief systems according to their level of parsimony or belief in monotheism, several Eastern religions would line up with the Western ones against some other Eastern ones. However, it is not my purpose to provide rich typologies or add more intercultural comparisons. I merely argue that, for several key issues at hand, the grouping of cultures into East and West suffices as a first approximation. I shall show that, on some points, there are two camps. This generalization will be followed by highlighting the differences within each camp.

A WESTERN EXCLUSIVE?

Francis Fukuyama advanced the thesis that the whole world is in the process of embracing liberal democratic regimes and capitalism, a process he famously called the "end of history." He recognizes that many nations are still "in history," but since the collapse of the communist bloc, he sees a trend toward an increasing and worldwide dominance of individualism. (Because the values and institutions involved are all centered around the respect for individual dignity and liberty of the person—protected from the state—to make his or her own political and economic choices, I refer to these concepts jointly and as a form of shorthand as individualism.)*

---

*The reader may wonder why I am taking on Fukuyama's half-truth and largely ignoring Huntington's clash-of-civilizations idea, given that many think the events of September 11, 2001 have validated the latter's approach. In a sense my whole book, which could be titled *The Dialogue of Civilizations*, is a response to Huntington's viewpoint.

Fukuyama's thesis (and those of others who developed related lines of argument, such as Mandelbaum and Zakaria) is that the whole world is in the process of embracing Western values. These scholars tend to see these individualistic values as "universal" ones that non-Western societies were slow to recognize but now are discovering as compelling.[9] ("The liberty we prize is not America's gift to the world; it is God's gift to humanity" is the way President George W. Bush voiced this idea.[10]) We also should note that reference is to a global trend of intranational developments, not to the development of some global society and government. Thus, China and India are said to be gradually liberalizing and opening their markets; the United Nations, the World Health Organization, and international nongovernmental agencies are not held to undergo such changes.

As I see it, the argument that individualism is gaining a growing worldwide following is valid, yet only half right. It is valid because, despite some setbacks (such as in Latin America), there is considerable and accumulating evidence that numerous nations gradually are inching—some even rushing—in this direction. It is only half true because the East, despite the fact that it is even more heterogeneous than the West, does bring several key values of its own to the global dialogue, and it lays moral claims on the West with even greater assurance of their universal validity than the West does with its claims on the rest of the world.

Before I proceed, I should reiterate that to speak about two normative approaches as if that were all there is, as many do, is of course merely a first approximation. Huntington lists nine civilizations; others have still longer lists. Recently much has been made about differences between European and American belief systems. A whole library of books just on the differences among various Eastern beliefs could be found. Nevertheless, there are significant commonalities among the various Western beliefs and among all the others. The fact that the West shares a commitment to rights, democracy, and capitalism—despite differences as to how raw various countries are willing to stomach capitalism—is common knowledge. These beliefs are cardinal to the West's view of itself and of others. They are central to its public philosophy and what it seeks to bring to others.

Similarly, although less clearly, non-Western belief systems, often referred to as the East, share some important commonalities. These commonalities may not encompass every single culture, but they do include most, including those of which many millions of people are a part. (Because, like many others, I use the term "East" to mean all that is not "West," I must find a place for Latin

America. For the purposes of this analysis, it is where geographers put it, part of the Western Hemisphere.)

The normative positions championed by the East might be called "authoritarian communitarianism." While the Western position is centered around the individual, the focus of the Eastern cultures tend to be a strongly ordered community. In its strongest form, the East's core tenets are not individual rights, but social obligations, toward a very extensive set of shared common goods and toward various members of the community; not liberty, but submission to a higher purpose and authority, whether religious or secular; not maximization of consumer goods, but service to one or more gods or to common goods articulated by a secular state.

These social order values are at the heart of Islam, at the core of several Asian philosophies and religions, and play a central role in traditional Judaism. The preceding observation is so widely held and has been so often documented that I merely provide a few quotations to evoke the flavor of these belief systems. For instance Lee Kuan Yew, former prime minister of Singapore, states:

> [A]s a total system, I find parts of it [the United States] totally unacceptable: guns, drugs, violent crime, vagrancy, unbecoming behavior in public—in sum the breakdown of civil society. The expansion of the right of the individual to behave or misbehave as he pleases has come at the expense of orderly society. In the East the main object is to have a well-ordered society so that everybody can have maximum enjoyment of his freedoms. This freedom can only exist in an ordered state and not in a natural state of contention and anarchy.[11]

Similarly, Hau Pei-tsun, former prime minister of Taiwan, notes:

> It is very important, I believe, for one to pursue success and to realize one's ideals, but it is even more important that individual successes are accumulated to make it the success of the nation as a whole, and the realization of individual ideals will result in the attainment of goals of the entire society. . . . Individuals in the society are like cells in a body. If the body is to be healthy, each cell must grow likewise. The aim of education is to make every citizen a healthy cell in the body of our society. . . . Everyone should know precisely one's place in the society, establish one's proper relationship with the society, then set up one's personal goals and begin working for them.[12]

Being part of a community is central to Islamic teachings: "Every Muslim is expected to feel and to accept responsibility for those who are near to him, and even for others who are outside his immediate circle."[13] (Much more about Islam follows.) In the Jewish tradition, initially founded in Asia, which has maintained some of its original communitarian elements, Rabbi Herbert Bronstein writes that the "interrelated cluster of terms (Torah, mitzvah, b'rit) implies a spiritual mindset that assumes an authority which transcends the individual ego and personal choice, fostering a sense of obligation to an 'Other' beyond the individual self. Torah, mitzvah, and b'rit, therefore, imply not only a strong sense of obligation to God, but since God's covenant is with the community of Israel, a communal consciousness as well, a sense of we: which transcends the individual self."[14] Thus, according to Jewish tradition, the poor are not entitled to welfare, and have no right to charity, but members of the community have a responsibility to attend to the poor.

These quotes provide the flavor of the main tenets found in Eastern belief systems.[15] Furthermore, from almost all these viewpoints, it follows that the West is anarchic, materialistic, hedonistic, and lascivious;[16] its citizens are self-centered and woefully bereft of community and authority.[17] When these criticisms are leveled at the West, its representatives and spokespersons often react as defensively as do those in the East when their lack of respect for rights and liberty is challenged. The West has a point, to the extent that it responds that Western society is not without a sense of responsibility, community, common good, and authority. But, as sociologists such as Ferdinand Tönnies, Emile Durkheim, Robert Park, Robert Nisbet, Robert Bellah and his associates, Alan Ehrenhalt, and I have pointed out—backed up by more data presented recently by Robert Putnam and Fukuyama—the trend in the West has been to delegitimate authority, to weaken communal bonds, and to diminish a sense of obligation to the common good in favor of individualism of both the expressive (psychological) and instrumental (economic) kind. *That is, what the East has in great excess, the West is lacking, and not merely the other way around.*

Because the United States has been leading the individualism parade (followed by other nations of Anglo-Saxon ancestry—the United Kingdom, Canada, and Australia—and trailed by the rest of the West), its history is particularly relevant to the point at hand. Some historians have depicted the United States as a society centered around Lockean values, those of rights, liberty, and individualism.[18] Actually, it is now widely agreed that the United States had from its inception both a strong communitarian and an individualistic strand, a synthesis of republican virtues and liberal values.[19] However, because communal institutions and authority, as well as a sense of obligation to the society, were strong and well-entrenched (indeed, as the American society evolved, the nation was added as an imagined community to the local and regional ones) during the first 190 years of the republic the main focus of attention was on expanding the realm of individual rights, democratic governance, and market forces. This attention was reflected in developments such as allowing people without property to run for office; extending voting rights (and, much later, a measure of social and economic rights), to women, minorities, and younger adults; expanding de jure and de facto rights of disabled persons, immigrants, and people of divergent sexual orientations; providing for the direct election of U.S. senators; curbing corruption in government; and deregulating markets. However, as has been often observed, over the last decades—roughly since the 1960s—the United States and increasingly Europe have developed what might be called a community deficit (or a social capital shortfall). The same holds for authority, as shown by a high level of distrust of leaders—from school teachers to elected officials, from generals to clergy.

Although the Western community deficit is a relatively new phenomenon, the absence of robust cultural and institutional foundations for individual rights, democratic government, and free markets for individualism has been evident throughout much of the history of the East, despite numerous variations over time and in different societies. Just as American historians correctly hold that the United States was not bereft of community and authority, so students of the East argue that it was not bereft of attention to individual dignity. For instance, Amartya Sen argues that scholars have been theorizing about freedom for many centuries in many different parts of Asia.[20] Very few, however, deny that as a rule these individualistic elements were weak, and often very weak.

In its relatively benign form, what might be called the liberty deficit is still found in Japan. At least until recently, the deficit took the form of very strong informal social controls, which are also very encompassing in terms of the scope of individual behaviors covered. ("The nail that sticks out gets hammered down," a widely held Japanese saying, captures the excessive communal pressures under discussion.) The Japanese often do not feel free to follow individual preferences, desires, or agendas because their lives are invested in heeding the prescriptions of their communities concerning responsibilities toward their parents, superiors, and the nation, among others. Those who violate these very elaborate, albeit informal, communal codes and traditional authoritarian normative claims are chastised and ostracized, the fear of which most times suffices to keep them in line.

A more common and less benign form of the authoritarian community, which is often found in the East, takes place when the community is invested in a state and its normative claims and strongly enforces the state rather than relying mainly on social bonds and elders. This is particularly evident in

Muslim-dominated countries, including Afghanistan under the Taliban and Iran under the Ayatollahs, and somewhat less extremely in other nations that heed the *sharia*, such as Saudi Arabia. Its secular version is found in nation-states that impose orders of their own, such as Singapore, Saddam's Iraq, and Asad's Syria, among others. Just as Western nations vary in the extent to which they suffer from a community deficit, Eastern ones differ in the extent to which they are burdened by lack of liberty. For instance, the liberty deficit is less severe in Tunisia, Morocco, and Qatar than in Burma and Malaysia. Still, it is obviously pervasive in the East.

In short, both West and East contribute to a new normative synthesis that moves their respective societies, their polities, and, as we shall see, their economies toward a better design than either individualism or authoritarian communitarianism provides. By bringing their "surpluses" to the table, elements will grow softer as they are blended with those of the other camp. To use the term "better" immediately raises the question: What is considered good? Before I can further advance the thesis that the East has major contributions to make to the evolving global normative synthesis and assess the validity of those values that the West is promulgating, I must first explicate what a good society is considered to be. The result provides a basis for communitarian international relations, a guide for the foreign policies of nations from all parts of the world. The vision of a good society ultimately has a role to play in narrowing the moral gap, a major step on the way to the establishment of human primacy. Progress on this front is best made with values that are shared rather than with those that clash or with one side claiming to have a monopoly on what is good.

THE GOOD SOCIETY

Before I can sort out what specific contributions the East and the West can make toward a core of shared values to be embodied in a new global architecture, and the ways that their respective contributions will have to be adapted, I need to lay out my criteria for what makes a society good. A liberal may suggest that the very introduction of the concept of a "good society" biases the discussion. Indeed, according to several key contemporary liberals, the formulation of what is good should be left to each individual, and decisions as to what is right versus wrong should be left to the private realm. In contrast, the very notion of shared formulations of the good is at the heart of the communitarian position. However, such an argument tends to overlook the difference between society and state. True, any extensive enforcement of shared formulations of the good by the state is incompatible with a strongly liberal society.[21] Liberals tend to oppose government imposition of the good because of its coercive nature. However, social fostering of the good—through informal controls—is not coercive. No force is exercised to impose the shared norms.[22] They are fostered by people encouraging one another to do what ought to be done and chiding those who do not.

Indeed, if we take into account that not all people will, out of self-interest, refrain from antisocial behavior all of the time, we realize that there are only two ways to undergird prosocial conduct: coercion or informal social controls. As we know from communities as different as Israeli kibbutzim and American suburbs, when these informal normative controls are intact, state interventions can be minimized. (True, in earlier periods and still in some parts of the world, communities became oppressive; but in modern societies, where there is a high rate of mobility and freedom of association, in which people choose which communities to join and are often members of two or more—such as at work and place of residence—communities' normative controls tend to be quite mild.) Jonathan Rauch, a libertarian who wrote in support of community controls, refers to this position as soft communitarianism. He explains: "A soft communitarian is a person who maintains a deep respect for what I call 'hidden law'—the norms, conventions, implicit bargains, and folk wisdom that organize social expectations, regulate everyday behavior, and manage interpersonal conflicts."[23] He goes on to point out that the shaming often involved is not attractive, but is vastly superior to what he correctly calls real-world alternatives: either social anarchy and anomie or government impositions.

With these considerations in mind, I draw here on a communitarian conception of the good society. As I have spelled out its features elsewhere (in a book entitled *The New Golden Rule*), I here mention only three essential characteristics of the good society. First, it is a society based on a carefully crafted balance between autonomy and social order. (I use the term "autonomy" to encompass individual rights, a democratic form of government, and free markets. By "social order" I mean both order based on government enforcement and informal, social, normative controls, so-called hard and soft power.) That is, it is a society that both vigilantly safeguards basic rights and liberty and one that nurtures a set of shared commitments to the common good, such as homeland security and the protection of the environment. (It does so even if this entails placing some obligations on the members of the society, ones that they might not wish to honor if left to their own devices. Hence the inherent tension between autonomy and social order.)

Second, good societies continuously reexamine the balances they have reached between autonomy and order. To maintain the balance, they tend to correct tilts that have developed in one direction or the other, adjusting as the historical context changes (as the United States did following the September 11, 2001 terrorist attack).

Finally, the more the social order is based on moral suasion and informal social controls ("normative controls") and the less on the state, and the more limited the scope of behaviors under the state's control, the closer the society is to a good one. In the United States, for instance, the ban on smoking in numerous public spaces, which relies almost completely on moral suasion and informal social controls, is vastly superior to bans that rely heavily on state imposition, as Prohibition did. Indeed, in a good society a great deal of social business is carried out because people have internalized certain duties—from taking care of their children to minding the environment, from giving to charity to helping the elderly and the sick—that they consider to be moral obligations. That is, the social order of a good, communitarian society is largely a soft one, both in the sense that it is respectful of its members' rights and preferences and in that it relies largely on moral and social ways to ensure that members will live up to their obligations to one another and to the common good rather than relying on state policing.

Specific societies, in particular historical periods, tend to upset this balance in one direction or another. Hence, in their quest to better themselves, to move toward the same basic societal design, they may well have to move in the mirror-opposite direction. Thus, from the viewpoint of the good-society design, the United States in the 1980s and onward needed to restore the bonds of community and trust in authority, while in the same period China had to make much more room for autonomy, both from those in power and from one another.[24] With this concept of a good society as a sort of a benchmark or evaluation criterion—applied to an evolving global society—we can proceed to assess the ways in which both the West and the East approach the global give-and-take on the values that should guide both future and existing international institutions.

Two hypotheses are implied in the preceding lines that I should state explicitly. I expect that some kind of a global model of a good society will continue to evolve gradually, one that many nations will favor although they will vary significantly in their detailed interpretation of its nature and even more in the extent to which they will progress to heed its tenets. I also suggest that for a global society to be good, it must—like a good national society—combine respect for individual rights with a commitment to the common good (e.g., the global environment), concern for the gradual development of political democracy (say, via a much-restructured United Nations) and for law and order (e.g., greater use of peacekeeping forces).

LIBERTY: VACUUM OR SOFT ORDER?

Western triumphalism tends to confuse autonomy with the absence of rules and norms—in plain English, with a moral vacuum. The record shows that when rigid, fiercely enforced Eastern codes collapse, they need to be replaced with some other basis for social order. The incontrovertible fact is that those societies that have given up on their strongly "Eastern" sets of beliefs and regimes and have moved sharply in the individualistic direction, but have formed few if any new shared sets of beliefs, experience sharp increases in anti-social behavior. Thus, in many former communist countries and in countries in which a repressive regime has been removed, we find exploding crime rates, drug abuse, high HIV rates, neglect of children, and a strong sense of power-lessness and ennui.[25] In some areas the disorder is so overwhelming (and un-employment is so high and job prospects so bleak) that millions say they yearn to return to earlier, authoritarian regimes.

Because of the importance of this point, and because its implications for the model of the good society often are overlooked, I next present some illus-trative data to drive the point home. In Russia, between 1989 and 1993, the total crime rate increased by 73 percent, or 1,180,000 reports. The murder rate rose by 116 percent and assaults increased by 81 percent. Indicative of how shredded the social fabric had become, in 63 percent of major criminal injuries the victims were relatives or friends of the offenders.[26] Alcohol abuse, already high, increased 39 percent from 1989 to 1997. In 1999 the Russian Health Ministry reported 2,500,000 "official" alcoholics in recognized treatment pro-grams. 2002 statistics show that deaths from alcohol-poisoning have increased by as much as 155 percent since 1991, to over 30,000 annually.[27] (The United States, with a population twice as large, averages 300 cases of fatal alcohol poi-soning per year.)

Drug abuse and HIV infection rates also have risen at a steady rate since the breakup of the Soviet Union. By the year 2000, 3 million Russians (2 percent of the population) were addicted to drugs, and HIV neared the 2 million mark.[28] Russia's suicide rate has increased 60 percent from 1989 to 2000.[29] (As of 2003, Russia had the second-highest suicide rate in the world, 37.4 per 100,000. The U.S. rate is 11.1 per 100,000.) There were also sharp increases in highway accidents, weapons and currency smuggling, and rob-beries. Similar developments took place in several other former communist countries, from East Germany to China, although there were significant dif-ferences in specific rates.[30] Of course, there was antisocial behavior during the preceding totalitarian regime, including alcoholism and corruption; the regime itself can be said to have been antisocial. Hence the desire of some citizens of these countries to return to the "good old days" is especially troubling. Yet we cannot deny that something beyond extolling liberty must be done about the new forms of antisocial behavior.

Early reports suggested that similar antisocial behavior is increasing in nations that have been de-Talibanized. In the first days after Kabul was liberated, the pedophiles were back, indulging their obsession. As further evidence of post-Taliban antisocial behavior, Afghan opium production leaped from 185 tons in 2000 to an estimated 3,700 tons in 2002, as compared with more than 5,000 tons produced before the Taliban acted to stop production. Afghanistan regarded the infamous title of "world's largest producer of illicit opium" in 2002.[31] The lack of law and order during reconstruction has generated fears that Afghanistan could easily turn into a "narco-mafia" state with a drastically reduced capacity to adopt democratic institutions.[32] In post-Saddam Iraq, vigilante justice was so commonplace that the country was said to have a "wild west lawlessness."[33] Increases in many other forms of antisocial behavior have been widely reported.

These sharp increases in antisocial behavior and anomie—and what must be done to deal with both beyond more policing—are not often discussed when increasing autonomy (or individualism) is extolled or exported; instead, they are dismissed as the cost that must be borne for being free, or, simplistically, the problems are assumed to vanish, after a transition period, as the standard of living rises. However, people have a greater range of choices than either living in an authoritarian society—whether governed by religious fundamentalists, communists, or some other state-imposed ideology—or living in a society in which antisocial behavior is rampant. *The synthesis of autonomy with social order, a synthesis based largely on moral codes and normative controls, provides a better way.*

Once the need for some shared beliefs is granted, the question of whether they can be secular or must include spiritual, or even soft religious elements, arises both with respect to the East and to the West.

For much of the second half of the twentieth century, leading philosophers and political theorists who had lived through the horrors of fascism and communism and who had considerable public voices, such as Hannah Arendt, Isaiah Berlin, and Ernest Gellner, focused on the danger of totalitarianism. Hence, these scholars adamantly opposed thick normative schemes and visions of a good society, which they derided as perfectionism or utopianism. These schemes were said to legitimize large-scale coercion when it came to the question of how to fashion a new societal design. Giving up on any such grand notions, and ensuring that each person will be free to formulate and follow his or her own moral lights, came to be considered a key guarantee against the return of a Hitler or a Stalin, of concentration camps and gulags. However, as these scholars and myriad followers were glued to their rearview mirrors, they did not see the giant pothole in front of them: the danger of a moral vacuum and the need to fill it with some moral content compatible with autonomy, lest it be occupied by content that is not.

FROM "EXPORTING" HALVES TO SERVICE LEARNING

The basic contours of the slowly evolving global synthesis are discernible if we draw on the good society design just outlined. As a crude approximation, it might be said that the West promotes one core element of the evolving set of shared values and global architecture—autonomy—and that the East promotes another—social order. Thus, the State Department, the National Endowment for Democracy, the Voice of America, and other champions of the Western way of life naturally do not concern themselves with the high crime rates in the West, the widespread drug and alcohol abuse, and numerous other forms of antisocial behavior that all reflect a weakened social order. At the same time, advocates of social order based on a rigid interpretation of Islam—the Ayatollahs of Iran, the moral squads in Saudi Arabia, and the promoters of strict interpretation of the *sharia* elsewhere—have little to say about the massive abuses of human rights, large-scale oppression and violations of human dignity, and the economic costs involved in maintaining their tighter social order. The same holds for several Asian authoritarian regimes such as Singapore, Malaysia, and Burma. Thus, each side extols the beauty of the two legs of the elephant dear to it, ignoring that it needs all its legs to maintain its balance.

Further development of the normative synthesis would be best served if both sides adopted what might be called a service-learning approach. "Service learning" is a term that heretofore has been used mainly for domestic policies. It calls on those who bring educational programs, religious teachings, and social services to the poor or minorities to recognize that these groups have contributions of their own to make; that we ought to refrain from approaching people of different subcultures as if one were bringing light to the heathens, but instead show our eagerness to learn from them as we share with them what we hold to be true.

It may be suggested that such a service-learning approach is merely a tactical move; people are more likely to accept whatever the staff of Peace Corps, Vista, AmeriCorps, and such dish out if the staff shows respect to those that they reach out to, indicating that they have something to learn from them, too. This may well be true; service learning may well provide a more productive posture than most, if not all, others. But it is far from being merely a posture. For instance, middle-class youngsters often are exceedingly naive about worlds outside their own. Learning from people of different backgrounds can provide them with reality testing and help prepare them for dealing with people from other parts of society (and the world) than their own.

Better yet, a service-learning approach calls on public leaders and elected officials to approach the world with a deep conviction (not merely a public relations posture) that they, their nation, and their ideology do not have a monopoly on what is good, that other cultures can make profound and true contributions to the emerging global synthesis.

As already suggested, both the end-of-history and the clash-of-civilizations arguments approach the non-Western parts of the world as if they have little, if anything, to offer to the conception of a good society—at least to its political and economic design—or to the evolving new global architecture. Indeed, there has been a tendency, especially by the economists of the International Monetary Fund (IMF), to pressure countries in the East to pursue purer forms of individualism than those that currently exist in the West, such as deregulating and opening their markets to outsiders. Also, both before and after the collapse of communism, the West actively sought to export recognition of individual rights and a democratic form of government to countries all over the world. As I already stressed, it tended to overlook that autonomy (rights, liberty, and democratic government) cannot be nurtured in a vacuum, that it rests, in part, on foundations of cultures and mentalities and, above all, on moral and social commitments. To push the point, the West has been exporting a model that reflects its weaknesses—its community and authority deficits. Similar points have been made with great force and much documentation by Thomas Carothers and Robert Kaplan, among others.[34] (In addition to the points made here, these authors stressed the absence of other noncommunitarian elements, such as a middle class, and the necessary levels of income and education.)

The East typically has mirror-opposite blinders. The fact that the ideologies and social designs that the East "exports" are order-centered and disregard autonomy has been depicted and denounced so often that it needs little discussion. Here I list briefly the major forms that the East's excessive focus on social order has taken and some differences among them. As others have pointed out, there are some striking similarities between religious fundamentalism and the great totalitarian movements, especially communism, an approach that the West has foresworn.[35] (Hence the term "totalitarian religions" is fully appropriate.) A major reason why communism—which for decades was promoted all over the globe as a state-imposed social order and command-and-control economy—fell apart was because it allowed little room for autonomy, including both political expression and economic initiatives and innovations. Troops or armed minorities often had to force communism on other people because—in the communitarian terms employed here—it was so unbalanced; it was basically unexportable, especially to countries that had had some experience with autonomy.

Recently, the main Eastern-exported societal design has been that of totalitarian religions, in particular a harsh version of Islam (especially in the Wahhabi tradition). The social order it imposes is particularly encompassing and severe, leaving next to no room for autonomy. Fundamentalism has an active expansionist agenda; it seeks to bring its extreme model of social order to other nations and ultimately to the world. As with communism, these attempts take many forms, including that of agitation (imams preaching in Western countries and gaining converts), armed imposition of the *sharia* by some groups over others (in Nigeria), and armed intervention of agents or troops of one country into another (the support by Wahhabi fighters of Muslim forces in Bosnia and Wahhabi support of Chechen separatists). These regimes, which are unbalanced in the sense that they tilt heavily on the side of social order and away from autonomy and that their order is imposed rather than based on informal normative controls, do not seem more sustainable in the longer run than communism. This situation can be seen in the growing opposition to the mullahs and their regime in Iran,[36] in the joy that greeted those who liberated the Afghan people from the Taliban regime, and in the movement of several republics to forms of Islam that provide more room for autonomy, as I report later.

In short, both West and East tend to "export" only half of what could make a good society if the two elements were synthesized (and adapted in the process), each making little out of their own respective deficits. Before I show that there is an actual global movement toward synthesis and indicate what the specific contours of the emerging synthesis look like, I present a few lines on what might seem like an exception: the exportation of civil society—a form of social order fashioned by the West, especially the by United States.

THE CIVIL SOCIETY: AN ELEMENT OF AUTONOMY AND SOCIAL ORDER?

Where does the civil society fit into the line of analysis here followed? The West, especially the United States, is making considerable attempts to export

civil society—voluntary associations, volunteerism, pluralism, and civic education—to the developing world, to former communist societies, and more recently to the domains of religious fundamentalism, especially Islamic ones.[37]
These social formations often are depicted as essential for building a free,
Western polity. Alexis de Tocqueville's well-known analysis is repeated often: a
rich fabric of voluntary associations protects the individual from state domina-
tion; they serve as training schools for democracy, as people who learn to lead
these associations are developing the political skills that democracy requires;
organizing political parties is similar to organizing voluntary associations; and
so on. Viewed in this way, civil society is merely one—albeit an important—element of the Western export of autonomy.

Actually, civil society also can provide a major foundation for social order;
one that is especially compatible with the good society because the order that it
fosters is based mainly on normative controls. However, its contributions to social order can be realized only if it is understood that a civil society entails much
more than volunteerism, tax exemptions for donations to good causes, interest
in public affairs, and other such autonomy-promoting features. The essence of
what is needed for a social order based largely on normative controls is a civil
culture centered around several communitarian values. First and foremost
among them is a willingness to make some sacrifices for the common good.

This sense of commitment to the common good is essential for societies to
be willing to avoid using violence in dealing with one another, to make compromises, to split the differences, and to tolerate people who pray to different gods
and have divergent subcultures. Individualists may try to explain such conduct
by self-interest; people make concessions in order to foster social peace. However, if such calculations would suffice, we would not have the kind of mindless
civil wars and bloodshed that have been so common in human history and that
we now witness in many parts of the world. Such violent attempts to deal with
the differences among groups of people (as distinct from those among individuals, such as a spouse who has offended) are best avoided when these groups see
themselves as members of one overarching community, for whose integrity and
good they are willing to make some sacrifices. (Civil culture thus stands in stark
contrast to those cultures that give much weight to tribal loyalties, or religious
or racial purity, or are centered around such concepts as demanding respect for
one's honor and approving of revenge when one feels injured.)

Aside from communitarian values and loyalties—which are much more
difficult to export or develop on cue than reliable voting machines, tax exemptions for charities, and even civic education—civil culture so enriched often requires major changes in personality, at least in the habits of the heart. For

people to become good members of a civil society, they need to practice considerable self-restraint. When they face people whose basic values differ from their own (an issue that more nations face due to immigration growth everywhere from Japan to Western Europe) or who have conflicting interests (such as between labor unions and management), or when they are called to sacrifice for the common good—for instance, to conserve water—self-restraint is essential. It is needed so that members of a good society will refrain from resorting to violence to get their way; be willing to make the considerable sacrifices involved in accepting the results of peaceful give-and-take; and not engage in free-rider behavior. However, self-restraint is not a natural instinct; people are not born with it, nor is there a gene for it. Indeed, in many societies throughout history, the needed order and sacrifices have been imposed either by the government or by religious authorities or both. Hence, if civil society is to be exported to places where it does not exist, those who are to receive it must develop self-restraint, a slow and difficult process. It is hard to say what is more foolhardy, to believe that one can generate self-reliance on demand or to believe that one can produce a civil society without it.

Thus, civil society can be exported as merely part of the West's autonomy promotion, or it can lay a foundation for a social order based largely on normative controls, a key element of soft communitarianism and the good society. The West has almost exclusively exported civil society in the first way; in order to foster the evolving global normative synthesis, both conceptions of the civil society should be advanced.

Another ground on which both East and West can meet, and are meeting, is the growing recognition of the three-sectorial nature of society. Far from being divided merely into a public and a private sector, government and market, the civil sector has a major place in any good society, including not merely voluntary associations and not-for-profit corporations, but also places of worship and communities. Most societies—East and West—are like a stool that has two long legs and one short one;[38] they would benefit if they would nurture the civil society and lessen the extent to which they allow the market and the government to dominate their members' lives.

GLOBAL HARBINGERS

A TREND UNFOLDS

The synthesis of core Eastern and Western values is slowly, but gradually, taking place.[39] It has been well documented, and hence needs no repeating here, that the "East" is slowly, in a crab-like walk, one step backward for every two forward, moving toward a relaxation of community and authority, slowly making more room for more economic freedoms and—much more slowly—for some political ones.[40] But this does not mean that the East—as so many are taking for granted—is moving toward a Western model; in effect, it is moving toward a middle ground. The same holds for the West; it is moving Eastward—not to the East, but toward the middle ground, by reducing the community (and authority) deficit. I am not claiming that East and West are converging; merely that they are moving toward the middle of the autonomy/social order spectrum, and that each has covered only part of the way. We also should note that the movement is not toward one synthesized model, but rather a variety of societal designs that share two profound qualities: a society more balanced than either individualistic or authoritarian ones, and a society whose social order is based more on moral suasion than either. Thus, societies reveal different balances between autonomy and order and the extent to which they rely on moral suasion. (Compare, for instance, the United States to Scandinavian countries. Compare China to Japan.)

A major reason it is difficult to discern with assurance where these global trends are leading is that the trend toward synthesis is rather new and the societies involved are very much in flux. Moreover, many nations, in both the East and the West, were so far apart in terms of the key values involved (and the institutions that embody them) that each can move light-years in the opposite direction before they reach a middle ground. (A simplistic metaphor highlights the synthesis hypothesis: The fact that someone left the West Coast and is traveling east does not mean he is going to end up on the East Coast, just as someone who travels west from New York may not end up in California. Whether they both stop in Omaha, or whether one will choose to stop in the relatively western city of Denver and the other in the more eastern city of Chicago is a secondary question.)

Whether the global movement is toward a society based on soft communitarian principles of the kind the global normative synthesis points to or toward an individualistic, libertarian model is being sorted out in several societies that are leading the change parade. Among communist countries, China is by far the most important one. There seems to be no way to predict at this stage whether China will continue to liberalize, especially on the political front, and continue to loosen its social bonds and respect for authority—moving ever more toward a Western societal design—or whether it will evolve into a new Asian-liberal synthesis. Still, over time, it has been moving away from its authoritarian communitarian past.

Japan has not only moved away from its authoritarian communitarian past, but it also has provided a distinct societal design, following the introduction of

Western political institutions after World War II. It has a fairly solid democratic regime (albeit a regime long dominated by one party) and a reasonable measure of individual rights (although women, minorities, and people with disabilities have not been fully encompassed). It also has a strong measure of economic liberty, although the economy is manipulated by the Ministry of International Trade and Industry (MITI), coupled with a very strong, indeed often overpowering, informal social order based largely on moral suasion, that is, on normative controls.

Several Islamic societies have taken a few baby steps away from their versions of authoritarian communitarian regimes by reducing reliance on the state to impose a religious code and by becoming less authoritarian. For instance, in 1998 Bahrain made its constitution the supreme source of its laws and legalized nongovernmental organizations.[41] In 2001 the emir freed political prisoners, granted amnesty to exiles, and repealed security laws used for punishing political dissidents.[42] In 2002 the first Bahraini national parliamentary elections since 1973 took place, the very first in which women were allowed to run for office and to vote.[43] Bahrainis formed their first labor union that year.[44] The government also revoked the harsh laws that had been used to punish dissenters, but it still denied people access to the Internet and even to Al Jazeera.[45] Qatar has freed its press, formed a "politically daring" satellite television station, and held municipal elections in which women were allowed to run for office and to vote.[46] In 2003 it undertook a massive reform of its education system with the help of the RAND Corporation, not only rewriting textbooks but also attempting to prepare young people for a more active role in government and economics through elected student councils in schools.[47] Lebanon and arguably Kuwait are other countries that have liberalized to some, often limited, extent. The direction is clear, as is the distance that remains to be covered. Saudi Arabia wins the prize for the smallest and most tentative step in the said direction: in 2003 it announced that it will conduct local elections—without setting a date.[48] Still, the move is in the predicted direction.

End-of-history devotees often depict these trends as if they constitute proof positive of the rising acceptance of Western values, as more and more people in more and more countries gain greater measures of autonomy. However, as we see next, other developments are taking place in the same countries that are directly relevant to the normative synthesis thesis: Several of these societies are struggling to find a religious foundation for their social order—but a "soft" one. They are seeking (not necessarily consciously) to adopt a moderate version of Islam, based on faith and informal controls rather than on the moral squads and flogging and stoning.[49] They differ in their interpretation of *sharia* as, say, reform Judaism differs from its ultra-Orthodox versions, Unitarianism from the more extreme forms of Christian fundamentalism, or today's American Catholics from those of fifty years ago. Such a soft Islam need not clash with the West, but it also would not be secular, libertarian, or individualistic. Instead, it would constitute a form of East-West synthesis. It combines a strong social and moral order based on religion with much respect for liberty and rights.

I delve into Islam for two reasons: Currently, it is widely considered to be the belief system that is the most antagonistic to Western ideas and hence the one that is "clashing" with the West. And if Islam can participate in the global normative synthesis, surely other belief systems can. It is a test by the hardest case. I first list the major attributes of a soft Islam and then cite places where its seeds have been planted.

THE FEATURES OF SOFT ISLAM

As I have already suggested, a major feature of the good society is that its social order relies first and foremost on moral suasion, not coercion. Hard Islam is notorious for relying on moral squads, stoning, whipping, and other extremely coercive measures, which are justified in religious terms.[50] The question of whether Islam clashes with the good society or provides one basis on which it can be erected hence rests on the answer to the question of whether a different Islam can provide the foundations for a soft communitarian social order. That the idea that religion has a key role to play in the postmodern world runs counter to the Enlightenment notions implicit in much of the Western, often mainly secular, positions should not stop us from recognizing its empirical validity and normative potential.

Because soft Islam is a much contested subject and because it is often confused with a related but different question—whether Islam can be made compatible with democracy—it is worthwhile to examine key features of a soft Islam. This is a subject on which much has been written in recent years, resulting in several typologies in which liberal, modest, modern, and Euro-Islam are contrasted with militant, virulent, totalitarian versions.[51] Naturally there also are considerable differences in the interpretation of relevant texts and traditions. To list several key features of a soft Islam, it is neither possible nor necessary to review this large body of literature.* Hence merely a few quotes and notes follow.

---

*Similarly, moderate versions of other religions also can play an important role in the emerging global normative synthesis.

Muqtedar Khan of Adrian College in Michigan captured well the vision of a soft Islam:

> Moderate Muslims aspire for a society—a city of virtue—that will treat all people with dignity and respect. There will be no room for political or normative intimidation. Individuals will aspire to live an ethical life because they recognize its desirability. Communities will compete in doing good and politics will seek to encourage good and forbid evil. They believe that the internalization of the message of Islam can bring about the social transformation necessary for the establishment of the virtuous city. The only arena in which Moderate [sic] Muslims permit excess is in idealism.[52]

Soft Islam differs from the fundamentalist version in that it draws on members of the community for consultations (*shura*) rather than relying on rulings from the mullahs.[53] The concept of *shura* has been traced to the pre-Islamic era, during which time tribal councils decided important public issues through consultation. Forough Jahanbakhsh of Queen's University in Canada adds that most modern scholars hold that such consultative bodies should be composed of representatives of the whole community and not just elites.[54]

In 2001 President Mohammad Khatami of Iran, the leader of the reformers, said that "the constitution [of Iran] states that the rule is Allah's . . . but it also states that this Divine rule is based on people's opinions. Man is Allah's representative on earth and the right to rule does not refer to any specific person. Rather, it refers to all those who participate in elections and set the government's agenda."[55] Others attribute to the Prophet the notion that "every *mujtahid* (the person exerting effort in deducing the law) is correct." This means that "one must search for the law without fear of failure . . ." and that while humans strive to discover the divine will, "no one has the authority to lay an exclusive claim to it."[56]

Iranian historian Hashem Aghajari addresses the nature of the authority of the mullahs, noting: "The Protestant movement wanted to rescue Christianity from the clergy and the Church hierarchy—[Christians] must save religion from the pope. We [Muslims] do not need mediators between us and God. We do not need mediators to understand God's holy books. The Prophet spoke to the people directly. . . . We don't need to go to the clergy; each person is his own clergy."[57] Others have stressed that the Quran is open to different interpretations rather than commanding one strict, rigid, by-the-book line. Khan writes:

Ijtihad narrowly understood is a juristic tool that allows independent reasoning to articulate Islamic law on issues where textual sources are silent. The unstated assumption being when texts have spoken reason must be silent. But increasingly moderate Muslim intellectuals see *Ijtihad* as the spirit of Islamic thought that is necessary for the vitality of Islamic ideas and Islamic civilization. . . .

For moderate Muslims, *Ijtihad* is a way of life, which simultaneously allows Islam to reign supreme in the heart and the mind to experience unfettered freedom of thought. A moderate Muslim is therefore one who cherishes freedom of thought while recognizing the existential necessity of faith.[58]

Khaled Abou El Fadl of the University of California at Los Angeles provides two examples of divergent interpretations. The Quran commands, "Do not take a life which God has forbidden unless for some just cause," yet what constitutes "just cause" is susceptible to debate. The Quran also commands, "And do not kill yourselves." Abou El Fadl says that whether smoking is a form of killing oneself is up for debate. Regarding the veil or headscarf (*hijab*) worn by many Muslim women, Abou El Fadl writes:

Most importantly, the historical setting and the complexity of the early context do suggest that the inquiries into the juristic basis of the *hijāb* cannot be considered heretical. In this sense, labeling the *hijāb* as a part of the *usūl* [the foundations of the faith upon which disagreement is not tolerated], and using that label as an excuse to end the discussion in the matter, is obscenely despotic. It might very well be that this is yet another legal issue where the law of God is pursuant to the convictions of the pious adherent.[59]

The last comment is particularly important. When religions become softer, whether it leads to praying in the vernacular or to allowing men and women to worship together, there is a common fear that the whole construction will unravel. Hence, drawing a distinction between an inviolate core and other elements is crucial for a sense that people can both reinterpret various religious dictates and maintain the religion's essence. Soft Islam builds on this distinction between the core and the rest; rigid Islam denies the very existence of such a difference.

A particularly important case of two interpretations of Islam, one antithetical to a civil world and one supportive of it, is found in the debate about the meaning of the word "jihad." Some Muslims interpret jihad to mean "holy war." For instance, a group of sheikhs in Cairo stated, "According to

Islamic law, if the enemy steps on Muslims' land, jihad becomes a duty on every male and female Muslim."[60] Iraqi Imam Omar Hussein Asengawy said, "Let's wage *jihad* together . . . to face the enemy and the infidel."[61] To the followers of this version of Islam, all nonbelievers are a lower grade of human beings, contemptuously referred to as *kuffar*.[62] However, in other, civil interpretations, jihad is conceived as merely a spiritual struggle. According to Abou El Fadl: "*Jihad* . . . means to strive, to apply oneself, to struggle, and persevere. In many ways, jihad connotes a strong spiritual and material work ethic in Islam. . . ."[63] Seyyed Hossein Nasr writes, "*jihād* is therefore the inner battle to purify the soul of its imperfections, to empty the vessel of the soul of the pungent water of forgetfulness, negligence, and the tendency of evil and to prepare it for the reception of the Divine Elixir of Remembrance, Light, and Knowledge."[64]

This brief discussion and few quotes from a huge body of literature are meant merely to illustrate the basic character of a soft Islam: It seeks to educate and encourage good conduct rather than coerce; it is open to reinterpretation on all matters but its core; it is open to participation by the members of the community rather than dictated by the mullahs; and its expansionism is spiritual rather than by the sword.

The question in this context is not whether Islam can be Westernized, but whether it can provide a foundation for a good society by curtailing its autonomy deficit, even if, in many details, it will support regimes that are different from secular Western regimes. This question is best settled not on the basis of Islam's past history (e.g., Islam is said to have been quite moderate in earlier ages) or examinations of its behavioral tenets and expansionist ambitions, but empirically, within contemporary sociological reality—that is, by examining the development in various countries that are trying to synthesize Islam with much greater measures of autonomy. We must pay attention to whole societies in which Islam plays a pivotal role in government. Doing this is preferable to drawing conclusions from Islamic minorities in places such as Europe and the United States, where the government is not based on Islamic law and Islamic communities are unable, as a rule, to use the government to enforce their code, whether they would prefer to do so or not.

Harbingers of a Softer Islam

The societies in which soft Islam is a vital part of government include Bangladesh, Indonesia, Malaysia, Mali, Sub-Saharan Africa, and some former

Soviet countries, among others. They differ greatly in the extent to which they are examples of a softer Islam. A recent survey of Muslims in Bangladesh, for example, found that 60 percent felt that a woman should have the right to decide whether to veil herself, and more than half disagreed with putting restrictions on men and women working in the same place.[65] In Indonesia, although moderate Muslims have not yet regained control of the government, a significant number of citizens follow a softer Islam, believing, among other things, that the *sharia* should be adapted to modern conditions.[66] Some in Indonesia have even gone so far as to argue that each person can design his or her own individual *sharia*.[67] Malaysia, with a majority Muslim but with significant minority populations, is also living by a somewhat softer version of Islam. The holidays of other religions are national holidays; there is power-sharing between Muslims and non-Muslims; and women are accorded some rights.[68] In Mali, 71 percent of people believe that education should "focus more on practical subjects and less on religious education."[69] South of the Sahara in Africa, where a number of countries have a Muslim majority or a significant minority, Islam is practiced with some moderation. Many African rituals and ceremonies continue to be celebrated, sometimes as Islamic ones; women's dress is not restricted; and alcohol is freely available and consumed.[70]

Developments in Iran are of special interest in this context. Since the mid-1990s, there has been a gradual, albeit slow, increase in political and economic autonomy in that country. While Iran was ruled by charismatic mullahs in the first years after the revolution, beginning in 1997 it conducted both local and national elections. The mullahs harassed and arrested some of the reform candidates, but the candidates repeatedly won a majority in both local and national elections. The mullahs, through the Guardian Council, have veto power over the parliament; nevertheless, it has become a source of opposition and protest. Oppression continues but has become significantly lighter. For example, the government often shuts down a newspaper but immediately grants it a license to reopen under a different name. Massive demonstrations, which often have been tolerated in recent years, further highlight the change. Access to the Internet is fairly widespread. On the economic front, in 1997 Iran opened its borders to tourism despite its fear (not without reason) that tourists would foster further social change. And, since 1992, Iran has allowed foreigners to make significant investments in the country. So far it would seem that Iran is merely increasing the scope of autonomy—that is, Westernizing.

I learned differently when, in 2002, I participated in a three-day dialogue with reformers in Iran. They left no doubt in my mind that they aspire to a soft Islam (as defined above) but reject a Western secular civil society. The most-often repeated theme was that once people are not coerced to heed the *sharia*, they will want to do so out of their free will. They favor that women would pray just as men do, but not for either to forgo their religious beliefs. Reformers supported the idea that Christians and Jews be treated with respect, especially because Christian and Jewish religious convictions are close to those of the Prophet, rather than viewed as inferior human beings, *kuffar*. The fact that fewer and fewer women wear the *burqa*, and more and more allow their scarfs to recede, or use lipstick, is less easy to interpret. It could simply mean that the influence of religion is lapsing and autonomy is increasing or that, at least for some of the women involved, less behavioral and more spiritual expressions of religion are being practiced.

Thus, I join with others in predicting that Iran may well succeed in becoming not only the most liberal and democratic society in the Middle East, but one with a strong sense of dos and don'ts, morally undergirded, and with informal normative controls of a much thicker scope than those in individualistic societies.[71] The new constitutions of Afghanistan and Iraq are especially important tests of my thesis. Afghanistan's embraces a mix of human rights and soft Islam. Iraq's constitution is still being drafted as these lines go to press.

In short, softer Islam is more than a way of thinking. It is a way of life for some, and a compelling vision for millions of others.

SOFTNESS: A KEY DIMENSION

At this junction, a brief conceptual digression is called for. I started by using East and West as a crude first approximation to highlight normative differences and respective contributions toward a global synthesis. However, by now my examination has been extended to recognize major differences within each camp. Among these differences, that which is by far the most important to the issues at hand is the question to what extent a belief system draws on coercion versus moral suasion—how "soft" is it. This distinction runs within each civilization rather than separating them from one another. Hence, for my purposes the key differences in the East are not between Buddhists, Hindus, Muslims and other civilizations, which constitute the basis of Huntington's analysis, but rather those differences that are found within each of these belief systems.

To illustrate: The two main political traditions in China are Confucianism and Legalism. Confucianism has tended to oppose heavy-handed rule. Confucians prefer rule by example and virtue rather than coercive law. The competing tradition has been termed "Legalism" (its most famous proponent is Han Fei Tzu). Legalists prefer rule by coercive law for the purpose of strengthening the state (the military in particular) and social and political control.[72] Other scholars have used different terms but drawn similar conclusions about the differences between what they call "soft authoritarianism" in East Asian belief systems and, by implication, hard or coercive power.[73]

Similar distinctions can be found in all other belief systems. The reason this analysis is of such cardinal importance for the values to be institutionalized in the new global architectures, is that belief systems that extol coercion (hard ones) cannot serve as a basis for a civil, let alone a good, society. They are beyond the pale. In contrast, those that extol moral suasion, it matters little if they come from Islamic, Hindu or African traditions—are particularly well suited to contribute to the evolving global synthesis.

The same holds for differences in Western belief systems. Radical libertarian belief systems, those that celebrate self interests and individual rights but have no room for social obligations and the common good, cannot find a place in the new global core of shared values.

And the West Moves Eastward

Although many may agree that Muslim countries, or more generally Eastern societies, might well be moving not toward a Western society but toward a soft, communitarian middle ground, few note that the United States has been changing as well, moving toward a similar soft communitarian middle ground, roughly from 1990 on. The United States had experienced decades of growing antisocial behavior and anomie; Fukuyama called this The Great Disruption.[74] Then, during the early 1990s, American society began to restore community and shared values and to draw more on renewed informal controls, such as those used to curb violent crime (via what has been called the Broken Window approach), to expand the involvement of faith-based groups in social services, to increase character education, and to provide some help to families (such as with a meager yet new Family and Medical Leave Act and a reduction of the marriage penalty in the tax code). At the same time, Americans rejected Christian fundamentalists' demands for the state to impose religion (such as banning abortion and homosexual activities and by requiring prayer in public schools). Above all, there has been a growing sense that individual rights entail the assumptions of social responsibilities (an issue flagged by the communitarian movement). As a consequence, most forms of antisocial behavior declined substantially (especially violent crime),[75] and others ceased to grow and began to roll back (like teen birth rates and drug abuse).[76] Similarly, after decades of business deregulation, various scandals (such as the Enron and Arthur Anderson accounting scandals) led to several measures of re-regulation and new regulation; these measures have subjected the market to a somewhat higher level of political and social guidance. These steps have begun to correct an individualistic tilt by according more weight to social order, largely of the normative kind, for which soft communitarian thinking provides considerable backing.

The American move toward stronger communal commitments in the 1990s was followed, after the 2001 attack on America, by a dramatic shift from emphasis on individual rights to social order. The United States moved significantly to enhance homeland protection, a prime example of the common good, even if this entailed curbing some liberties. This development is best viewed in historical context. In the 1970s, the FBI was reigned in after it was established that it had engaged in numerous abuses, including spying on civil rights leaders and nonviolent political dissenters. Firewalls were erected between the CIA and the FBI (as well as other law enforcement agencies) to ensure that the agency entitled to spy overseas will not apply its methods to the homeland. As a result, FBI agents felt that they risked their careers if they even asked to put a suspected terrorist under surveillance, and the CIA did not share information about terrorists with the FBI. In short, it might be said that in the matters at hand, the government had a strong individualistic tilt between the mid-1970s and 2001. After the September 11, 2001 terrorist attack, especially following the enactment of the USA PATRIOT Act and other such measures, a balance was restored; in some areas, the opposite tilt was introduced, which will need to be corrected next in a continuous endeavor to find the proper balance between autonomy and social order. All said and done, the United States has become, over the last years, significantly less individualistic and more social order oriented.

Other Western societies have been seeking to find their own point of balance between autonomy and social order, including many in Western Europe, Canada, and several Latin American countries. I discussed elsewhere their place on the continuum from excessive autonomy to excessive social order, and their movements on that continuum.[77] It suffices to say that they are not all marching in unison toward a perfect balance, nor do I claim that the balance must take only one form. However, several of these societies such as Canada were closer to the zone of balance for decades, and hence their movements are less notable than those of outliers. Several others have been moving in the "right" direction, closer to the balance zone (such as Germany over the last two decades).[78]

All of this suggests that various societies are moving toward a middle ground that reflects the evolving global normative synthesis. Their changing value systems will support not merely domestic changes that move them closer to each other, but also a global society that is based on the same principles. Just as those who favor democracy at home want to see it on the global level, those who embrace other values increasingly apply them to the global society. This trend will be accentuated as this new global society will become, for reasons to be discussed, more prominent.

Developments concerning the UN Universal Declaration of Human Rights provide an interesting case in point for the study of the evolving synthesis. The Universal Declaration has gained considerable following all over the world. Elie Wiesel went as far as to call it a "sacred document."[79] Bilahari Kausikan of Singapore, although supportive of the idea of Asian difference, embraced the cardinal notion that, at the heart of the Universal Declaration, states "can and do legitimately claim a concern" about human rights violations in other states.[80]

At the same time, critics, many in the East, consider the Universal Declaration a "Western" document[81] given both that it was formulated when the United States dominated the world after World War II and that it focuses primarily on rights. In response, over the last years, several attempts have been made to recast the declaration, not by curtailing rights but by adding a declaration of one's responsibilities.[82] (The thesis that strong rights presume strong responsibilities is a key theme of soft communitarianism, and it directly reflects the overarching idea of balancing autonomy and social order.[83]) The most noticeable of these attempts was the move by twenty-four former heads of state, many from the East, to draft such an amendment and to seek its adoption by the United Nations. The difficulties that the group, the InterAction Council, encountered are telling.[84] Its members found it difficult to agree on issues in which rights and responsibilities clash. Thus, early drafts suggested that journalists ought to act responsibly, which critics saw as endangering freedom of the press and the public's right to know, all of which are essential to a free society. Moreover, despite several reworkings, the group has been unable to gain enough support to have its planks added to the Universal Declaration. All of this illustrates the direction that the evolving synthesis is taking; the kind of difficulties that are being encountered by those seeking to advance it; and the fact that the evolving synthesis is still in an early stage of growth.

Chapter Two

Specific Elements of the Global Normative Synthesis

So far, our examination of the global normative synthesis has focused on a high level of generality, as it dealt with basic core values. The discussion now turns to show that the evolving shared formulation of the good can be relied on to derive fairly specific moral guidelines above and beyond the general ones.

Particularism within Universalism

At first it may seem that the Western commitment to individual rights and liberty and to legal and political equality cannot coalesce with Eastern commitments to strong community and authority. This seemingly irreconcilable opposition is encountered in several ways. Political theorists and sociologists refer to the difference between "universalism," according to which all citizens (or people) are to be treated in the same manner, and "particularism," according to which people are to be treated differently based on the group to which they belong, whether it is racial, ethnic, religious, political, or a caste. Others refer to the "rule of law" and contrast it with cronyism, nepotism, and various other forms of corruption in which civil servants, judges, law enforcement agencies, and regulators treat people differently on the basis of irrelevant criteria (say, personal relations rather than merit). The same seemingly polar opposition is said to be faced when people are charged with various racial, ageist, or some other form of discrimination based on social criteria rather than on merit. Still others hold that a person is either a cosmopolitan or ascribes to parochialism.[1]

Moreover, for centuries the West regarded the rise of universalism as key to progress, economic growth, efficiency, and justice, while particularism was associated with traditionalism, tribalism, and parochialism. The concept that the king, and by implication no one else, was above the law was a major tenet of the bourgeoisie rising against feudalism and its estate-bound laws. Hence, even today, many in the West oppose exemptions from various laws, say for immigrant groups, such as those banning forced marriage.

Nevertheless, the two approaches can be reconciled, although hardly without difficulties or tension. A societal design that accords priority to universal rights over communal bonds and particularistic values but legitimates these bonds and values in areas not governed by rights provides such a synthesis, indeed a very powerful one. Concretely this means that communities cannot violate people's rights to free speech, to vote, or to assemble. However, other matters—from the amount of taxes levied to the kinds of houses that people may build—are proper domain for communities to be the final arbiters, as long as community rules are not indirect ways of violating rights (such as levying higher taxes on people who engage in what the community considers undesirable speech).

In addition, if we follow the model that universalism takes priority over particularism but leaves ample room for it on matters not encompassed by universal rights but subject to democratic political resolutions, the more encompassing bodies (national and supranational) trump local ones. (These rights are called for because universal rights typically are enshrined in the national constitution and not in local laws and regulations. Exceptions to this rule need not be explored here.) However, these bodies can leave considerable room for particularistic preferences and decision making by the entities they encompass. Typically, federal systems of government, and constitutions that grant to communities all powers not enumerated to the federal government in the constitution, accommodate a synthesis of universalism and particularism. In contrast, unitary states such as France find it more difficult to accommodate such combinations. But even in these states, cities and regions are growing more autonomous. Moreover, particularism need not be geographic. European states are learning, albeit grudgingly, that they can respect legitimate differences among various religious and ethnic groups and cease treating all matters of dress, schooling, burial, and animal slaughter as universalistic matters in which all have to abide by one code.

Having the most encompassing polity take precedence on matters of universal rights and democratic decision making but not preempting all particularistic rulings has an additional major design benefit: It helps to ensure that communities will not be overbearing, as they were in earlier periods and still are in many parts of the world. Communities so contextualized cannot prevent people from leaving, from traveling and returning, from forming associations including oppositional ones—all of which makes these communities radically different from traditional villages. Amy Guttman once chided communitarians for seeking Salem without witches.[2] This is exactly what the synthesis between universal rights (favored by the West) and particularistic bonds (cherished by the East) favors and what it is being brought forth in both.

I cannot stress enough that I am not talking about doing a "reverse Tönnies." Ferdinand Tönnies was a leading sociologist who saw the modern society as moving from *Gemeinschaft* (community) to *Gesellschaft* (society).[3] Many others joined him and depicted this trend in a positive light. The march of history from community to society was viewed as liberating. Then a neoromantic reaction set in, which characterized the community as a warm, supportive place and modern society as generating anomie. Communitarians sometimes are viewed as favoring a reverse Tönnies—seeking a return to the womb of community. I hold that a good society can find ways to combine the closer associations of a community with a respect for rights and autonomy that a free modern society provides.

Last but not least, I differ from the social capital, civil society advocates in that I hold that a good society shares not just bonds of affection, but also a moral culture. Social capital can be found in gangs, militias, and other closely bonded but antisocial entities; good they are not. That is, we must administer an additional test to that of closeness and intimacy in judging what makes for a commendable societal design. For the first approximation, a carefully crafted balance between autonomy and social order, and an order based primarily on moral suasion rather than on coercion, will serve. Additional specifications follow.

TOWARD A MORE AUTHORITATIVE USE OF POWER AND A SOFTER MIX

I hypothesize that as the global normative synthesis advances further, the current trend to render the uses of power more legitimate, both on the domestic and international fronts, will be extended. It may at first seem that this thesis is the same as the argument that a nation, especially a superpower, should rely more on soft power and less on hard power than has the Bush foreign policy. The term "soft power" has been introduced by Joseph Nye, Jr.[4] and it is very widely used. It is defined as the power of attraction. Attractions though can be of two different kinds: One is based on generating an interest, often by providing an economic incentive (or lifting an economic penalty); for instance, when the United States offered billions to Turkey if it would send troops to Iraq to help with peacekeeping. The second occurs when the leaders of one nation convince the leaders and people of other nations of the normative merit of the first nation's course of action, often by appealing to values that citizens of that other nation already subscribe to, sometimes by first persuading these citizens to buy into these values. Thus when the United States rolled back Saddam's troops in 1991 after they invaded Kuwait, most nations recognized the legitimacy of this action and agreed that for one nation to occupy another is a violation of values they hold dear.

The difference between what I have previously called utilitarian (or economic) power and normative power (persuasion or influence)[5] is that the first kind of power generates a convergence of interests and the latter a convergence of normative judgments. Although both are soft powers, economic power generates unstable attraction because those subjected to it have not been converted and hence need to continue to be paid off, bribed, or otherwise "incentivized." If a higher bidder comes along, those courted will turn to support the other side in a heart beat. The exercise of economic power also often generates, I have shown, at least a residue of resentment because those subject to it were made to change course when they still preferred to follow their original course.[6] (That resentment is much higher though if they are coerced).

In contrast, normative power is based on true persuasion, which profoundly alters that which the given people or nation seek. Thus if a people in an Islamic country such as Iran are convinced that a democratic way of life is preferable to that of the *sharia*, then they will support a homegrown regime change with all their hearts. As a result, the benefits of the application of normative power tend to be much more reliable and stable and less costly than that of economic power, albeit much harder to attain. (In economic terms, normative power generates not a change in prices but in preferences). I will use from here on soft power when it does not matter which kind of attraction is at issue and normative power when the focus is on legitimation. Indeed, most of those who use the term "soft power" employ it in this way.[7]

My thesis that in the near future the ratio of coercive power to normative power will *decline* should not be read that I expect it to disappear as some liberals, especially in Western Europe, presume is possible.[8] My starting point is the assumption that the exercise of force cannot be fully avoided, that it is an essential feature of an ordered life and a good society, but that the more legitimate the use, the better for all concerned, both for those who wield the power and for those subject to it.

This idea is captured by the term "authority" (as distinct from power), which is best defined as legitimate use of power.[9] This definition starkly contrasts with one provided by Herbert Simon, wherein authority is simply "power to make decisions which guide the actions of another."[10] ("Authority" is a more parsimonious term than characterizing an agency as combining both the hard and the persuasive forms of soft power, which amounts to the same thing.) But if authority is used in this way, the concept is dichotomous: The exercise of power is or is not legitimate. I use the term "authoritative" as a continuous variable, as it allows one to state that the mix is changing to become more (or less) legitimate, hence making the application of power more (or less) authoritative. Rendering relationships and institutions more authoritative is in line with a core thesis of soft communitarianism: to make social order relatively more dependent on moral persuasion than on coercion. The global normative synthesis informs us which exercises of power are highly legitimate or more authoritative, as compared to others that are less so.

The pressures to act more legitimately are evident in the fact that governments in more and more nations are modifying their political institutions to "open up," to become more "democratic." It is also evidenced in growing respect for the United Nations and in demands on nations to abide by human rights and much else. The importance of legitimacy was dramatized when the Bush administration, which initially held that the United Nations was of no import, first decided early in 2003 that it would be desirable to gain UN approval for its invasion of Iraq. When the United Nations' blessing was not forthcoming, the Bush administration again discussed the United Nations in dismissive terms—only to be forced to return to it, hat in hand, to ask for legitimation in order to draw troops and funds from other nations.

Extreme neo-conservatives consider international law so pliable that they see little if any value in heeding its tenets to obtain legitimacy for forthcoming actions. Robert Kagan, for instance, holds that it was America's defense of other nations that lent legitimacy to U.S. policy during the Cold War, not "obedience to the dictates of international law or to the manifestly dysfunctional UN Security Council."[11] Other neo-conservatives consider the United Nations a mere debating club or worse; George F. Will writes that the "crucial function" of the United Nations is "to enmesh America in inhibiting procedures."[12] And the same neo-conservatives hold that might—and the will to use it—is what cuts it on the international level. Charles Krauthammer bluntly states that "the way to tame the Arab street is not with appeasement and sweet sensitivity but with raw power and victory."[13]

The reactions to the 2003 U.S.-led invasion of Iraq from many American allies, former allies, and most other nations were so negative, and exacted such high costs (detailed in Part II), that acting more legitimately has gained considerable support.[14] That weak nations in the East and the West will urge legitimate conduct is not surprising; after all, it tends to protect their interests. However, the United States found in the wake of the second Iraq war that paying more mind to due process, international law, and evolving global values serves its own purpose as well. Its approach to North Korea and Iran, at least so far, has been much more consistent with the application of international authority rather than brute force. (Critics will say that there were practical rather than principled reasons for the multilateral approach employed, but the result is the same.) The fact that there is such a trend does not mean that there will be no setbacks, but the trend seems unmistakable.

Although there are numerous differences about what is considered legitimate, some kind of a shared understanding is evolving. It favors respect for international law and treaties (e.g., the Treaty on the Limitation of Anti-Ballistic Missile Systems and the Kyoto Protocol), international institutions (especially the United Nations), and above all, limiting the use of force. The focus of the evolving synthesis, as is typical when shared normative principles are still thin, is on procedure rather than on substance. This fact, however, does not make the evolving synthesis meaningless; as time passes, substance is being added (for instance, on matters concerning human rights and the grounds for humanitarian interventions).

In the storm of criticism over the United States as the rising imperial power,[15] the point that has been overlooked is that acting authoritatively means not only drawing on soft, normative power—acting legitimately—but means also using force legitimately. Although the concept that force can be used legitimately may seem self-evident, it is not to many Europeans, especially German intellectuals who hold semipacifist positions and who believe that everything should and can be achieved through negotiations and mediation. For them, the term "just war" is an oxymoron. Nor is it self-evident to those liberals who hold that the way to avoid violence is to give everyone in the world a decent standard of living and an effective vote (to "empower" them), not to mention those remaining on the left who hold that U.S. corporations breed the problem and that restraining them is mainly what is required to appease the world. This is not the direction that the global normative synthesis is taking. Its focus is on the authoritative use of coercive (or hard) power—which in turn entails that it be used rarely and only when all other measures have failed—and not on relying only on soft power, however this is defined.

Much less advanced is the communitarian idea that the more that social order is based on persuasion and the less it is based on coercion, the closer we are to a good society. For persuasion or the moral voice to work, people need to have a shared moral culture and bonds of affection—my definition of community. Nations do acquire some attributes of communities, but it is widely assumed that any notion of a global community is a visionary dream. I shall return to this question later in Part III, but suffice it to say here that there are numerous signs that a thin, but far from meaningless, transnational community is beginning to form. This evolution is one reason why the global exercise of power can become more authoritative. Other reasons include well-known factors such as the ease of communication, spread of education, opening up of societies, and the rise of a de facto shared language. Most important is the increasing entrance of the masses into politics. There are too many involved citizens to be bought off or held at bay by force. Increasingly, for a regime to last, it must gain both domestic and international legitimacy.

LIMITED BUT NOT THIN

The evolving normative synthesis is also bringing East and West closer in terms of the scope of behavior that they are seeking to regulate by the state or by informal normative controls. In the past, communist societies as well as religiously fundamentalist societies still sought to regulate, often closely and in great detail, people's work and consumption, the music they listened to (e.g., the communists, the mullahs, and other religious fundamentalists have banned jazz), the movies they watched (banned are Western, X-rated, or English-language movies), whether or not they danced, their sexual conduct, and much else. Moreover, they have all tried to shape not merely behavior, but also what people feel and think.

In contrast, the liberal design favors a thin collective agenda (including a very limited set of shared formulations of the good). Although no Western society fully implements this design, opposition even to informally enforced moral norms is much stronger in the West, especially in the United States, than in other societies. Two major reasons are given. The first is that informally fostered, shared moral formulations may lead to state-imposed ones. The second is that even if these formulations are enforced merely informally, such normative controls also violate a person's autonomy.

In opposition to the notion that the world is or should become Westernized—which, in this context, would mean minimizing the collective moral agenda of societies—the synthesized design calls for a thicker layer of morally defined issues undergirded by normative informal controls. However, how thick it is going to be and what the range of behavior is that the shared pre-scriptions seek to encompass are questions whose answers are lacking at this early stage of the development of the global normative synthesis. It seems safe to suggest, though, that the synthesis would not be nearly as thick as that of many Eastern societies and not as thin as that of the American society.

Indeed, even a cursory examination will show that numerous Eastern soci-eties exempt ever more areas of behavior from their formal and informal con-trols, including, for instance, which television stations people watch, what radio programs they listen to, and even which web pages they access via the Internet. At the same time, in the West there is a slowly growing recognition that areas which have been exempted from public scrutiny may need some form of public guidance, if not regulation. These areas include, for instance, the cultural ma-terials to which children have access or to which they will be exposed, as well as transactions on the Internet. In other areas, a measure of re-regulation is called for—for instance, the accounting practices of corporations. (Further progress on this front can be expected to result from cross-cultural moral dialogues, dis-cussed later in chapter 4.)

A SELF-RESTRAINED APPROACH

The Western, especially American, worldview reflects a combination of opti-mism and a belief in progress and social engineering mixed with a sense of tri-umphalism. It leads the West to presume that one can readily introduce autonomy (respect for rights, democracy, and free markets) into various East-ern societies. It has led Western consultants to urge countries to jump from the Stone Age, or at least from very underdeveloped conditions, into an American-like polity and economy. These nations were strongly advised that they could do so if they would only cut their deficits, open their markets, and carry out a few other such changes by a stroke of the pen. Beyond advice, the International Monetary Fund, the U.S. Department of State (especially the U.S. Agency for International Development), and other such bodies exerted considerable pres-sure to the same effect.

Eastern worldviews—despite all of the differences among them—tend to combine pessimism, in some cases even fatalism, with a long sense of history. (The Chinese, especially, have a thousand-year perspective). Such a worldview leads people to expect that social change will be slow, difficult, and full of unan-ticipated consequences. Communism, which as an ideology was fashioned in the West, was in this sense especially ambitious, seeking to re-engineer both the society and the personality of its members. When neither yielded, millions were slaughtered in desperate attempts to accelerate change and maintain control. However, at the end of the day, the old Eastern foundations prevailed. These regimes, while still intact, increasingly accepted society the way that they encountered it—for instance, allowing farmers private plots and people to trade—rather than trying to change them in line with their master designs.

In this area, the East–West synthesis best leans in an Eastern direction in the sense of recognizing the severe limits under which social reengineering must labor. Such a tilt would prevent disappointment and cynicism, not to mention the massive application of coercion, which all too often arises when hyper-optimistic normative plans yield little social change.

I refer to this approach as one of self-restraint. Others call it humble, or berate nations for their hubris. Such an approach recognizes that our powers are more limited than we often realize, and that promises to deliver more than we can will backfire. Moreover, a restrained approach argues that we all are better off when we hold back, when we apply less power than we command, in order to win the collaboration of others and build institutions that will serve us in the longer run, even if they entail some holding back in the shorter run.

CHAPTER THREE

CONTAINING CAPITALISM

SETTING LIMITS

THE TENDENCY OF THE WEST TO FOCUS ON EXPORTING ONLY ONE element of the good society—autonomy—and to be much less attentive to the foundations of the social order is particularly evident when the virtues of free markets are extolled and urged upon countries that have as yet missed its blessings.[1] To the extent that we view these measures as much-needed corrections to state-controlled economies—rather than as actual prescriptions for unfettered markets—often they are justified. For instance, the economies of China and India flourished as they curtailed their extensive command and control systems. However, in most of the former Soviet republics—in which the unleashing of the market was much more extensive, and in which the needed social foundations were particularly lacking—the result has been devastating.

The exported free-market model failed to take into account that successful economies presume some legal (e.g., state) as well as moral and social underpinnings. Bribery, corruption, and nepotism must be kept at low levels—either by the law or, best, by morally based self-restraint—if capitalism is to work. Respect for the right to own and control private property is not naturally available, nor can it be produced or sustained by the market itself. Citizens and captains of industry initially must be willing to save and invest more than they consume, which—as Max Weber has shown—is the spirit of capitalism: They are compelled to do so out of moral convictions rather than by promises of higher returns in the remote future. A modern, efficient economy cannot function if the parties do not respect the law and if they do not trust each other. In addition, society must be protected from market excesses or it will lose its legitimacy. All of this often is ignored when Jeffrey Sachs and others urge countries to "jump" into capitalism to make the transition as quickly as possible.[2] Such a transition is more likely to take decades. Above all, it must be understood that the market does not rest on its own foundations, but rather it must be embedded in a social order. Exporting freedoms—without the social order on which they are based—is like exporting cars with a steering wheel but no chassis.

Free markets, which, according to economic theory, entail perfect competition, have never existed in human history. The United States, which has the relatively freest economy of them all, regularly and extensively "interferes" in and regulates the economy in the name of a variety of social goods. These goods include the protection of children, workers, and consumers; preventing unfair competition both domestically and overseas; enhancing national safety and the environment; safeguarding endangered species; and much more.

On some specific items, it might be said that a given regulation (or other form of market containment) actually benefits the economy—for instance, industrial standard setting. However, most of the laws and regulations reflect other public needs, normative considerations, and political pressures. American advocates often export the free market ideal as if it means an unfettered market, but both historical and current experience shows that what is actually at issue is the *level and scope* of market regulation and control—not whether there should be any. That is, the United States itself is much closer to some kind of compromise between autonomy and order in the economic sphere than is implied when individual economists, the State Department, and the International Monetary Fund pressure other societies to embrace "free markets" or chastise them for various limitations that they put on imports, competition at home, and the like. These pressures are best not taken at face value but should be interpreted as seeking less state control and less managed economies—not free markets.

Indeed, as compared with the United States, many societies (for instance, in Western Europe) have chosen to have significantly larger welfare states and laws to contain the market. It is surely premature to assume that various Eastern societies will want to have markets managed as little as those of the United States and not try to find their own balance between laissez-faire economics and state management. True, the East is moving the management of its economies toward a Western model; however, this move does not entail a disregard of noneconomic values and institutions, but rather a quest for a middle ground between excessive, extremely detailed, and tight state controls and a free-for-all void of government guidance. And even if here and there, say, in some sectors of the Russian or Chinese economy, we see a rough-and-tumble form of raw capitalism, these instances might well be transitional phenomena as these societies seek their own form of balance, overshoot the mark, and then try to establish how far to pull back. In short, one of the important specific issues that the East and West have to sort out as part of the quest for a carefully crafted balance between autonomy and social order is the extent to which market forces will be given free rein versus being contained by the requirements of the social order, which advancing human primacy requires.

It is true that many nations in the East are passing through a period of relatively free-for-all, raw capitalism, as the United States did in the nineteenth century. But we must expect that, based on the total of historical experience, such a period is very likely to be followed by the introduction of new measures of market containment, as we have seen already in Russia under Vladimir Putin. The human and social costs of raw capitalism are too high to be tolerated, and as the same societies become relatively more democratic (I should say, less authoritarian), these costs tend to find a political voice. "Containment" refers to both sets of values and government controls that combine an assurance of considerable free rein to market forces while setting clear and enforced limits. (The fact that larger corporations tend to support some measure of state regulation for their own reasons enhances the political feasibility of such containing developments.)

I am not referring to a return to command and control, planned economies, but to one version or another of a social market, of the kind Western Europe has had for many decades. It might be argued that the Western European model is flawed because the combination of high social costs and high labor costs makes it difficult to sustain. It may well have to be adjusted to reduce labor costs to some extent (as has already been done in Britain) and to trim social costs—that is, the mix might be changed to include a bit more market and a bit less "social." However, it does not follow that Europeans are going to give up on the basic social market concept, even if keeping it means somewhat lower economic growth rates than might be achieved if the market were less contained.

Thus, both East and West are moving, from very different parts of the spectrum to be sure, toward a middle ground in which markets are neither tightly controlled nor unfettered. It follows that some containment of the market should be viewed not as deviation from the Western model but as an integral part of the global model of a good society. The normative issue is to what extent the market should be contained and what are the best ways to contain it, not whether it must be contained.

LIFE'S PROJECTS AND MEANINGS

Rarely discussed in this context are questions concerning life's projects, but they are very much at issue. The term "project" refers to what a person or a group (even as large as a society) is seeking to accomplish, the vision projected into the future that provides benchmarks for progress and the criteria for choices. Thus, if a person projects herself as a physician in the future, her chosen project will affect the classes that she chooses to take in college, the amount of debt she is willing to assume, whether she should defer having children, and much else. Viewing people as what they project themselves to become is radically different from treating them on the basis of where they are coming from (inner-city Detroit or Appalachia). Above all, projects give meaning to life. They tell people why they should make an effort, defer gratification; why they should get up in the morning, so to speak. Although many projects are individual or corporate ones, they reflect the culture and society in which they are embedded. Most relevant for the issue at hand is that societies can also be viewed as centered around projects.

There are great differences between the projects that many in the West, as opposed to those in the East, pursue. Millions of people in the West center their projects around the affluent way of life; they work hard to make consumer goods (and services) in order to gain the means they need to purchase them.[3] Prestige, self-esteem, and sense of purpose for many millions are closely wrapped around their achievements in this area. They measure their progress in terms of how much money they earn and what kind of goods they are able to purchase. The source of their motivation to exert themselves is their high production/consumption project. True, the same people also strongly favor keeping their society safe, free, and democratic, but most days these commitments do not entail any particular efforts on their behalf. Hence such commitments are not part of their defining, main project. Production and consumption are.

To highlight the nature of the high production/consumption project, which for many is so self-evident it is often not examined, it might be useful to mention other projects that some people center their lives around. These include serving the Lord as one's dominant activity (e.g., missionaries), making culture one's project (e.g., struggling artists), or political action (e.g., organizers). Typically these people scoff at maintaining an affluent way of life. They tend to make less money than others with similar qualifications, and they tend to be much less interested in purchasing the most fashionable clothes or cars, nor do they mind the absence of these objects. Instead they find other sources of meanings for their effort, other criteria for their decisions, and other benchmarks with which to assess their progress.

Currently it may seem, as millions upon millions in the East are rushing to join the high production/consumption project, that it will become the one around which most people in the East and in the West will center their lives and from which they will derive meaning. Many prominent tracts about economic development as well as programs promoted by the World Bank, United Nation's Development Program, and numerous other agencies as well as national governments assume—although it is rarely explicitly stated—that people of the world aspire to an affluent way of life. They hold that all people of the world are (or ought to be) willing to put in the work and scale back other competing commitments—for instance, family and the spiritual life—in order for them to be able to gain more income. A cursory examination of former communist societies,[4] India, and newly liberated Islamic countries (see Afghanistan and Iraq) seems to indicate that there is nothing that the people of these countries aspire to more than getting their hands on ever more consumer goods. (For some it is merely bicycles, for others motorcycles or cars; for some merely new sneakers, for others satellite dishes, CDs, and cell phones.) Whether they are willing to submit to the rigors of the market economy is less obvious, but they are surely told, and quickly find out, that if they wish to live an affluent life they will need to follow its economic logic. Accordingly, it would seem that in the future the whole world will increasingly aspire to look like an American suburb. Indeed, as various developing countries grow in wealth—Singapore and Taiwan, for example—they tend to imitate American suburbs in housing styles, traffic patterns, and much else. In short, at first it may seem that, at least in economic matters, the Western ideals will dominate.

There is, however, a great deal of social science evidence that shows that human contentment ceases to increase as income grows beyond a fairly modest level. To cite but a few studies of a large body of findings: Frank M. Andrews and Stephen B. Withey found that the level of one's socioeconomic status had a limited effect on one's "sense of well-being" and no significant effect on a person's "satisfaction with life-as-a-whole."[5] Jonathan Freedman discovered that levels of reported happiness did not vary greatly among the members of different economic classes, with the exception of the very poor, who tended to be less happy than others.[6] David G. Myers and Ed Diener report that while per capita disposable (after-tax) income in inflation-adjusted dollars almost exactly doubled between 1960 and 1990, 32 percent of Americans reported that they were "very happy" in 1993, almost the same proportion as did in 1957 (35 percent). Myers and Diener also show that although economic growth slowed between the mid-1970s and the early 1990s, Americans' reported happiness was remarkably stable (nearly always between 30 and 35 percent) across both high-growth and low-growth periods.[7] Richard A. Easterlin's work found that happiness remains generally constant throughout life cycles. Typically, income and general economic circumstances improve throughout one's life until retirement, but happiness does not experience a comparable level of growth; nor is the leveling off of income during retirement accompanied by a decrease in happiness.[8] In other words, once basic needs are satisfied, the high production/consumption project adds little if anything to human contentment.

There are several reasons to expect that maximization of income and consumption will not constitute the economic and certainly not the social agenda at the heart of the evolving global normative synthesis. Many millions of people (even in the West) already show that they are not as willing as most Americans are to pay the social and human costs that maximizing wealth entails.[9] This fact is reflected in their strong support for a social market, a thick welfare state, and large amounts of time free of labor—even if it entails a relatively lower level of consumption of goods and services. And there seems to be some increasing awareness that the affluent way of life project is not truly satisfying and that it is accompanied by a wide range of neuroses; that the pursuit of ever higher levels of affluence is not conducive to human flourishing.[10] Moreover, there is a growing recognition that the more that people across the world become involved in the high production/consumption project, the more the environment is undermined. We can hardly assume that the Earth can sustain an ever-growing population at ever-higher levels of production and consumption and that alarms sounded earlier about various shortages, especially about oil—proved to be false—will not turn out to have been merely premature.

The preceding analysis suggests that the higher (and more secure) people's income will become, all over the world, the more they will be inclined to search for other projects, although to do so they will first have to break out of the social obsession to gain ever more means (or resources), despite the declining marginal utility of these goods. I am not arguing that, because affluence is not truly satisfying, to protect the environment, and so on, the poor should accept their poverty or that less developed countries should remain so. For the affluent, however, after what Abraham Maslow calls "creature comforts" are well sated and securely provided for,[11] capping one's income and expenditures, embracing "voluntary simplicity,"[12] and freeing one's energy to engage in other projects are sources of more profound meaning and containment than consumerism.

Economist and Nobel laureate Robert Fogel shows that throughout history, periods of affluence are followed by what he calls Great Awakenings, which entail an examination of life's purposes and their priority over instrumental matters, and he predicts that the world is due for another one in the near future.[13] Accordingly, we would expect that more and more people, especially in affluent parts of the world, are likely to realize that the pursuit of well-being through ever higher levels of consumption is Sisyphian, and that when it comes to acquiring material goods—where enough is never enough—the project in the end is inherently unsatisfying.

In China it is now fashionable to refer to a "moderately well-off society," a concept drawn from Confucius.[14] It denotes a level of material success in which basic needs are sated with something left to spare, but contains no ambition for still-higher levels of consumption. Instead, the ambition is to move toward another concept of the great philosopher—a "great community": a society without crime, selfishness, war, or social divisions. The concept far from dominates Chinese thinking, but the very fact that it is popular and promoted by the government shows the appeal of a project different from maximizing wealth, work, and consumption.[15]

I believe that once basic material needs are satisfied, more and more people will break out of the obsession with consumer goods and increasingly will find that profound contentment rests in other projects and activities, especially in ends-based relationships; in bonding with others, in community-building and public service, and in cultural and spiritual pursuits. This is not an idle forecast. In recent years there have been numerous reports, albeit about a relatively small number of people, who are engaging in what is called voluntary simplicity; that is, people who can afford a more affluent way of life but choose to adopt a less object-rich one. Some merely moderate parts of their lives (perhaps clothing): Others change their professions and move to the countryside.[16] I expect that, as the income of people in many countries rises, more and more in the East and in the West will ask themselves (although rarely in the terms here employed): How much they should worship mammon, and how much of their lives they should dedicate to other pursuits?

Aside from making people more profoundly content individuals, a major and broadly based upward shift on Maslow's scale is a prerequisite for addressing the means/ends imbalance, for establishing human primacy. Such a shift entails a growing number of people being willing to relate to one another as members of families and communities, and thus as ends in themselves, and not mainly or exclusively as means, employees, people to whom products must be sold or with whom one makes economic transactions. This shift, in turn, would help create the social foundations for a society in which ends-based relations dominate while instrumental ones are well contained.

Also, such a change in the core project must take place before the world can come into harmony with the environment, which is a major common good and human purpose. The higher human needs in Maslow's scale put much less demand on scarce resources than do the lower needs. Involving oneself more deeply in human relationships and spiritual activities is much more compatible with protecting the environment than an ever higher consumption of goods and services.

In short, when we focus on the implications of the global normative synthesis for the economic realm we find that there is a worldwide quest for a higher degree of economic autonomy from political and social pressures, and an intensive quest for affluence, for a high production/consumption project, as the center of life's meaning. However, there are empirical, social, environmental, and moral reasons to hold that the more affluent people become, the more meaning they find in other core projects, which in turn serve the common good (e.g., protection of the environment) and are closer to ends considerations (e.g., family and communal bonds) than the celebration of resources, that is, of means.

How much of the new blend will draw on Eastern spiritual sources (as do New Age followers in the West as well as converts to soft versions of Islam) and how much on Western religious and spiritual traditions of social activism is far from clear. The basic direction, though, is clear. The high production/consumption project will find its place as one activity that has an important role in human life, as one way to sate basic human needs, and as one that serves other noneconomic projects. However, this project will have to leave increasingly more room for other meaningful but less instrumental projects, if human primacy is to be advanced.

RESPONDING TO A MORAL AND TRANSCENDENTAL HUNGER

Beyond the question of how much weight to accord to the economic project lies a whole set of even more profound normative issues. To proceed we must differentiate between responding to moral versus transcendental questions. Moral values define what people consider right versus wrong: what we owe our children, what elder children owe their parents, what our obligations are to our friends and neighbors and to the communities of which we are members. Responses to transcendental questions attempt to explain why we exist, why we are cast in this world, and why we are born to die.

Why explore such profoundly personal questions in this context? For two reasons: They are part and parcel of the evolving global normative synthesis, and they affect the kind of new global architecture that may be erected.

As a first step, we must take into account the fact that society and state, the private and the public realms, do not exist in separate worlds. Hence, if moral values are weak or eroding, matters that otherwise are attended to by families and communities fall into the lap of the state, whether national or transnational, at great public and human costs. For instance, if families neglect their children, they become wards of the state, raised in foster homes or orphanages or "warehoused" in juvenile detention centers. As a result, many children do not grow up properly and resort to drugs and crime, thereby expanding social disorder and increasing public costs. In short, there is a strong inverse relationship between the scope of society, ordered by moral values and informal controls, and the scope of the coercive elements of the state. Hence, whether there are shared moral values and how compelling they are, even when they merely concern what are considered to be private matters, has a direct impact on the autonomy versus social order balance as well as on the nature of the social order as a whole. The most effective antidote to the explosion of antisocial behaviors that often follows the collapse of totalitarian and theocratic governments, and undermines extant democratic and free societies, is found when citizens embrace a rich set of moral and prosocial values—a main thesis of soft communitarianism.

Regarding transcendental questions, people may well be unaware of the need to address them or they may consider them of concern mainly to philosophers, adolescents, and New Age gurus. However, when these profound questions remain unanswered, they gnaw. They directly affect the extent to which people are basically content versus the extent to which they seek new sets of values and regimes that reflect those values. The reason that charismatic and religious movements, as well as various cults—including totalitarian ones—are in constant demand is that the individualistic, secular worldview is not addressing these basic questions effectively.[17]

The tendency in the West has been to associate individualism with secular ways of thinking. The stress on free choice, rights, and autonomy typically is grounded in philosophers whose bodies of thought are secular (John Locke or Immanuel Kant) even if the philosopher himself personally were not. Religion, for many, used to be associated with tradition and those "reactionary" forces that were opposed to autonomy. Moreover, it was long assumed that as modernity evolved religion would recede. Elizabeth Shakman Hurd supports this point: "The benefits of secularization were long ago accepted as a basic prerequisite for entry into the modern world. Challenges to secularism represent little more than the last gasp of a dying era in which religious identity, practices and institutions represented the center of gravity in many societies."[18]

Religion, however, did not die out. In fact, as Peter Berger puts it, "the assumption that we live in a secularized world is false."[19] The experience of the Soviet Union is particularly telling in this context. For more than seventy years the USSR fully controlled education, most culture (from books to movies), and the media, but still it was unable to suppress the religious urge. And this is despite the fact that the USSR provided an elaborate ideology and actively fought religious expression, which it considered a debilitating addiction. Even in its heyday the USSR could not overcome the appeal of religion. After seventy years of antireligious campaigns, communism is gone but millions attend churches in Russia and other former Soviet republics and religious beliefs play a considerable role in people's lives. The number of adherents of the Russian Orthodox Church nearly doubled from 1970 to 2000,[20] and other former communist nations in Eastern Europe have seen an "outpouring of pent-up religious [fervor]."[21]

Former Soviet Union states have seen significant growth in religious adherence. Uzbekistan, in which Muslims made up 50 percent of the population in 1970, has seen its Muslim population grow since the dissolution of the USSR, reaching 71 percent in mid-1990 and 76 percent in mid-2000. Turkmenistan experienced an even greater growth, from 50 percent Muslim in 1970 to 83 percent in mid-1990 and 87 percent in mid-2000. Similarly, Azerbaijan grew from 61 percent Muslim in 1970 to nearly 84 percent in mid-2000.[22]

The intense quest for more robust normative treatments to quench moral and transcendental hunger is evident in the rise of religion in the East, particularly in Eastern societies that opened up and have become somewhat "less Eastern," so to speak.[23] We are witnessing an explosive growth of Christianity in East Asia.* While between 1950 and 1970 adherents of all religions in China declined under the influence and pressure of the Communist Party, since 1970 religious following has increased significantly. The number of Christians has grown from 665,000 in 1970 to 14 million in mid-2000. (The followers of Islam in China declined in the same period, however, from 21 million in 1970 to 19 million in mid-2000.)[24] In South Korea, nearly a quarter of the popula-

---

*Note that all numbers taken from the *World Christian Encyclopedia* include only "professing" Christians, or those known to the state. Adding "crypto-Christians," hidden or secret Christians usually known just to churches, significantly increases the numbers.

tion is Christian, a 4,000 percent increase from the early part of the twentieth century.[25] In Thailand, Christians have increased from 23,000 in 1900 to nearly 800,000 in mid-2000. Christianity has also grown in Indonesia, from 9.9 million in 1970 to 21 million in mid-2000. In all of these countries, the growth is not just in numbers of followers, but also in numbers of followers as a percentage of the population.[26]

Other areas are also experiencing a religious resurgence. In Africa, there were more than 350 million Christians in 2000, compared to about 8 million in 1900. Currently about 45 percent of Africans are self-identified Christians, up from 8 percent in 1900. Christians in India grew from 14 million in 1970 to 40 million followers in mid-2000. Muslims in India also grew, from nearly 63 million in 1970 to nearly 123 million in mid-2000, although in terms of percentage of population this increase is slight.[27] Worldwide, Mormons have more than doubled their membership in the last twenty years, currently reporting more than 10 million adherents.[28]

Above all, the rise of religious fundamentalism (not just in the Islamic world, but also in countries as different as India and Israel) is a major reaction to the same moral and transcendental vacuum.[29] José Casanova writes that "what was new and unexpected in the 1980s was . . . the revitalization and the assumption of public roles by precisely those religious traditions which both theories of secularization and cyclical theories of religious revival had assumed were becoming ever more marginal and irrelevant in the modern world."[30]

Of special interest are recent developments in Turkey, which is moving back toward Islam after its government diminished its role for decades.[31] Since the days of Ataturk, Turkey moved significantly in the Western direction, arguably more so than any country in the Middle East, more than many countries in Africa, and more than quite a few in Asia. This movement is evident in its separation of mosque and state and the secularization of the private realm. (Turkey's constitution serves to "prevent any public display of religion by parties and politicians, and designates the military as the guardian of secular democracy."[32]) To a considerable extent, Turkey has been democratizing, although the military continues to play a significant role in domestic politics. Individual rights have been strengthened, although not very extensively. If a Western-like secularization, leaving transcendental matters unattended to, would suffice as the march of history, the people of Turkey should be spiritually quite content. Instead, in recent years millions of Turks have re-embraced Islam. As a result, some may view Turkey as a political battleground between totalitarian Islam and the secular West, and score is being kept to see which side is gaining ground. However, if my analysis is valid, neither will win in the longer run. As the world is moving to embrace the normative synthesis just outlined, millions of Turks will find totalitarian Islam too restrictive and Western secularism lacking in spirituality, and they will seek a third alternative, most likely some form of a soft Islam.

Not all responses to the transcendental hunger are religious. In Russia in recent years, a youth group called Walking Together has emerged. This group holds summer camps, educates its members and other Russians about Russian history, organizes rallies against communists, and lives by a strict moral code. Members work to create a sense of Russian history and culture by requiring participants to "attend six concerts or plays a year, visit four historic cities, check out six books from the library and volunteer at least once a month at orphanages or senior citizen homes."[33] The group believes that these activities and its moral code are needed to fight the evils of post-Soviet Russia. In still other former Soviet republics, the rise of nationalism benefits from the same moral and transcendental vacuum. (I am not suggesting that Walking Together and nationalism are wholesome responses to the transcendental void, merely that they serve as more examples of the void to which I am pointing.)

Most of these developments are taking place in the East, but the West also continues to seek ways to quench its moral and transcendental hunger. For instance, in the United States, various religious and spiritual cults are on the rise—fundamentalist, pagan, New Age, and Satanic, among others.[34] At the same time, more established religions and those that are more compatible with the evolving core of globally shared values continue to play in the lives of many millions of Americans.

True, in quite a few countries, including several in Western Europe (especially in the largely Protestant North), there are large majorities who are, at most, minimally religious or completely agnostic.[35] They avoid facing the transcendental issues by keeping themselves preoccupied with work and consumption, by resorting to mood-modifying and awareness-suppressing agents (alcohol or drugs), and by attending psychotherapy sessions—all ways to paper over their underlying anxiety. These unsatisfactory responses are indications that these unresolved issues continue to gnaw at them. As Christopher Lasch put it, people are "haunted not by guilt but by anxiety. . . . [They live] in a state of restless, perpetually unsatisfied desire."[36]

Whether this void can be filled only by religion or also by secular sets of beliefs is unclear. It is clear, however, that both kinds of beliefs carry within them risks for the good society. Both may turn authoritarian, or both may become so attenuated that they are no longer able to provide guidance for moral decisions nor address the transcendental questions.

The synthesis blends "hard" religions, especially the totalitarian version of Islam, with Western ideas of autonomy to make for soft religions. It blends Eastern spiritual notions with a Western commitment to liberal social action (in the Mario Cuomo, Hubert Humphrey sense and not in the traditional sense of the word "liberal"). Fabianism would serve as an example. Because neither camp is bereft of what the other in effect champions, the combination is generally smooth, albeit gradual.

Before moving on I feel compelled to address a curious case of tunnel vision that I find in some of my most learned and sophisticated colleagues, an observation of which is highly relevant to the issues at hand. These individuals cannot see, or maybe just refuse to accept, that there are hundreds of millions of people whose ultimate conceptions of the good are profoundly different from theirs. In other words, at conflict are not merely some narrow, highly specific agendas but rather whole worldviews. A fair number of my colleagues implicitly assume that when all is said and done, "everyone" wants the same thing that they desire—an affluent and free way of life. Hence when faced with a bin Laden (or another true believer) these colleagues focus on policy differences and ignore the deep conflict that is built into totalistic belief systems.

Typically these colleagues used to suggest that the United States should try to meet three demands of Muslim fundamentalists: get out of the holy places in Saudi Arabia; lift the sanctions against Iraq; and lean more heavily on Israel to yield to Palestinian demands. More recently they have argued that now that the United States has responded to the first two of these three demands; it should correct the American pro-Israeli tilt and then the Arab world would treat the West with much greater favor. They hold that such a move would remove a major source of the motivation that feeds anti-American feelings in general and terrorists in particular.

My point is that whatever the merit of the three suggested moves (and the newer demands, for example, to let Iraqis run Iraq without an American presence and interference), these moves will not appease fundamentalist Muslims any more than Christian fundamentalists would be satisfied if abortion would be made illegal, evolution taught in public schools, and abstinence preached from all the rooftops. The basic reason is that while these specific demands are the current front they are hardly what the battle is all about. Fundamentalists find that the basic Western way of life, in fact practically every aspect of it, deeply violates all that they hold sacred. Indeed from their viewpoint they are right. The spread of the Western way of life does directly endanger most everything that they believe in, from the way to treat women to how to spend one's day, from the importance of prayer to that of commerce. There is no way to appease a fundamentalist. They are beyond the synthesis here outlined. Only to the extent that they will be converted to softer religions or some mixture of secularism with soft religion can they become good citizens of the new world. Hence policy changes should be made but only on the basis of their inherent merit and not with the expectation that they are a kind of magic offering that will satisfy an angry opposition. Thus, moving American bases from Saudi Arabia to Qatar may have been a wise move but not because it will satisfy the followers of bin Laden. To deal with such true believers, above and beyond holding them at bay in the old-fashioned way, one must fill the moral and transcendental vacuum in which they thrive and address their concerns of what is right and wrong for the whole person, not just some fragments of this or that policy.

Chapter Four

Moral Dialogues

Beyond a general trend to develop a global normative synthesis of a set of core values, a process has developed that enables people of different nations, both from the East and the West, to come to shared moral understandings on specific issues. These issues range from values that drive the movement to ban land mines, to the quest to curb the warming of the Earth, the condemnation of child pornography, and the opposition to invading sovereign countries. These shared understandings, in turn, serve to feed a worldwide public opinion. This does not mean that everyone is informed or involved, let alone in agreement with one another. Even in developed and democratic nations what is called the attentive public—those who follow public affairs and form judgments about public policies—does not amount to more than a fraction of the population, and consensus is never complete. Still, the overwhelming majority of the attentive public can lean in one direction or another and have an effect on the course of public affairs. What follows are a few lines about the processes involved, which I refer to as moral dialogues.

Moral dialogues occur when a group of people engage in a process of sorting out the values that should guide their lives. The values involved are not necessarily such personal values as veracity, modesty, and honesty, but values that affect what public policies people favor, either in their own country or in others. These matters include affirmative action, the treatment of asylum seekers, the recognition of gay marriages, whether the death penalty should be imposed, and much more.

Moral dialogues are often messy; they meander and have no clear beginnings or endings. They are passionate and often contentious. Nevertheless, over time they often lead to new shared understandings, which in turn deeply affect not merely what people believe but also their actions, not only what people consider virtuous but also the habits of their heart. Among the most telling examples are the development of a moral commitment to the environment following moral dialogues initiated by the publication of Rachel Carson's book *Silent Spring;* the change in the ways people viewed relations between men and women following moral dialogues initiated by the publication of Betty Friedan's *The Feminist Mystique;* the changes in race relations that followed moral dialogues initiated by the civil rights movement in the 1960s; and the nearly self-enforcing ban on smoking in public in the United States after prolonged moral dialogues about the ill effects of smoking on nonsmokers.

It is easy to demonstrate that such dialogues take place constantly—and often productively—in well-formed national societies, which most democracies are, and that frequently they result (albeit sometimes only after prolonged dialogues) in a new normative direction for these societies. But can such moral dialogues take place transnationally, and, if so, to what effect? It is these dialogues that are most relevant to both the general development of the global normative synthesis and to the formulation of specific shared moral understandings that can undergird specific public policies. Granted, transnational moral dialogues are much more limited than their intranational counterparts in scope, intensity, conclusion, and result. Nevertheless, they are beginning to provide a wider shared moral understanding, political culture, and legitimacy for transnational institutions than existed until recently. For example, transnational dialogues have concluded that "we" ought to respect women's rights, promote democracy, and prevent superpowers from acting without "our" consent.

True, such dialogues are affected by numerous nonnormative considerations, often dressed up as normative claims. Nevertheless, these dialogues do affect what people of different nationalities consider to be morally appropriate. Thus, one reason most countries try to avoid being perceived as environmentally irresponsible is that they do not wish to be seen as acting illegitimately in the eyes of other nations.[1] Moreover, transnational moral dialogues occur on three levels: Should the people of one culture "judge" those of others? If yes, which values should guide such judgments? And, what means should be employed, beyond speech and symbolic gestures, to implement these values? (For instance, there is much stronger transnational agreement that terror should be curbed than there is about which means are best used to do so.)

Of all the global dialogues, particularly significant for the issues at hand are those that concern the developing new global architectures. Currently, the most important dialogue along these lines focuses on the key question: Under which conditions it is legitimate—that is, in line with shared values, mores, and laws—for one nation (or a group of nations) to employ force in order to interfere in the internal affairs of other nations? Few observers still accept the principle that what happens in a nation is of no matter to others; that nation-states are sovereign in their own turf; that the principle of *self*-determination should be upheld; and that no other nation has a right to apply force to intervene. The growing recognition of basic human rights has led many to believe that other nations, the United Nations, and, in a sense, the world community have not merely a right but also a duty to encourage, if need be, pressure, and, if all else fails, use force to protect these rights.[2]

There is growing worldwide moral support for intervention for humanitarian purposes. Various powerful nations, and some that are not particularly powerful, have been roundly chided for not having intervened to stop the genocide in Rwanda in which some 800,000 people were killed and many others maimed. This has also been true of genocide in the Congo and elsewhere.[3] There is a growing transnational normative brief for a court that would try individuals who commit the most serious violations of international humanitarian law such as genocide; specifically, for the International Criminal Court.

In addition, there is a surprisingly strong shared opposition to unilateral action. Many in both the East and the West prefer action by groups of nations ("coalitions") in which all the members are consulted and each has a veto power (as occurs in NATO). Further, many support action that has been endorsed by the United Nations and is in line with international law. The motivation that leads many heads of states and citizens alike to favor such positions often may have little to do with moral considerations. Rather, their motivation may reflect the desire of weak powers to curb the more powerful ones, especially the superpower; or the desire of nations that were once major players on the world stage, such as France and Russia, to regain influence on the global scene or to win an election at home (as Chancellor Gerhard Schroeder did in Germany in 2002 and as Roh Moo Hyun did in South Korea in 2003). Nevertheless, the fact that those opposed to unilateral activity can find huge audiences that are receptive to claims that the United Nations should be respected (despite its numerous and serious limitations), that multilateralism is preferable to unilateralism, and that compliance with international laws is important (despite their vagueness and fungibility) shows the direction in which shared moral understandings are evolving.

To argue that there are evolving transnational shared moral understandings that in turn affect what the public is willing to accept as legitimate acts and institutions is not to suggest that global public opinion is all-powerful or even that it is highly effective. Military force still plays a key role and can be applied in defiance of worldviews. Economic factors also play a key role, as evidenced when national governments change direction after they are promised large amount of loans, grants, foreign aid, tariffs, concessions, and the like. Still, public opinion is one significant factor that affects how much normative power a nation-state commands and which acts and institutions are considered legitimate. Flying in the face of this opinion has both short- and long-term costs. Moreover, if the developments of global institutions explored in Part II follow their current course, the effect of world public opinion on the future direction of global public affairs will grow further in importance.

Followers of what might be called the Madison Avenue school believe that public opinion can be manipulated through a series of clever ads, Voice of America broadcasts, and colorful brochures.[4] Advocates of this view for instance "believe that blitzing Arab and Muslim countries with Britney Spears videos and Arabic-language sitcoms will earn Washington millions of new Muslim sympathizers."[5] Ads can be used to change people's attitudes from favoring one brand of consumer goods to another, say from favoring Pepsi to Coke, especially when the difference between them is minimal and many millions of dollars are spent on such campaigns. But when it comes to moral issues, many factors drive public opinion, including religious upbringing, education, communal pressures, and independent media sources. True, public opinion sometimes can be misled and misdirected. However, a superpower, or for that matter any power that proceeds on the assumption that it can shape public opinion by Madison Avenue devices, often will find to its chagrin that people's views have an independent force of their own. Hence the importance of the evolving global synthesis not merely for general normative purposes but also as a key element in developing what is considered a legitimate new global architecture.

Western policy makers should disregard reports such as that issued in 2003 by the United States Advisory Group on Public Diplomacy for the Arab and Muslim World, which holds that: "The United States must drastically increase and overhaul its public relations efforts to salvage its plummeting image among Muslims and Arabs abroad." It reported that the Bush administration had made some efforts to improve public relations abroad, including "a series of television commercials showing that Muslims in the United States lead lives of dignity and equal rights." But, tellingly, "the advertisements were suspended after several Arab countries refused to show them." Edward P. Djerejian, the head of the advisory group, said he was struck during a recent visit to Cairo when he saw a panel discussion on Al Arabiya television in which "Americanization" was a code word for corruption of Islam—a keen observation. But what lesson did he draw from this? The problem, he told a reporter: "Woody Allen said 90 percent of life is just showing up. In the Arab world, the United States just doesn't show up." Accordingly, the major recommendations of the group, "besides creating a new White House director of public diplomacy, were to build libraries and information centers in the Muslim world, translate more Western books into Arabic, increase scholarships and visiting fellowships, upgrade the American Internet presence, and train more Arabists, Arab speakers and public relations specialists."[6] That is, to make Muslims more aware of a message that offends many of them. A group of moderate Muslims told the same advisory group panel in Indonesia, a message that the panel largely ignored, that "*the basic problem is policy, not public relations.*"[7]

The lesson is that unless the West approaches the world in ways that show that it will respect both Western and Eastern values, both secular and soft religious positions, both liberty and community, and that this synthesized approach will be reflected in special policies, public relations will do very little good and will, quite likely, backfire.

CHAPTER FIVE

IMPLICATIONS FOR AMERICAN (AND WESTERN) FOREIGN POLICY

STRONG REALISTS (NEO-REALISTS INCLUDED)[1] BELITTLE THE USE OF normative power in international relations if they do not dismiss it altogether, focusing instead on the use of economic power—such as trade privileges and sanctions—and military threats and applications. Strong idealists accord values, and thus, persuasion and supreme power.[2] As I see it, normative principles are best treated as one significant factor among a handful of others especially important in determining what is considered legitimate.

I turn next to examining the implications of the global normative synthesis for relevant foreign policies. The implications are far from earthshaking and hardly novel, but they grow in importance and acquire additional meanings in the context of the evolving global synthesis. I cannot stress enough that my intention is to list the implications of communitarian thinking for foreign policy and not to present a set of prescriptive "dos" and "don'ts." Each specific foreign policy decision is and ought to be influenced by numerous complex considerations: No one principle can determine whether this or that line of action should be followed. To give but one example from the days when I served in the Carter White House; Carter strongly supported human rights. He was, however, regularly criticized for not following this principle "consistently," by which critics typically meant that he did not allow human rights to trump all other considerations, although they hardly put it in those terms. The facts of life are that as long as the United States was (as it still is) dependent on Saudi and Nigerian oil,

Carter's administration could not simply overlook the national interests in-volved in order to advance human rights. It does not follow, though, that articu-lating the normative principles that have foreign policy implications is a useless exercise. These principles add one significant consideration to the mix. They in-form us in which direction we should move and they inspire us to work to make it more feasible for that movement to occur. Although I discuss these principles one at a time, they obviously all come into play simultaneously.

IMPLICATIONS OF THE
SERVICE LEARNING APPROACH

I defined a transnational service learning approach as one that holds that the West has no reason to imply, whether in word or in deed, that with regard to po-litical and economic institutional designs and core values the East has little, if anything, to offer. On the contrary, the West ought to openly and readily ac-knowledge that there is much that the East, like the West, has to contribute. The West should recognize that the evolving global normative synthesis includes ele-ments from all parts of the world, although the original elements will be modi-fied significantly in the process. The more that a people and their elected officials embrace the shared formulations that arise out of the *global* synthesis, the farther we will move away from confrontational posturing toward a global community.

Reference is to rhetoric by officials; surely I do not suggest that we should deny academic professors or public intellectuals the right to write and say what they believe, even if some of them highly offend other cultures' sensibilities, as Salman Rushdie did in *Satanic Verses* and Samuel Huntington did in *The Clash of Civilizations*. But such voices should not be treated as if they are de facto spokesmen for the West if we adopt the service learning approach rather than one of arrogant Western triumphalism. The same holds for the consultants that the U.S. Agency for International Development is sending to countries from Russia to Afghanistan. Those countries should be spared the enthusiastic cheerleaders of capitalism who do not worry about the need to contain it. The West's own interest would be best served if it adopted the service learning ap-proach and forewent the language of superiority or confrontation in the fram-ing of speeches, declarations, and presentations by Western leaders, officials, and diplomats, as well as the messages of the Voice of America and the public affairs sections of embassies overseas.

Furthermore, the West might acknowledge that, just as societies in the East are woefully short of the institutions and values that the West cherishes, so is the West deficient in other departments in which the East is richly, indeed excessively, endowed. We can learn from one another.

FIRST: OPEN AND DETYRANNIZE

The global normative synthesis finds many nations short on one key element or another. Moreover, there is some pressure to move nations, and the relations among them, closer to the evolving shared moral understanding. The restrained approach, whose value I have already indicated, leads to the question of which elements of societal change involved in such a movement ought to be promoted first.

Initially, the collapse of the communist bloc led to Western triumphalism, well captured in the end-of-history thesis. It fed hyper-promises and arrogance, such as the futile promise that the West would democratize scores of countries, most recently Afghanistan and Iraq.[3] When democratization turned out to be much more difficult than promised,[4] Western politicians rushed to certify as democratic countries any nation that merely held elections, even if the freedom of the press was very limited, respect for the law was severely compromised, the power holders were corrupt and authoritarian, and other elements essential for democratic formation were missing.[5]

This propensity to define down democracy, and in the process cheapen it, intensified after 1989, but was far from unknown before. Western politicians have pronounced as "democratic" countries in which the military has effective veto power on all that the elected officials do (Turkey), in which the monarch dissolves the parliament at will (Jordan), and in which opposition parties have no effective chance of election (Venezuela). To paper over the democratic gaps, various euphemisms have been introduced, such as "guided democracy" (Indonesia), "managed democracy" (Russia), and "electoral democracy."[6] These are word games that allow one to maintain American triumphalism, but they have several ill effects: They generate a mixture of cynicism and contempt and, in some cases, feed into a desire to return to the old regimes. The same holds with vengeance for vacuous promises to "reconstruct" or develop the economies of Afghanistan, Somalia, Haiti, and Niger, among scores of other countries.

These faux democracies not only greatly devalue democracy's currency, but they also pervert Western foreign policy as governments fall prey to their own overblown rhetoric.[7] One hardly needs a more telling and troublesome example than President Bush's claim that a major reason why the United States invaded Iraq (a reason played up when other reasons turned out not to be credible) was to provide its people with democracy. Once Iraq was liberated, the United States established a government from handpicked people it believed would do its bidding. When some of the leaders the United States imported either did not follow its cues or were widely disrespected, the United States replaced them at will. An American administrator in effect acted as Iraq's president. When the most influential Iraqi spiritual leaders, supported by many others, called for general elections to established a legitimate democratic government, the United States demurred, insisting that power had to be turned over to an Iraqi government by July 1, 2004—and then used this tight deadline (which it is said was non-negotiable) to argue that there was not enough time to conduct democratic elections. Instead the United States favored some convoluted caucus system, the obvious purpose of which was to form a government that will not turn Iraq over to a Taliban-like government, to a group to which the bitter slogan, "one person, one vote, one time" might well have been applied.

The United States did not come out openly and state that Iraq was far from ready to form a truly democratic government. Hence, the United States would either have to conduct a long-term occupation and implement a very difficult and expensive conversion to democracy or let the Iraqis duke it out in any way or form they desired, just as long as they understood that the United States and its allies would accept any results—even some kind of moderate autocrat (like Putin), king (like in Jordan), or three-way division of the country—as long as that leader would respect basic human rights and ally him- or herself with the West in key matters such as suppressing terrorism and not seeking weapons of mass destruction.

In Afghanistan the United States declared a second victory early in 2004, when, following its previous miliary victory, a democratic constitution was adopted and hence presumably the country was well on its way to form a democratic form of government, another pin to be stuck on the End of History map on the wall in the State Department. Actually, the government of Hamid Karzai barely controlled the capital. It survived only because it was defended by Western miliary forces and supported by shiploads of Western funds. Karzai himself—handpicked and imported by the West—had to rely on around-the-clock protection from American bodyguards because he was unable to trust his own people. Most important, the rest of the nation basically continued to be governed—as it has been for centuries—by unelected tribal war lords.

As this book goes to the press these matters are still being sorted out. One thing, however, is clear: The claim that an outside power can democratize nations on the run, with little preparation for a democratic form of protection, flies in the face of longstanding evidence from previous experience, reinforced daily in Iraq and Afghanistan.

If we grant that societal change is slow and onerous, and that there are great limitations on the extent to which one nation can promote significant changes in the polity and economy of another, then the normative question for Western foreign policy is which elements of autonomy should be promoted first? To reiterate: If we accept the severe limits of social engineering, especially by outsiders, the approach to deliberate social change should be highly restrained; that is, it should recognize that even given large amounts of resources and prolonged commitments, there are severe limits on what foreign policy can accomplish in this area. Given that a gradualist approach cannot be avoided, which elements ought to lead and which ought to follow?

This issue is faced often by those who argue that economic development should precede political development and that freer markets should precede the introduction of democracy and greater respect for rights.[8] Others have suggested that the institutionalization of rights should take precedence over democracy.[9] I hold that when facing traditional, authoritarian societies—such as Iran, Saudi Arabia, Sudan, Libya, Cambodia, Laos, and Burma—it would be best if the West initially focused on opening and detyrannizing these societies as well as the remaining communist, closed societies, North Korea and Cuba.

Opening societies entails promoting—in negotiations, in give-and-take, in public opinion campaigns, diplomatic pressures, as a condition for admission to various international bodies—free travel to and from the countries, a free flow of goods and services, and a free flow of cultural materials, including access to the world wide web. Societies that already have opened up to varying degrees should be encouraged, pressured, and receive incentives to open up further—for instance, by pressuring or creating incentives for their governments to remove limits of the kind that Singapore and China have imposed on access to the Internet. Opening is essential for the development of the three elements of autonomy (rights, democracy, and freer markets); and promoting autonomy in societies in which it is lacking is essential for the movement toward a good society.

Opening societies is a much more restrained and achievable, and in this sense credible, goal than democratizing or introducing a full array of human rights (although opening entails the introduction of some of these values). Promoting democratization becomes more achievable after the society has been open for a considerable period of time, sometimes a decade or longer. I am not against fully democratizing and liberalizing Sudan or Libya from the first day they open up. I am just suggesting that overreaching will backfire and that laying the foundations first—regrettably, slowly—is unavoidable in many countries with little historical, cultural, or sociological preparation.[10] As Jessica Mathews put it, a "crusade on behalf of democracy is arrogant, blind to local realities, dangerous, and ignorant of history."[11] When the legal and cultural foundations are absent, premature democratization and the rush to create a free market exacts numerous social and economic costs that are as a rule much higher than they would be if change proceeded more gradually.[12] Moreover, both democracy and free markets lose credibility when their aggressive promotion results in a kind of robber baron society, such as what emerged in Russia after 1989 (and Russia was significantly better prepared for the massive societal changes involved than many other countries).

Once a society begins to open up there is room for the promotion of all three elements of autonomy, as the experience with Russia suggests. Whether one element should be promoted at this advanced stage more vigorously than the others and whether there is one optimal sequence for all societies are questions that have long been studied but over which little agreement exists.[13] A self-restraint foreign policy best focuses first on promoting whatever element that a given society is leaning toward building up (say, economic liberties in China) instead of insisting that the society has to make more or less equal progress on all three fronts at once (e.g., boycotting trade with China—undermining both engagement and opening up—because of a lack of sufficient progress in human rights, as some advocate). The approach outlined here is further supported by the observation that often progress on one front gradually leads to progress on other fronts (e.g., China's respect for rights and democratic development are lagging and, indeed, it occasionally suffers a setback, but still it is progressing significantly beyond what it was when it first began scaling back command and control of the economy).[14]

Such promotion, however, should be limited to nonviolent means (from student exchanges to increased trade). None of the preceding argument justifies the use of military might for the advancement across international lines of what might be called Lockean goals—human rights (beyond some very elementary ones such as the right to live) or the installation of representative governments. The notion that what happens in someone else's country is nobody else's business has limited and failing legitimacy in an age of diminished national sovereignty. However, unless massive bloodshed is involved, armed interventions—of the kind the United Nations authorized in Haiti—are not justified. The notion that God has chosen the United States to impose democracy on those who do not know its name, as some extreme neo-conservatives argue, as a sort of renewed "white man's burden," is without moral and empirical foundations. No earthly power is capable of changing the world to such an extent. To claim otherwise invites disappointment, breeds cynicism, wastes resources, and generates a political backlash on the home front.[15]

The 1994 U.S.-led intervention in Haiti to restore exiled President Jean-Bertrand Aristide to power received the blessing of the UN Security Council on the grounds that the military regime was in breach of Security Council resolutions. The Security Council also expressed its concern that the military regime was violating civil liberties and exacerbating the plight of Haitian refugees. Deplorable, yes; worthy of economic sanctions, maybe. But the situation did not rise anywhere near the level of genocide or ethnic cleansing that justifies military intervention. Scores of nations engage in civil rights violations similar to, or worse than, those with which Haiti was charged. The sheer number of violations makes it nearly impossible for armed enforcement of the protection of human rights. Moreover, in many cases, including those of Saudi Arabia, Egypt, Pakistan, Jordan, the Ivory Coast, and many others in Latin and Central America, the offending regimes are propped up by the West.[16] The West cooperates with governments in Pakistan, Turkey, and Chile in which the militaries veto many decisions made by the parliament or prevent such decisions from being reached in the first place. And the West supports such military governments by providing financial and technical resources and training to police and the military, which severely limits democratic developments in these nations. Thus Arab authoritarian regimes are well in place, and despite some powerful speeches by President Bush, the United States has hardly moved to ally itself with democracy-seeking opposition groups in these countries. Instead, the United States continues to find it necessary to thank governments of countries such as Algeria and Tunisia for their help in the war against terrorism and Egypt's autocratic government continues to receive millions of dollars in financial and miliary aid, while not a penny is allotted to reformers. Despite occasional oblique critical comments of the Saudi regime, its autocratic rulers are handled with kid gloves rather than undermined by the United States.[17] In short, claiming that one nation's foreign policy is to protect rights and export democracy at the point of a gun is both hypocritical and impractical. It follows that *human rights and democratization should be vigorously promoted, but by the use of nonlethal means—and we must recognize that the process will be slow.*[18]

As previously suggested, the use of force is justified to save a large number of lives that would otherwise be lost to violence—but not merely to make people's lives better. A large number of people die from starvation, AIDS, and other nonviolent causes—no marshaling of troops or invasion will cure these malaises. They certainly deserve our attention, but the treatment ought to be nonviolent; and we must admit that these problems are much more tenacious than overcoming ethnic conflicts and civil wars, as difficult as these are to curb.

Using the promise to democratize as a reason for invading a country is a particularly poor argument, given that the record shows that democratization rarely follows. A study conducted by the Carnegie Endowment for International Peace found that out of the eighteen forced regime changes to which American ground troops were committed, only five resulted in sustained democratic rule.[19] These countries include Germany, Japan, and Italy, in which conditions prevailed that are lacking elsewhere, including a high level of education, a high income per capita, a sizable middle class, and national unity, among other prerequisites for democratization.[20] Two other countries listed as democratized—Panama and Grenada—have yet to earn this title. The difficulties that the United States and its allies have experienced in democratizing Afghanistan and Iraq are but the most recent examples in a long list of failures.[21] The notion that if the United States just provided a Marshall Plan to umpteen countries, they would all become democratic (and/or that their economies would be "reconstructed"), repeated like a mantra,[22] has little sociological validity.

If and when troops are sent into a country for a good cause—stopping a genocide, for instance, in Congo, Burundi, Kosovo, or Bosnia and Herzegovina—the most effective foreign policy following pacification still is not the promotion of democracy, but detyrannization, which encompasses removing the secret police, death squads, hanging judges, and gulags, and hauling the leaders before criminal courts. I am using this awkward term because it serves to highlight the world of difference between de-Nazification or de-Baathification and trying to install a competitive party system, a free press, independent judges, noncorrupt civil servants, respect for law, and other delicate but essential elements of democracy. To reiterate, I am not arguing that it is undesirable to achieve much more than detyrannization, but merely that, in many countries, all that can be achieved in the short order is opening up and detyrannizing, and that rushed drives to establish democracies lead to faux ones.

The West should draw here on Eastern spiritual concepts. The Buddhist concept of the Eightfold Path provides people with a vision, hope, and steps to get to the golden end state, but no illusion that one can rush there. The Hindu concept of reincarnation, of suffering in this life but returning in the next one at a higher state, provides comfort from the harshness of life in this world. The West would benefit if it would apply such a concept to the process for democratization and, more generally, to autonomy building. Nations could state that they had completed this or that step and are making progress on the next one, rather than claim to have democratized when they merely covered some of the distance required for them to become a genuine, free society.

In this way, opening up and detyrannizing are stages 1 and 2 in an eightfold path to democratization. Introducing basic laws and respect for those laws might be stage 3, and so on. Introducing fully competitive political parties might be placed late in the sequence; Japan and Mexico are still struggling with this requirement.

A seemingly unrelated point is very much at issue here: The costs of a new global architecture. Many have questioned whether the United States is willing to shoulder the costs of running the empire it has formed.[23] These costs, however, are not set in stone; they greatly depend on what ordering the world entails. Enhancing safety, removing tyrants, and opening a country incurs substantial costs, but they pale in comparison to what democratization and development or "reconstruction" require. American taxpayers and those of other Western nations that share in absorbing these costs are indeed very unlikely to be willing to shell out scores of billions year in and year out, especially once they become more aware of how unlikely it is that these outlays will deliver the desired results. Critics of U.S. foreign policy who have long predicted that the nation's demise will result from its being overstretched, such as Paul Kennedy[24] and more recently Chalmers Johnson,[25] may turn out to be right, not because the United States will implode or become vulnerable (as they have predicted), but because it may once again retreat from the world like a tourist who finds that overseas accommodations are too expensive.[26]

To sum up, keeping down the costs of ordering the world is a prerequisite for the taxpayers of a democracy to be willing to continue to foot the bill. I re-iterate that I am not arguing that we should not democratize and develop the world because it costs too much. Rather, I contend that because in most places democracies cannot be advanced by outside powers in the first place, vain at-tempts to do so would alienate the citizens who must pay for the effort and squander the resources needed to maintain global order and those goals that can be achieved, especially opening and detyrannization.

This issue is now being sorted out in Afghanistan and Iraq. The costs, in casualties and resources, are rapidly leading to a level that the American elec-torate is unwilling to bear. There is good reason to doubt that Americans would be willing to foot the bill if the United States chose to play a similar role in one more country, say Iran, not to mention others. (Note that the costs of maintaining American forces in other parts of the world are also far from trivial and they are rising). The United State may well be forced to declare victory and retreat, all because of an excessively ambitious formulation of its goals. If this occurs, the United States will lose its credibility as a superpower that can order the world.

The discussion so far has focused on implications of the evolving global normative synthesis for the West. What are the implications of the same syn-thesis for Eastern foreign policies, especially as they seek to promote more so-cial order—and of the kind they favor—in the West? In the past, coercion was the earmark of such policies—for instance, when members of the Saudi Ara-bian royal family and the Iranian government financed terrorism in Europe, the United States, and Israel to promote their totalitarian, religious vision of social order. And these policies have been expansionist to boot. This last point deserves emphasis because the fact that Islam is expansionist has not been suffi-ciently recognized. Various Muslim countries have helped, with funds and fighters, insurgent Muslim forces in Lebanon, Saddam's Iraq and post-Saddam

Iraq, Kyrgyzstan, Kashmir, East Timor, Uzbekistan, Tajikistan, the Xinjiang province in China, and Chechnya, among others. Such policies are completely incompatible with the normative synthesis and they have been counterproductive for those who offer them. For Eastern countries to embrace the new shared normative principles, they must drop expansion through the use of force as an element of their foreign policy.

In contrast, there is no reason to oppose Eastern societies that seek to do what the United States does: Pay for student exchanges, send books, invite leaders, and arrange for broadcasts to promote their vision of the good society. One major exception does apply: All of these seemingly suitable tools of foreign policy can be rendered counterproductive if they are used to promote fanaticism and hatred, as did the Saudi financing of religious schools, *madrasas*, in Pakistan, Afghanistan, and Indonesia.[27] To be good citizens of a society and a world in which there is a carefully crafted balance between autonomy and social order requires people to be tolerant of differences and to think critically rather than to adhere rigidly to dictates based on an age-old text.

A Pro-Engagement Tilt

Those who favor isolating authoritarian regimes (North Korea, Cuba, etc.) and those who favor engaging them often have similar goals—to make more room for autonomy and all that it entails—although typically other policy goals are involved as well, such as efforts to stem the proliferation of weapons of mass destruction or open markets to foreign corporations. (The term "engagement" is used to refer to fostering travel, trade, cultural exchanges, visits from leaders, and diplomatic relations, while "isolation" indicates the curtailing of all of these.) Although neither camp sets out to advance the normative synthesis that is laid out here, increasing autonomy in authoritarian societies would move them in that direction.

Both camps argue for the policy approach they favor in the name of normative principles. For instance, those who favor engagement argue that it is more conducive to peace; those who favor isolation claim that it generates the needed pressure to advance human rights. The debate would benefit from a greater reliance on empirical evidence, which strongly suggests that under most conditions, engagement is much more effective than isolation. Richard N. Haass has pointed out that sanctions are not only costly and counterproductive, but they can be circumvented by elites in the target country and hence rendered uneffective.[28] Although there are significant differences among the various societies involved, it is almost enough to list the regimes that have been isolated and those that have been engaged (or to compare the periods in which they were isolated versus engaged) to support the point.[29]

The United States isolated Castro's Cuba for four decades, banning trade with and travel to and from the island, as well as exerting pressure on other societies to follow the same course. However, containment of Cuba, for more than a generation, failed to grant its people more rights, introduce democratic reforms, and open its markets. Saddam's Iraq and North Korea are two other authoritarian regimes that were isolated; still they persisted for decades. China was first isolated and yielded little, but following Nixon's "opening" in 1972, it gradually changed, making much more room for economic, as well as some political, autonomy.[30] The same holds true for North Vietnam. The fifteen Soviet republics changed even more, including on the political front, largely after they were engaged rather than isolated.

The dramatic and very important change in Libya that occurred in 2004 may at first seem an exception. In 2004, Libya dropped its plans to develop WMD, promised to dismantle its facilities, and invited the West to participate in the process. Indeed one of the first steps was for the United States to remove large amounts of equipment from the country.[31]

There is a world of difference between maintaining nuclear facilities and allowing their inspection and disassembling them. In the first case, cheating can occur and inspectors can be kicked out following a change in policy or regime. In contrast, once dismantled, it takes years and billions of dollars to rebuild weapons and such moves are hard to conceal. I shall refer to this difference as that between arms control and deproliferation. By following the second track—deproliferation—Qaddafi set a model for other nations to follow, for which he should be award the Nobel Peace Prize (perhaps to be issued with a demerit badge for his continued disregard for human rights). Qaddafi has done much more for global safety than many others who have received the prize in the past. (Those who will say that his motives were impure should consider the motives of others who have received the prize, including Yasser Arafat.) But how did he get there? A detailed examination, which I cannot reproduce here, shows that the turning point came when the United States attacked Iraq. The sanctions were long in place and did take their toll, but they did not get him to turn over the keys to his program of building weapons. Whether engagement would have brought this day earlier is doubtful, but sanctions per se clearly did not do the trick.

U.S. Senator Jesse Helms, a strong supporter of the isolationist tactic, lists Switzerland, Nigeria, the former Soviet Union, Poland, and Guatemala among the countries that have modified their behavior in response to actual or threatened U.S. sanctions.[32] However, a detailed examination of these situations will show that in most cases the isolationist measures, and their effects, were limited (e.g., getting Switzerland to change its banking laws), while engagement had much more encompassing effects. Moreover, engagement does not mean that no sanctions can be imposed. An engagement policy can tolerate a few sanctions, limited in scope and in time span, like those exacted by the World Trade Organization when trade agreements are violated.

The reasons why engagement is often so much more effective, and why it neither entails a violation of principles (such as commitments to human rights) nor endangers security (as nations learn to screen much better to whom we grant entry), need not be explored here. The only point relevant to the current analysis is that engagement has, and we must expect it will continue to, encouraged authoritarian societies to introduce more autonomy and thus move them toward the global synthesis. The proper measure of progress, though, is not whether they become facsimiles or even close copies of the American regime, but whether they find their own balanced combination of autonomy and social order, based to a significant extent on persuasion.

SUPPORT MODERATE RELIGIOUS GROUPS AND VIRTUES, NOT MERELY SECULAR, CIVIL ONES

Many westerners, Americans, and French citizens in particular, hold that the separation of church and state is an essential feature of democracy and many doubt that a free society can thrive if these two entities are not kept apart. Such a separation, however, does not exist in most countries that are commonly considered solid democracies; indeed, many democracies flourish despite various forms of established churches, including Britain and the Scandinavian countries. U.S. foreign policy (with few notable exceptions) has supported the development of civil society in former communist countries and other nations by implicitly equating civil society with a secular society. (A revealing detail: A World Bank official pointed out that in the two-thousand-page history of the Bank, which covers its various endeavors and achievements, religion is mentioned only once—in regard to some meeting held in 1962. The reason: Many in the bank consider religion to be an obstacle to development and thus to be a negative influence.[33])

Therefore, although I already explored the nature of the moral and spiritual hunger that exists throughout the world, the question still remains: How can Western foreign policy address this need and combat the religious fundamentalism that gains adherents as it addresses the same hunger? One effective way to counter religious fundamentalism is for outside nations to encourage moderate Islamic groups and those of other religions, not merely secular groups. One example will stand for all of the others that could be given. In 2003, the United States came across as if it adamantly opposed attempts by Shia mullahs in Iraq to introduce a Taliban-like regime and instead favored a secular approach. Next to no thought was given to promoting soft Islam. As Anshuman A. Mondal asked: "Must they [Islamic societies] choose only between western secular-liberalism and an increasingly recalcitrant Islamic fundamentalism?"[34]

A major reason to favor promoting not only secular foundations of a civil society but also the soft religious ones is that it is easier for true believers to become more moderate than to give up the faith altogether.[35] In earlier periods, taking into account what might be called the convergence distance led by the West to support social democratic parties to compete with communists instead of supporting merely conservative parties such as the Christian Democratic Union in Germany and others in southern Europe and Latin America.

In the evolving global normative synthesis, the West should recognize that although all voluntary associations (or producers of social capital) are created equal from a Tocquevillian perspective, this is not the case from the viewpoint of the good society. Associations that promote rights and liberty have their place and are especially important in the many nations in which these rights are scarce and in which autonomy is lacking. However, to advance the synthesis, those associations centered around virtues and especially those that favor the soft, communitarian social order must be equally nurtured.

Closely related is the need to reframe many issues that have been characterized in the past as rights issues and recognize that they also promote virtues. For example, a transnational banning of child pornography is not only or even mostly a children's rights issue (especially when dealing with virtual child porn). Rather, it is a matter that concerns the well-being of children, whose protection and nurturing is an important common good. The same holds for protection of the environment; it is intended to ensure not the rights of this or that group, but of the community as a whole, including generations yet to be born. Trying to force every normative issue into the procrustean bed of what Mary Ann Glendon called "rights talk"[36] or considering the approach illegitimate is incompatible with promoting synthesis; recognizing that there is also a set of shared substantive values, favors it.

I now turn to illustrate the implications of promoting a soft Islam in concrete institutional and policy terms. I used soft Islam as an example. The same applies to other belief systems. School systems provide an especially suitable place to start to examine the third way between theocracy and secular civil society. Education in several Islamic countries is carried out in *madrasas*. These are often places where young people are drilled in Wahhabi Islam and anti-Western values, and inundated with rigid interpretations of religious texts, learning by rote, with next to no exposure to science and liberal arts. *Madrasas* are common in theocracies such as the Taliban's Afghanistan, Iran, Saudi Arabia, and northern Pakistan. If the dominant Shi'ites in Iraq have their way, such schools are likely to be introduced in that country. In place of these schools, Senator Joseph R. Biden, Jr. has suggested that the United States should instead promote secular, American public school-like institutions.[37]

A third alternative is to provide two tracks of education within public schools. One track is basically secular (although children do learn about religion), and the other dedicates a significant proportion of the teaching, say 20 percent, to religious subjects. In Malaysia, where there is a large but relatively moderate Muslim population, the government provides both secular and religious education; Muslim children may attend secular school in the morning and religious classes in the afternoon.[38]

To ensure that the religious part of public schooling is used for what are called here soft religious teachings rather than for fundamentalist indoctrination, the teachers—although as a rule from a given religious group, say Shi'ites in southern Iraq—need to be qualified and selected by the school, not by religious groups, and teaching material must be approved by the department or ministry of education.

This is a sound educational system for several reasons. It prevents fundamentalist education; it ensures that all children will get the rudimentary knowledge of modern culture; it allows those parents who seek religious schooling to secure a significant amount of such instruction for their children with the costs covered by the state; and it ensures that children of different backgrounds, both secular and religious, will mix, which is prevented when some children go to segregated five-day-a-week religious schools. Above all, such a two-track system allows a government to promote moderate religions without preventing anyone who wishes it from procuring a secular education. Such a solution, thus, is a prime example of how a government can promote religion, ensure that it will not be fundamentalist, and yet still provide access to a secular education to those who desire it.

Another way in which the institutionalization of a civil society with religious elements can proceed is through the provision of social services. In several parts of the Islamic world—in southern Iraq, for instance—various religious bodies provide social services. Conversely, in France, social services, including health care, welfare, and child care, are provided largely by secular arms of the government. A third way would be to continue to draw on whatever governmental and secular voluntary social services are available and expand them, but also to draw on religious ones, as it is done in the United States.

Despite the strong American commitment to disestablishment, the U.S. government relies to a significant extent on voluntary religious groups to provide many social services.[39] The government does this either by contracting with various religious groups for the provision of services or by allowing religious institutions, such as Catholic or Jewish hospitals, to receive Medicare and Medicaid payments via individuals who choose to be served by the hospitals. For instance, 75 percent of the funding for the Jewish Board of Family and Children Services comes from government sources;[40] Catholic Charities' programs receive about 66 percent of their funding from government grants and contracts;[41] and Lutheran Services in America gains more than 33 percent of its annual budget from government funds.[42] Moreover, the United States has expanded its reliance on faith-based institutions following the charitable choice provisions of the 1996 welfare reform law, and since the inauguration of the 2001 Bush administration. The same approach could be applied to Afghanistan, Iraq, and other countries, which would then rely on what amounts to two-track social services, those provided by government agencies and those provided by faith-based institutions. Here too the government would impose some limitations on the ways in which religious groups can use public funds. Specifically, it would require that the funds be used fully for social services and not for political action or authoritarian indoctrination.

Finally, a government keen on promoting a two-track civil society might pay the salaries of the Muslim clergy and pay for the maintenance of mosques. To Americans this may seem highly controversial and a gross violation of the separation of church and state, but paying religious functionaries is a common practice in many democracies—in Catholic countries such as Spain and Italy, in Scandinavia, and in Germany. (In some countries this is done indirectly, by the government collecting a special church tax from those who attend church, but the net effect is that the clergy are publicly supported and not dependent on passing the plate.) Once the government pays for clergy, it is free to determine who qualifies as such. A group of moderate clergy may advise the government on who is qualified to serve in the public-religious sector. Fundamentalist preachers surely will not be banned from practicing, but they will not do so on public dollars.

We may ask, "But what about Christians and other religious groups?" The same arrangements would apply to them. These religious communities could provide social services, their clergy could be compensated, and two-track education could be provided. In short, it is high time that foreign policy outgrows

sociologically invalid and morally misguided Enlightenment notions and real-
izes that religion is not a relic of previous historical periods nor an obstacle to
rationality and progress, but rather, it is a key element of a good society. Religion can be fully compatible with a free society as long as its soft versions are
advanced—as holds true for secular belief systems.

MULTILATERALISM OR COMMUNITY BUILDING?

From a communitarian viewpoint, multilateralism is a procedure that, like
other processes, can help legitimate the outcome of the issues that are being
processed, but the resolutions must be assessed substantively, in this case
against the normative principles that evolve out of the global synthesis.[43]
This observation requires some elaboration. Many liberals in the United
States—and critics of the United States overseas—have been extolling multilateralism for years. The term is used in a variety of ways,[44] but it has become
a code word for respect for the United Nations (and other international bodies), international law and mores, and working with one's allies. A major argument in favor of multilateralism (out of many) that is particularly germane
for the issue at hand runs as follows: If a nation acts in a participatory way
then it helps to build institutions that in the longer run—as no superpower
lasts forever—benefit all, including the nation that currently could act on its
own. Few if any demand or expect that the United States—or for that matter
any other nation—will, under all circumstances, disregard a truly vital interest in order to please its allies or abide by UN rulings. However, in many situations, working in ways that strengthen institutions is strongly favored.
Joseph S. Nye, Jr. writes: "Multilateralism involves costs, but in the larger
picture, they are outweighed by the benefits. International rules bind the
United States and limit our freedom of action in the short term, but they also
serve our interest by binding others as well. Americans should use our power
now to shape institutions that will serve our long-term national interest in
promoting international order."[45] In contrast, many neo-conservatives see
submitting to multilateralism as an admission of weakness and as unduly
cumbersome.

Those who are committed to multilateralism (and other procedures) are
right—up to a point. To the extent that the procedures involved are considered legitimate, studies of a number of political situations show that people
will, as a rule, accept the outcome even if they otherwise would have ob-
jected.[46] However, what is far from obvious is that the institutions that are
now celebrated, especially the United Nations, have anything like the legiti-

macy that was attributed to them during the controversy over the 2003 U.S.-led invasion of Iraq.

Many confuse the United Nations as an ideal and the way it is currently composed and performs. The United Nations is a body in which Libya chairs the Commission on Human Rights. It is an institution which is free to pass scores of resolutions with the full realization that most of them will be ignored. (Eighty-eight UN Security Council resolutions were being violated as of February 2003, including resolutions condemning the Armenian occupation of Azerbaijan and calling for the cessation of nuclear weapons' development by India and Pakistan.)[47] For long periods the Soviet Union had a choke hold over the Security Council; it blocked numerous resolutions that most would now consider highly legitimate, including the membership applications of Australia, Ireland, Portugal, Spain, and Finland. Between 1946 and 1965, the USSR used its veto 106 times. (The next closest country was France, with 4 vetoes.) Although the United States did not use its veto at all between 1965 and 2003, the United States used its veto more than 70 times, greatly exceeding vetoes by the USSR/Russia, at fewer than 20 vetoes.[48] Because of such deadlocks, the United Nations was unable to act against the Soviet Union's 1965 invasion of Hungary and 1968 invasion of Czechoslovakia. Why, critics ask, should a free society submit its foreign policy to scrutiny by the likes of Syria, Iran, Malawi, Yemen, Libya, and Sudan, among others? Moreover, it is repeatedly stated that the UN General Assembly is basically a debating society and that it is unable to make its resolutions stick. Indeed, countries as different as India, Russia, Turkey, Sudan, and Israel have simply ignored them with impunity. NATO has its own procedural defects that are typical of multilateral institutions: It is a very cumbersome machine whose action requires consensus, which means that small members can hold up action for capricious or self-centered reasons.

Above all—to return to my main point—the outcome of any procedure must be assessed not just in terms of the legitimacy of the process but also in terms of the content of the outcomes. In Rwanda, the United Nations was unable to mobilize itself to act in a timely fashion to stop the genocide despite the fact that its own staff reported that a genocide was forthcoming months before it took place.[49] Few would consider this outcome acceptable in moral terms, although it was reached in line with UN procedures. The United Nations was slow to react to the massacre of the people of East Timor, which continued for months before the United Nations finally authorized action in 1999. To push the point, if tomorrow there were signs that another genocide were beginning in some part of the world and France or

Russia or China vetoed an intervention, would it therefore be morally wrong to intervene anyway?

The values that people bring to bear in making these assessments are those that emanate out of the global synthesis and the moral dialogues that help elaborate and extend it. Multilateralism is compatible with the evolving global normative syntheses, albeit only once the specific steps involved in multilateralism pass the moral test just indicated. It follows that under some conditions unilateral steps are justified, such as to stop a genocide when the United Nations is deadlocked. Under other conditions, multilateral decisions can be unjustified; for instance, when NATO decided to delay intervening in the ethnic cleansing in Kosovo due to the narrow political calculations of this or that member state. Hence, both procedural and substantive considerations must be taken into account, although granted that if the substance of the decisions is the same, as a rule multilateralism is to be preferable because of its longer run, institution-building side effects.

In addition, a communitarian finds that multilateralism is not too restraining but it is an insufficient basis for community building. To proceed on this higher level of building a new global architecture entails acting in ways that build transnational bonds and a sense of shared fate as well as the creation of shared values. Bonds can be advanced by welcoming multiple citizenships and transnational citizenship,[50] student and leaders exchanges, and an enlarged Peace Corps, among other measures. Shared values can be advanced by moral dialogues.

NOT DESTINY, BUT RESPONSIBILITY

Several keen analysts of international relations, especially Max Boot, argue that it is America's "destiny" to police the world, to impose a Pax America, and to bring democracy to failed states and oppressed people.[51] Joshua Muravchik maintains that the United States has an imperative to lead the world.[52] Robert Wright's study of history leads him to conclude that "the case for a kind of manifest destiny is stronger than ever." The concept is a long way from the notion that America's empire was accidental or reluctant, as others have suggested.[53] To the extent that one takes "destiny" simply to mean that it is the job of the United States, the only superpower, to foster peace worldwide, it does not raise many hackles, although critics would prefer for this task to be the work of the United Nations and that it be promoted as much as possible by nonviolent means.

The term "destiny," however, has strong normative, even religious, overtones. As the dictionary informs us, it suggests that the United States has been ordained, by a power greater than that of any person or a combination thereof, to undertake a mission. The notion that the United States has been sent by God to do whatever it chooses to do is dangerous. It implies that the United States is not accountable to any worldly body; that it need not justify itself to any earthly public; that the United States takes its directions directly from the Almighty; and that it has been chosen, from all the people, to bring order to the world. Hence the storm of criticism when President Bush referred to America's war on terror as a "crusade" and when a top Pentagon official said that America's war against Islamic terrorists was like battling "Satan."[54] Not only is the term "destiny" best avoided, so too is all that it brings to mind.

There is, however, a kernel of moral content that can be salvaged from such a self-aggrandizing notion. The United States and all other powers, by the very fact that they are endowed with a great many economic assets and military might, have a moral responsibility to help others. The obligation is similar to that of a rich and powerful member of a community. It matters little whether such a person or country has made their fortune only on the up and up or whether they exploited others to achieve their riches. It doesn't even matter if all the poor are deserving or if some are self-indulgent. Those who can readily prevent children from starving, administer to the sick, and curb violence have—by practically all religious and secular bodies of ethics—a responsibility to serve. This responsibility is a reflection of the basic moral worth of all human beings, all of whom are God's children.

The concept of responsibility draws on strong normative roots. Hence, from this viewpoint, it may be considered no different from the concept of destiny. However, there is nothing in the concept of responsibility that gives those who live up to it a license to proceed in any way that they deem fit or that exempts them from accountability to their fellow human beings. To put it more bluntly, there is no sign that God has chosen the United States to do anything, but there are strong moral reasons to hold that all big powers have a responsibility to respect the basic moral worth of all human beings and all that this entails.

PART II

A NEW SAFETY ARCHITECTURE

CHAPTER SIX

THE WAR AGAINST TERRORISM AND SADDAM'S IRAQ: CONTRASTING DESIGNS

LIKE THE CLASH OF TWO DISHARMONIOUS MUSICAL THEMES, as normative global principles are gradually synthesizing to provide a shared core of moral understanding, global projections of power are marching to a different drummer. The resulting tension leads one to expect that either the ways in which power is exercised will become more legitimate or that those who wield it will confront ever tougher opposition until they finally yield. Those who will argue that the preceding statement is an all-too-optimistic view of human nature and political systems should note that all empires the world has known have collapsed, albeit after long periods of time and after they had caused much grief (and some good). Moreover, *history is accelerating*, as is public involvement in politics, as a direct result of democratization trends. Illegitimate structures that once could survive for centuries now find that their lifespan is measured in generations, if not decades. Such regimes include those in nations as different as Saudi Arabia, China, and the American semi-empire.

I use the term "semi-empire" to mark the difference between other empires, which occupied the territories they regulated, and the American empire, which avoids this particular form of entanglement (with some notable exceptions). Others have responded to the need to distinguish this empire from others by calling it neo-imperial,[1] a "benevolent hegemony,"[2] "virtual,"[3] or "lite."[4]

Many call it a "unipolar system," which does not quite capture the overbearing use of power involved in the new global order. Whether the American semi-empire will collapse under its own weight or be converted into a lasting new global architecture—one less hierarchical and more legitimate than any empire—is the question explored in the pages that follow.

The discussion thus turns to the second element required for establishing human primacy, from exploring shared formulations of the good to identifying the political institutions needed for us to guide our joint fate rather than be subject to forces that we do not understand nor control.[5]

Ironically, the cornerstone of the new global architecture was laid by bringing down a huge tower, indeed two. The construction of the American semi-empire was greatly accelerated on September 11, 2001, although many of its building blocks had been put into place much earlier. Many people who do not live in the United States fail to appreciate the profound effect that the September 11 terrorist attack had, and still has, on the American psyche, polity, and international posture.[6] Some have argued that, after all, the United States loses many more citizens each year to garden-variety crime than the 3,000 people killed by terrorists in the 2001 attack. (John Muller listed lightning, deer, and peanuts as more dangerous than terrorists, which led Walter Russell Mead to quip that Muller considered Bambi more dangerous than bin Laden.) A left-wing leader exclaimed that the attack was, after all, on the *World* Trade Center and on the military—the Pentagon—and not on the American people.

Such comments disregard the fact that the attack primarily killed civilians who were working peacefully at their desks. It showed for the first time since 1812 that the American homeland (as opposed to a peripheral military base such as Pearl Harbor) was very vulnerable; that the enemy was capable of carrying out a well-planned and meticulously executed attack on targets of great American symbolic importance. The fact that the fourth airplane was poised to crash into the White House or the Capitol further shocked the American people.

Between 1989 and 2001, the United States was deeply conflicted, as it had often been before, about its role in the world. It shifted between neo-isolationist and neo-interventionist orientations depending on whether it was concerned about oil, human suffering, or some other cause. The September 11 terrorist attack greatly diminished this ambivalence. The United States committed itself to promoting a world order by using the superior might, status, and resources that it commands as the only superpower. (As Michael Hirsh put it, "Today, Washington's main message to the world seems to be, 'Take dictation.'"[7]) It is this global projection of power that has led many to view the United States as an "American empire."[8]

The dramatic alteration in the U.S. posture toward the world is reflected by the way President George W. Bush conducted himself following the attack. He transformed overnight from someone who was unsure of his purpose, reluctant to act, and doubtful that he was suited to be president into a leader on a tear, surefooted, and disinclined to share power with others.[9] Since the attack, the U.S. government has acted as if it was always crystal clear that it has a profound national interest, legal right, and even moral duty to bring order to the world, from North Korea to Iran, from Afghanistan to Yemen, from the Philippines to Colombia, from the seven seas to the skies above.[10]

My analysis of the new world order that the United States is fostering, and how it might metamorphose in the face of unprecedented global opposition, proceeds by comparing two very different designs that the country has employed since September 11, 2001. They reflect two profoundly disparate ways in which the new global architecture (and the United States' role in it) may be constructed in the future, and hence they deserve special attention. I first examine the 2003 war in Iraq and then the post–September 11, 2001, American-led global antiterrorism coalition.

The discussion then turns toward the future of this coalition—what additional missions it might embrace, whether it could become both more legitimate and less hierarchal, and whether it could serve as the basis for lasting global authority. Thus, the discussion focuses on matters concerning basic safety, especially massive terrorism, weapons of mass destruction (WMD), and genocide, and then on the institutions that now cope with other transnational problems, including the environment, welfare, and the reallocation of wealth.

It matters little that we may wish that a new world could have been initiated under different circumstances. It was born out of terror and launched by a global use of force. There is no wiping the slate clean, going back to the drawing board, as if the world were a tabula rasa and there were no terrorists, no WMD, and no superpowers. The key question, therefore, is what new institutions (broadly understood to include mores, values, and international law and structures—what some people call "regimes")[11] are developing, and how these might be improved so that out of the application of imperial might the sweetness of a just and lasting global order may one day arise.

THE WAR AGAINST SADDAM'S IRAQ: A GLOBAL VIETNAMESQUE EFFECT

In preparing for the 2003 war against Iraq, the Bush administration initially planned to confront what the president called the "axis of evil" on its own.

When the proposed unilateral action against these three sovereign states—Iraq, Iran, and North Korea—encountered criticism overseas, including among close U.S. allies, and raised doubts within the United States (and even within the administration), Secretary of State Colin Powell succeeded in persuading the administration to seek the approval of the United Nations for its plans to use military force against Iraq. The result is well-known: The United States encountered strong objections from three of the five permanent members of the UN Security Council—France, Russia, and China. The invasion of Iraq was also fiercely opposed by numerous American allies and scores of other nations, and it generated unprecedented and coordinated worldwide demonstrations and collective outrage, which fed into and were fed by rising anti-Americanism and a growing opposition at home.

True, not every nation opposed U.S. plans; several governments, including Britain, Spain, and Poland, supported the United States (although they ignored their own national public opinion). And there were minorities in many other countries who favored the U.S. course of action.[12] But, when all was said and done, worldwide opposition was monumental.

In Europe and beyond, nations that had been key allies in the war on terrorism balked at the idea of aiding a U.S.-led invasion of Iraq, and they refused to provide even noncombatant military support. French president Jacques Chirac called the invasion "illegal."[13] German Chancellor Gerhard Schroeder equated the Bush administration's policy to saying "[w]e are going to do it, no matter what the world or our allies think."[14] The forty-five-nation Council of Europe condemned the war in Iraq as "illegal and contrary to the principles of international law."[15] The German press proclaimed that the Iraq war was "a capital crime in modern international law"[16] and accused President Bush of sparking a "worldwide race for weapons of mass destruction."[17] A poll conducted in March 2003 found that 69 percent of Germans, 75 percent of the French, and 87 percent of the Russians opposed an Iraq war.[18] The reaction in Russia was so harsh, in fact, that one poll found that a majority of the country actually wanted to see an Iraqi victory. The same poll also showed President Bush's unpopularity in Russia at 76 percent, compared to 17 percent for Saddam Hussein.[19] Similar views, though not nearly as extreme, were also expressed in Belgium and in Greece, where 95 percent of the public opposed the war.[20] Andrew Kohut, director of the Pew Center for Research, summarized a poll of European public opinion on the war by stating that "[t]he war has widened the rift between Americans and Western Europeans, further inflamed the Muslim world, softened support for the war on terrorism, and significantly weakened global public support for the pillars of the post–World War II era—the U.N. and North Atlantic Alliance."[21]

The United States lost favor in the eyes of many.[22] For instance, in Indonesia, where 60 percent of its citizens held a favorable opinion of the United States in 2002, a mere 15 percent felt this way in May 2003.[23] In Turkey, 30 percent had a favorable view of the United States in 2002, but that number fell to 15 percent in May 2003.[24]

In February 2003 a quarter of a million Australians took to the streets to protest against a war in Iraq—the largest protest in that country since the Vietnam War.[25] In late March 2003, just after the invasion of Iraq began, an editorial in the Swedish tabloid *Expressen* stated "Today We're All Iraqis."[26]

In response to Thomas L. Friedman's column concerning why much of the world is upset with America, a Chinese graduate student wrote:

> The question you posed about hating America is the burning question . . . because USA has been the beacon of hope [this] past half a century to the disenfranchised, the wounded, the refugees (yours truly among the zillions), the hopefuls of the world. . . . More important USA, until now, has been seen as the FAIR ARBITER OF THE WORLD—a fair judge, and despite its unsurpassed muscles, a fair and unfeared policeman. . . . Nearly all imperial powers in history have been just the opposite. . . . The world is saying USA has become a self-righteous, self-centered Master of the Universe. . . . The world does not want to see you morph into just another imperial power. We know that movie too well. We all walked out, remember . . . ?[27]

Prior to the commencement of the war, large segments of the American public also shared the distaste for unilateralism.[28] In February 2003, only 38 percent of Americans believed that the United States should push forward with war on Iraq without their allies (up from 28 percent a month earlier),[29] and 56 percent preferred waiting for a UN endorsement of the U.S.-led attacks.[30]

Global opposition to U.S. policy had some very real consequences. Anger with U.S. plans to go to war with Iraq led to the reelection of Chancellor Schroeder in Germany, as well as the election of Roh Moo Hyun, a previously unknown politician in South Korea, both of whom rushed to oppose U.S. policies, first with regard to Iraq and then with regard to North Korea. Public opposition to the war also prevented the United States from opening a second front through Turkey. It resulted in a drop in the purchase of American products overseas, and many shifted from holding dollars to hoarding euros. During the 1991 Gulf War, a number of other nations sent their troops and picked up about 80 percent of the war's cost.[31] This time around, the United States is stuck with most of the bill. As these lines are written it is not possible to assess the costs of the Iraqi occupation and "reconstruction." However, the military bill has amounted to at least $4 billion per month.[32] Paul Bremer, the U.S. administrator in Iraq, estimated in August 2003 that the total costs of the war and reconstruction are likely to exceed $100 billion.[33] The Center for Strategic and Budgetary Assessments estimates that the costs will reach nearly $600 billion over five years.[34] In September 2003 President Bush petitioned Congress for $87 billion towards rebuilding Iraq and Afghanistan,[35] adding to the previous appropriation of $79 billion. The United States has found these costs so burdensome that it has repeatedly applied for help from other countries. An "international donors conference" was held in October 2003,[36] though it yielded only a fraction of the funds for which the United States hoped. And, as American casualties have mounted, so have the requests for other people's troops. In a humiliating U-turn, after claiming that the United Nations "risked irrelevancy" in late 2002, by September 2003 the Bush administration was seeking a UN blessing for its administration of Iraq in order to gain more support from other nations, claiming that the United Nations carried out "vital and effective work every day."[37]

The greatest "cost" of the occupation of Iraq lies in the future. It concerns the credibility of the United States as a major power. It is commonly understood that the best way to lead is not to actually apply one's power, but rather to merely imply that it might be exercised. The ability to draw such leverage out of one's forces and resources—which allows one to advance policy goals without actually sacrificing lives and assets—in turn depends on one's credibility; that is, when a nation threatens or promises action, others must assume that it has the wherewithal to deliver.

In Iraq (as well as in Afghanistan), U.S. credibility as a global power is being tested. This may seem like a ridiculous statement given the ease with which the United States won the military rounds of these conflicts. However, in both countries, the United States is facing guerilla attacks. These are of the kind that drove Israel, after years of losses, out of South Lebanon, which in turn led to the second intifada, during which Palestinian forces openly hoped to accomplish the same feat in the West Bank. They led the United States to abandon Lebanon and Somalia, and arguably Vietnam. It remains to be seen whether the United States will declare victory and leave Iraq or Afghanistan while under attack, or whether it will persevere. (Various intermediary strategies, such as turning the governing of Iraq over to Iraqis while maintaining a sizable military force in the country, must be judged on their own merits. How-ever, that judgment will not depend on the spin the White House will put on such moves, but rather on how they will be perceived by those who must re-spect American power in order for it to be credible.)

The bar of credibility[38] is set particularly high, as the United States has re-peatedly declared that it will turn these countries into peaceful, prosperous democracies. If it leaves these countries to fall apart and engage in ethnic and religious wars or to establish some new kind of authoritarian regime, U.S. credibility—which it put on the line first by invading these countries and then even more so by promising the sky—will be no better than that of a second-hand car dealer.

The rationales of those who opposed the U.S. invasion of Iraq deserve at-tention because they concern the design of the emerging new global order. Some critics merely wanted the war to be delayed, to give Iraq more of a chance to peacefully disarm, for force to be used only as a last resort. Others did not agree that Iraq provided an imminent threat in the first place, holding that it could be deterred just as other nations with weapons of mass destruction had been in the past. Still others believed that the United States had no right, under the UN Charter, to attack Iraq. (The charter states that "[a]ll members shall refrain in their international relations from the threat or use of force against the territorial integrity or political independence of any state.")[39] And some critics held that a U.S. war against Iraq reflected deep flaws in its role as a superpower, that it showed the United States to be arrogant, moralistic ("dress-ing the business of power in the garb of piety," as Simon Schama put it[40]), overbearing, and out to serve narrow self-interests, especially its need for oil.

When a number of American intellectuals issued a letter trying to justify the war against Iraq,[41] only nine of the sixty intellectuals who endorsed a simi-lar letter on the war against terrorism endorsed it.[42] (I endorsed the original letter, but not the second one.)

Viewed in terms of just war theory, the U.S. invasion of Iraq fails to meet the two main criteria that the war against terrorism did meet: There was no imminent danger to innocent people (or even to others), and the United States did not exhaust all available options to deal with whatever dangers the Saddam regime posed.[43] Moreover, the claim that Iraq possessed WMD was not sub-stantiated. The connection drawn between Iraq and Al Qaeda was so tenuous that it was reminiscent of the Gulf of Tonkin resolution used to justify the war in Vietnam. By September 2003, the Bush administration had begun to stress that Iraq was the "central front in the war against terrorism" and that fighting terrorists was the reason war had to be waged against Iraq.[44] At first, the daily attacks on Americans would seem to bear out this claim. However, there had been no terrorist attacks in Iraq until the United States invaded it. The claim that the United States was out to democratize Iraq—added late in the process when the other claims did not take—proved weak given that the United States so often supports authoritarian governments. Furthermore, military interventions for the purpose of democratizing a nation do not meet the standards set forth in the UN Charter and international law, and surely do not require such a hasty attack before things can be sorted out in the Security Council. The democratization claim fails by another key test: True democracy cannot be imposed on ill-prepared countries.

Nor was there a convergence of interests. Russia and France had given Iraq huge loans, to the tune of $8 billion each.[45] They feared that these obligations would not be respected by a new Iraqi government. French oil companies had negotiated exclusive contracts allowing them to control 22.5 percent of Iraq's oil imports, while Russian corporations maintained 5.8 percent. Both countries had good reason to fear the loss of these contracts.[46] Nor did they view Iraq as a threat to their security. All things considered, these nations had much to lose and little to gain if the issue is examined from a narrow national interest perspective.

In short, the majority of governments and attentive people considered the 2003 U.S.-led invasion of Iraq to be a sheer exercise in the use of naked power, as highly illegitimate, and not in line with their own interests.[47] The U.S. action in Iraq stands as a symbol of a superpower that seeks to govern the world unilaterally. It is about as contrary to building a sound new global architecture as empire is to community.

If, as the United States faces future challenges, it follows the Iraqi model, a strongly neo-conservative strategy of basically going it alone, the result will be a Vietnamesque effect in several parts of the world.[48] Numerous articles have been written about whether the situation in Iraq is or is not akin to the experience in Vietnam. There are obviously some very important differences, above all the absence of a USSR and a China, which supported the communist forces in Vietnam. But there are also some significant parallels that should not be ignored. In using the term "Vietnamesque," I do not claim that the situation is identical, only that there are some similarities, and enough of them to generate Vietnam-like effects. These similarities include: (1) being mired in local guerrilla-like wars, which will result in rising casualties and costs; (2) facing growing alienation and opposition overseas as well as at home; and (3) finding that this kind of strategy is ineffectual and in the longer-run cannot be sustained.

In Vietnam, it took several years before the United States finally yielded to a small Third World nation that used terrorist tactics (in U.S.-controlled areas) and mobilized intense global and American public opposition. Perhaps this time the United States will be able to pacify Iraq and Afghanistan, as unlikely as this seems now. However, it is hard to imagine that a global architecture can rest on what is, in effect, basically a policy based on the exercise of brute force.

I should add, from my personal experience as a Special Force (commando) fighter in Israel, that most of those who cite U.S. military force as the reason for its being the only superpower in the world misunderstand its strength and, more generally, the use of power. Much has been made of the easy victories that the United States tallied in the Gulf War, Afghanistan, and Iraq. However, *power is sectorial*. The United States can readily defeat an army that fights it conventionally. However, it is likely to have a much harder time when faced with guerrilla tactics in a country that is supportive of the guerrillas. Thus, despite its enormous resources and technological advantage, the United States had a hard time suppressing a few hundred members of the Abu Sayyaf group in the forests of the Philippines; was defeated in Somalia; and has been unable to make much progress in the jungles of Colombia. I have already discussed the other costs of relying first and foremost on brute force. Hence, the following analysis presumes that the Bush administration, or at least the one to follow it, will realize the merit of a course that engages allies and friends, that is compatible with a system of international institutions and international law (even if these are modified in the process), and is viewed as legitimate by the majority of the attentive public.[49] The only question, as I see it, is whether the United States will change course on its own or will be forced to do so when faced with multicontinental Vietnamesque effects and the mounting costs of an empire that its citizens are unwilling to support.

I turn next to examine the antiterrorism coalition, which offers a more promising model for the U.S. role in the world. I am not suggesting that everyone favors this model, or that those who support it have no reservations, just as I do not claim that the invasion of Iraq is antagonizing everyone. Nor do I suggest that the alternatives are limited to these two approaches. However, they serve as bookends between which a variety of more graded options can be located.

THE ANTITERRORISM COALITION: A FOUNDATION FOR A GLOBAL SAFETY AUTHORITY

Shortly after September 11, 2001, the United States invited all the nations of the world to join it in forming a coalition to combat terrorism. Numerous nations joined, and not just nominally. In fact, it is accurate to say that the re-sulting coalition has been significantly more global in scope than many, if not all, of the coalitions that have preceded it, including those that were formed during the Korean War, the Gulf War, and the peacekeeping missions in Bosnia and Kosovo. It is, of course, more inclusive than the Allied Forces of World War II, and it is much more global than the Western alliance that was formed to counter communism during the Cold War.

The scope of the antiterrorism coalition can be measured in two ways. One is fairly mechanical—simply comparing the number of nations involved to the number of those that did not sign on. By this measure, almost all the nations of the world, including those that previously supported terrorists, such as Sudan, Syria, Iran, and Yemen, have agreed to participate and have made actual contributions to the coalition's work. For instance, Sudan has provided the United States with intelligence about terrorists.[50] Iran reportedly has re-called seven hundred intelligence agents and advisers from Lebanon, Sudan, and Bosnia, where they were accused of aiding terrorist groups.[51] Yemen pre-viously refused to cooperate with the United States in the investigation of the bombing of the USS *Cole*, but since the September 11 terrorist attack has "opened its files," providing the United States with documents that shed new light on the bombing.[52] Former Soviet states helped the coalition, as Kaza-khstan and Tajikistan gave the United States fly-over rights and Kyrgyzstan and Uzbekistan allowed American military bases to be located within their territories.[53]

Fifty nations, including Egypt, Saudi Arabia, and Jordan, often working closely with the CIA, have arrested suspected terrorists at the behest of the United States,[54] Turkey has supplied troops for the fight against the Taliban, and Indonesia has also offered to contribute troops.[55] Pakistan, once a major source of support for the Taliban, has provided significant assistance to the coalition. NATO, for the first time in its fifty years of existence, agreed to act outside of Europe.

Members of the global antiterrorism coalition have also made several sig-nificant and especially rapid and synchronized changes in domestic laws and policies in their own countries. The European Union introduced a commu-nity-wide arrest warrant.[56] Germany tightened its surveillance and immigra-tion laws.[57] Britain expanded its antiterrorism act.[58] Japan passed legislation that will allow its Self-Defense Forces to assist the United States.[59] France adopted a law that provides the police with greater search powers,[60] and the In-dian government passed an ordinance that granted the police sweeping new powers.[61] These changes have occurred in a fairly coordinated fashion in many nations more or less simultaneously.

Most important, the U.S.-led antiterrorism coalition acts, in effect, as a worldwide agency, as if it were some kind of global Interpol, with limited respect for national borders and sovereignty. During the war on terrorism, the United States has established a military or semimilitary presence in at least 137—some say 170—countries.[62] In accordance with what Max Boot has called "Globocop,"[63] the United States has divided the world into five military commands, each under the direction of a four-star general. The United States has "forward operating locations" in places most Americans have never heard of, and surely could not find on a map, including Manta, Ecuador, and Comalapa, El Salvador.[64] American Special Forces action in Djibouti were revealed only after several members of the unit died there during what was described as a training exercise.[65] The U.S. military took over the island of Diego Garcia, after removing its entire population.[66] There is no place beyond the reach of the global antiterrorism operation led and orchestrated by the United States.

U.S. ships patrol the seven seas. There are few e-mails, faxes, or phone calls anywhere in the world that U.S. computers—or those assisting them—do not screen.[67] CIA and FBI agents, and the local agents that they recruit, span the world. The intelligence services of scores of nations and their antiterrorist forces, police, and border agents are working closely and directly with various U.S. agencies, often without processing their contacts through their respective state departments (as is customary in other international contacts) and occasionally circumventing national laws.[68] Terrorists caught in one country are shipped to another before national courts can review extradition. (In Malawi, a judge ordered the charging or freeing of some Al Qaeda suspects who were arrested at the request of the CIA, only to find out that they had been spirited out of the country.)[69] Suspects who do not cooperate are turned over for interrogation to police forces in countries where the governments are less respectful of human rights than those of Western countries. (The United States has been accused of engaging in such behavior. In September 2002 American officials arrested Canadian citizen Maher Arar and exported him to Syria, where he was reportedly tortured for a year before being released to his home.)[70] Cooperation is not always seamless, but the relationships between U.S. agencies and those in Britain, Jordan, Israel, Australia, and scores of other countries are closer than the relationship between the FBI and the New York City Police Department.

The effort to capture Hambali, one of the world's most lethal terrorists, provides a telling illustration of the transnational cooperation that has been a hallmark of the antiterrorism coalition. The process of nabbing Hambali began when Thai officials arrested Arifin bin Ali, a leader of the Jemaah Islamiah terrorist organization. Bin Ali was then sent to Singapore for an interrogation, the results of which led officials to three more Jemaah Islamiah members on the Thai-Malay border. Months later, in August 2003, Hambali was located while attempting to reach an Indonesian telephone that was being monitored by American and Australian intelligence.[71] Following his arrest by Thai police officers, the Thai government willingly surrendered Hambali to the CIA for a confidential interrogation.[72]

The arrest of arms dealer Hemant Lakhani, which took place during the same month, followed a similar pattern. Lakhani, who attempted to smuggle an S–18 Igla missile into the United States, was captured due to the joint efforts of American, British, and Russian intelligence—a collaboration that took place despite Russian opposition to the war in Iraq.[73] Khalid Shaikh Mohammed, whom many view as one of the masterminds behind the September 11 attack, was captured in one of several joint efforts of the FBI and Pakistani officials.[74] He was handed over to American authorities and questioned, which led to the arrest of another potential terrorist who had assisted Al Qaeda members in planning an attack on the Brooklyn Bridge.[75]

Viewed this way, the antiterrorism coalition is a new global architecture, a de facto Global Antiterrorism Authority, formed, led, managed, and largely financed by the superpower. In exploring this structure, I employ "authority" in both meanings of the term: institutional, and hence lasting rather than temporary or transitional (as we speak about the Port Authority), and legitimate (as we speak about someone's authority to rule).[76]

It might be said that the current level of cooperation is primarily ad hoc, not institutional, with limited legitimacy. Moreover, one might argue that cooperation is often the result of "adhesion," of smaller players going along with the 800-pound gorilla for fear that they will be punished if they do not. Such questioning results in part from the difficulties that the terminology imposes rather than the facts on the ground. We tend to discuss authority as if it were a dichotomous variable: either we face one, or none exists. As I see it, the antiterrorism authority has reached a fair level of institutionalization in the sense that it has now been working for years, and routines of cooperation have been well-established and followed even during the period in which the participants were deeply divided on the Iraq issue.

Legitimation is also far from absolute—especially with regard to the specific tactics employed by the antiterrorism authority—but it is nonetheless substantial, as the United Nations and practically all the governments of the world not only denounced the 2001 attack on America and terrorism in general, but have also, in essence, continued to support the war against terrorism.[77] Finally, it should be noted that even bodies recognized by one and all as authorities must employ assets and power to gain support. Call the antiterrorism coalition a nascent authority or an institution under construction, but it does have the elements that an authority make.

The Global Antiterrorism Authority, a first step that may lead sweetness to arise out of might, is much less than a world government, but much more than another intergovernmental organization. And, as experience with terrorism shows, it tends to endure. The work of the American led Global Antiterrorism Authority will not be completed in the near future. It is not merely an ad hoc coalition.

True, the Global Antiterrorism Authority is not an amalgamation of independent nations whose representatives democratically deliberated and found a shared purpose. It has been composed and fostered by one superpower, the United States, which used a mixture of diplomacy, normative appeals to global public opinion, covert operations, and the promise of economic aid and loans (or the threat of withholding such funds) to form and sustain authority.[78]

Importantly, the antiterrorism coalition has met the interest convergence test: It serves not merely American national interests, but also the significant national interests of many other nations, including key coalition members. (Reference is to national interests as perceived by the governments of these nations.) For example, Russia has been seeking approval for its fight against Muslim insurgents in Chechnya, whom it considers terrorists. China is concerned about Islamic radicals in its Xinjiang region. Egypt is among the score or more of nations struggling to control radical Islamic groups that resort to means of violence—terrorists, to these regimes. The Philippines consistently faces violence from two radical Islamic groups. Malaysian and Indonesian Islamic political groups are generally not militant, but some militant groups in these countries aim to create Islamic governments.[79] India and Sri Lanka are also threatened by militant Islamic groups.

In addition, the goals of the antiterrorism authority are considered to be legitimate, given the nature of the attack on the United States and similar attacks by other terrorist groups elsewhere, even though the same cannot be said about all the tactics employed. The September 11 terrorist attack on civilians, the overpowering images of victims leaping to their deaths from the towers to avoid dying by fire, and accounts of bereaved families commanded the sympathy of people around the world. The heads of many nations expressed their outrage and promised to assist in preventing future attacks. A large gathering of Iranians held a sympathy candlelight vigil in a public square in Tehran, where Iranians "mourn[ed] the death of [America's] innocent beloved ones."[80] In China, e-mails and phone calls of sympathy flooded the U.S. embassy, and flowers were laid before its doors.[81] In Germany, 200,000 mourners filed in a procession towards Berlin's Brandenburg Gate.[82] Bells tolled at Paris's Notre Dame Cathedral.[83] At the Rome mosque, Italian Muslims prayed for the victims of the attack. One of the clerics at the mosque explained, "The tragedy has hit us all."[84] On September 12 *Le Monde* printed the headline, "We are all Americans."[85]

In the month following the tragedy, these countries continued to express solidarity with the United States by supporting its invasion of Afghanistan—the beginning of the war on terrorism. France sent soldiers and advanced combat aircraft to aid in the military campaign and humanitarian relief.[86] Germany's chancellor resisted opposition from the left-wing fringe of his own party and from the Green Party (his coalition partner), and convinced the German parliament to support the deployment of troops in Afghanistan.[87] The Russian foreign ministry released a statement which referred to Afghanistan as an "international centre of terrorism and extremism" and said that they should be "taken to justice."[88] Japan went beyond what in the past it would have considered its constitutional limit on involvement in foreign military conflicts, and it sent warships and troops to be used in noncombat zones—the country's first wartime military deployment since World War II.[89] Turkey sent special forces to provide reconnaissance, training, and support.[90]

Although populations in some of these countries were wary of involvement in the U.S.-led Afghan campaign, a sense of solidarity with the United States and support for its war on terrorism remained strong. In May 2003, 60 percent of the French supported the U.S.-led war on terrorism, as did 60 percent of Germans, 51 percent of Russians, and 63 percent of the British.[91]

All fifteen members of the European Union supported a military strike in Afghanistan and evinced support for the wider war against terrorism.[92] Many other countries, such as Pakistan, Hong Kong, and the twenty-one nations of the Asia Pacific Economic Cooperation, also endorsed the war against terrorism.[93] Two UN Security Council resolutions legitimated the campaign—and implicitly supported the military strike in Afghanistan—by calling the September 11 terrorist attack a security threat and recognizing the need to combat these threats "by all means."[94] Although in later days some of the means used in the worldwide campaign against terrorism came under growing criticism, the main purpose and approach remained widely endorsed, especially as compared to the war against Iraq.

As mentioned earlier, in 2002 a group of sixty American intellectuals including Samuel Huntington, Francis Fukuyama, and myself issued *What We're Fighting For: A Letter From America*, in which we stated that the response to the 2001 terrorist assault against America met the criteria needed to justify a war set forth by St. Augustine in the *City of God* and many other deliberations on the subject that followed.[95] (I refer to a "justified war" rather than to a "just war" because some Germans argued that there can never be a just war, but there may be wars that can be justified. So be it.) Many since have embraced these criteria.[96]

One of the criteria is that you ought to die rather than kill if you are under attack. That is, self-defense is not a valid justification. However, when other innocent people are under attack, you should act. The second is that all other courses of action must be exhausted. Here it is relevant to note that the United States had been attacked by the same group of terrorists several times before and responded meekly, if at all. These attacks included the 1993 bombing of the World Trade Center; the bombing of the U.S. military complexes in Riyadh and Dhahran in Saudi Arabia in 1995 and 1996, respectively; the 1998 bombings of U.S. embassies in the Kenyan and Tanzanian capitals; and the 2000 attack on the USS *Cole* in Aden, Yemen. In total, more than 270 people lost their lives in these attacks and 6,500 people were injured. Only once, after the African embassy attacks, did the United States respond militarily, firing seventy cruise missiles at a presumed terrorist training camp run by bin Laden in Afghanistan. Moreover, bin Laden openly called for continued and escalating attacks—a holy war—against the United States.[97] Hence, the American response did meet those two criteria. The contrast with the situation in Iraq is particularly stark: There was no immediate danger and all other options clearly were not exhausted.

The Importance of Being Legitimate

Because a whole school of international relations scholars—the realists—and a fair number of policy makers and "people on the street" scoff at the notion that what the "world" thinks or considers legitimate should be of significant concern for a superpower, a few words on the importance of legitimacy in general, and in this age in particular, are in order. Much has been written about the importance of ideals as well as "norms" (I prefer the term "moral values") and law in international relations.[98] I agree with much of what has been said, although occasionally some writers overstate their case to the extent that it sounds as if military power and economic assets matter little.

My main focus is on a related issue. I am not concerned so much with the way that the international realm is composed, but with the ways that it is changing: It is becoming more focused on legitimacy than it was in earlier generations, when most foreign policy was the purview of small groups of power elites and diplomats.

As education and communication are spreading, more and more people—the "masses"—in growing parts of the world are becoming increasingly involved in politics in terms of following public affairs and reacting to them. In earlier generations, even in democratic nations, candidates for public office could be selected in smoke-filled rooms by power brokers, and elections could be won by "machines" by handing out coal and whisky to immigrants or by fixing traffic tickets. The "people" were largely inattentive, unaware, and uninterested in public affairs. Many had no political map in their head. Typically in those days, when a working man was asked about what makes a good citizen, he responded: "Someone who takes care of his children."

Since World War II, however, and to some extent even before, the size of the attentive public in free societies has grown and become more ideological. Self-interest still plays an important role, but moral values, and hence legitimacy, have grown in importance. It is enough to simply mention the war in Vietnam to realize the power of public opinion. Public rejection prevented the otherwise popular President Johnson from even running for a second term, forced the United States to accept a rare defeat on the battleground, and resulted in a sharply divided nation. Cynics will say that the opposition was led by young people who feared being drafted and killed. However, millions of others—including the author—who had no personal stake in the outcome, held that the war was morally inappropriate and was being fought in immoral ways, and acted on these beliefs.[99]

Over recent decades the masses have been entering politics in many parts of the world in which they previously were largely excluded. This has not been happening in all countries, nor to everyone in those countries that have opened up, but nevertheless, attentive publics are growing rapidly worldwide.[100] And they mind global, not merely local, affairs. They play an increasingly significant political role even in nondemocratic nations such as China, Pakistan, and even Kuwait. Moreover, worldwide communications (from CNN to Al Jazeera), the Internet, social activists, network organizers, and others link these publics to one another, and often move them in similar directions. (Of course, there are always minorities that do not move along.) In this limited sense one can speak meaningfully of a global public opinion, which tends to favor the environment, the United Nations, reallocation of wealth, and much else. Data from sixty-one countries representing each region of the world, collected by Shalom H. Schwarz and Anat Bardi, supports the idea that there is a worldwide consensus on several key values.[101] A survey of forty-four countries in different regions of the world also provides support for the idea of an emerging worldwide consensus. A majority of people in every country surveyed believed that moral decline was a "very big problem" or a "moderate big problem."[102] When asked whether differences between their country and the United States were due to different values or different policies, most respondents answered different policies, and in only a handful of countries did a majority pick different values.[103] Michael Walzer and Frances Harbour have also found that people in many different societies have a shared moral sense.[104]

I do not claim that whatever the emerging worldwide public opinion considers legitimate is necessarily morally right. However, because attentive publics often are not swayed by whatever the political leaders claim to be the right course, public opinion does play an important role in foreign policy. Hence the importance of convincing the various publics, and not just their political representatives, of the merits of one's case. As we have seen, most of the attentive public basically views the antiterrorism authority as legitimate, and this contributes to its effectiveness. As the years have passed since the September 11 terrorist attack, there has been some increased disaffection, especially as reports about collateral damage to civilians in Afghanistan have increased and criticism of the U.S. policy toward Iraq has spilled over into this policy area to some extent.

The Global Antiterrorism Coalition generated such a level of legitimacy—and not just a convergence of interests of big and small powers—that the coalition continued to function effectively despite the global falling out over the use of military force against Iraq. France and Germany, the leaders of the anti-U.S. opposition to the invasion of Iraq, and a host of other nations who vociferously opposed the U.S. treatment of Iraq, continued to participate actively in the war against terrorism. The justice and interior ministers of the Group of 8 met in

Paris in May 2003 to announce their continuing commitment to fight the war on terror. The ministers "seemed at pains to stress that the trans-Atlantic sniping over Iraq had not damaged the cohesion of the international alliance against terrorism."[105] In particular, the French interior minister noted that "French and American cooperation never stopped because it concerns the security of our citizens."[106] In support of the war against terrorism, the government of Saudi Arabia—which did not permit the United States to launch attacks against Iraq from its air bases—is cracking down on groups that are suspected of funding terrorists.[107] In 2003, after a terrorist bombing that targeted Saudis, the Saudi government established a joint task force with the FBI and Internal Revenue Service for the purpose of investigating terrorist funding inside their borders.[108] Saudi forces were also responsible for killing two Al Qaeda members in July 2003.[109] In early summer 2003 Iran's intelligence minister announced that his government had arrested a number of Al Qaeda operatives in support of the war against terrorism,[110] and by the end of August, Iran had extradited several of these terrorists to Saudi Arabia.[111] Yemen continued to act similarly.[112] There were many more indications that a number of nations continued to cooperate in the war against terrorism, while even U.S. allies continued to oppose its invasion of Iraq. All this shows the resiliency of a properly constructed Global Authority and points to how new institutions may be fashioned in the future.

The war against terrorism has become so "old hat" that we expect every other week a relevant item of news as part of the ongoing global campaign. We should not overlook, however, that it is very much an East-West operation. Led by the United States, Thailand is no less important or cooperative than Spain; Pakistan plays no less of a role than Australia; the Philippines and Indonesia are part of the operation, as are Germany, Britain, and Colombia. Norway even restructured its armed forces to fit into the global needs of the American military apparatus, by specializing in mountain warfare and mine clearing.[113] In that sense, there is a stark difference between NATO, yesterday's Western alliance, and the Global Antiterrorism Authority, in which the West works with the East. Although the United States is playing a commanding role in both NATO and the war against terrorism, the informal and floating directorates of both are quite different. NATO is governed largely by the United States in conjunction with Britain, Germany and—to a much lesser extent—France. The Global Antiterrorism Coalition is directed by the United States in cooperation with Russia, Britain, and a floating variety of partners that include China, Japan, and an ad hoc assortment of other nations, depending on the front.

A Designer's Lesson

One can view the U.S. response to the September 11 terrorist attack on its homeland and its 2003 invasion of Iraq as a competition between two designs for U.S. posture as a superpower once it resolved to engage much more actively on the global level than it had before. The differences are stark, although not complete. Not everyone favored the antiterrorism drive, and the war in Iraq had some supporters outside the United States. But, by and large, the continued drive against terrorism was considered legitimate and generated a considerable convergence of interests among those involved, while the opposite was true of the war in Iraq.

To the extent that the occupation of Iraq reflects a semi-empire design and the war against terrorism a global authority, one can safely conclude that the American empire was the shortest in human history. It failed by all three of the criteria on which an empire is based. Military might, which the United States used to justify its policy of going it alone whenever the spirit moved it, turned out to be insufficient to win the peace. Moreover, the U.S. military was stretched so thin that the reserves and the National Guard had to be relied upon to a very considerable extent. And when consideration was given to other members of the axis of evil, especially North Korea, there was considerable doubt that the United States could tackle it militarily without the North Koreans responding with an assault on South Korea. At first it may seem absurd to argue that the U.S. military is stretched thin, given the ease with which the United States won the wars in Afghanistan and Iraq. It would seem that it could readily overrun half a dozen other countries. However, the Taliban have still not been suppressed in Afghanistan, nor has the opposition in Iraq. And if the U.S. military were to leave these countries (and if no other outside force were to take over), they would very likely become rogue states again. Hence the United States maintains a military presence in these countries, which ties up eight of its ten active duty divisions as well as 156,000 member of the Army National Guard and Reserve. *Ergo, precious little military force is left to ensure peace and change in other countries once they are occupied.* Theoretically, the United States could greatly increase its military force (albeit hardly overnight), but the political will is not in place. Moreover, the U.S. military tackling North Korea is likely to prove a dangerous undertaking, given North Korea's well-shielded weapons systems and their chemical, if not nuclear, capabilities. In short, far from showing friends and foes alike that the United States can act on its own to reorder the world by the use of might, Afghanistan and Iraq have shown the great limits of its military force.

In March 2003, when the United States marched into Iraq in disregard of the United Nations, some observers wrote that the United Nations had become irrelevant, or at least of little consequence. When, a few months later, the United States was in effect forced to come back and seek UN endorsement, the earlier debacle turned into one of the United Nations' greatest victories, significantly enhancing its stature and normative power and reinforcing its position as the source of global legitimacy.

And instead of continuing to act unilaterally, the United States has found that it needs more help from allies, not merely to deal with the occupation of Iraq and Afghanistan, but also to bring about a policy change in Iran and, above all, in North Korea. Indeed, the United States has refused to deal directly with North Korea, insisting on six-nation talks. The reasons the Bush administration has followed a much more multilateral approach in its dealings with North Korea and Iran, including a close collaboration with the International Atomic Energy Agency (IAEA), a UN agency, are numerous. They are not necessarily tied to a recognition of the error of its previous ways or a new profound respect for multilateralism, but the result is nevertheless a major shift in strategy.

I am not arguing that the United States or other big powers will never again act unilaterally or refuse to wait for the United Nations, allies, and worldwide public support before crossing national borders if they believe that their vital national interests are at stake. However, in contrast to a widely held belief that the lasting effects of the way in which the United States invaded Iraq have undermined the evolving global regime, I suggest that the world has evolved from a place in which a superpower acted imperially to one in which the United States (and other powers) will be significantly more reluctant to do so. Thus, in effect, the respect for the evolving global regime—one in which negotiations, the United Nations (and hence, legitimation), and multilateralism play key roles—has substantially increased. True, this community-building effect will not continue to develop in a straight line; history rarely does. Some setbacks are to be expected. The longer-run trend, however, will strengthen transnational institutions rather than weaken them, as has often been the case in instances of nation building that started with the application of force before community building took off in earnest. (For a more detailed discussion of this point, see chapter 11.)

As I have indicated, I do not believe that the U.S. approach to Iraq can provide a sustainable design for the new global architecture. I hence focus in the following chapters on the other design, which is growing out of the antiterrorism coalition, and ask: Where do we go from here?

CHAPTER SEVEN

HOBBESIAN VERSUS LOCKEAN GLOBAL AGENDAS

MISSION APPETITE: SECURITY FIRST

IN DISCUSSING THE EFFECTS OF A NATION—ESPECIALLY A SUPER-POWER—becoming involved (some say entangled) in the internal affairs of other nations, critics often invoke the danger of "mission creep."[1] This notion refers to the inadvertent expansion of missions, and it is viewed negatively because new missions and tasks are adopted without deliberation and conscious decision making, and presumably in conflict with the interests of those who proceed so irrationally. In contrast, I use the term "mission appetite" to refer to an increasing willingness and ability to assume additional missions as the "taste" for them grows.

The United States, long an ambivalent global power, has acquired much more of a taste for international intervention since the September 11 terrorist attack. Given that it is the power behind the new Global Antiterrorism Authority, I ask which additional missions would be considered legitimate and could be carried out effectively on a sustainable basis if the United States were to continue to assume the role of a superpower. In order to avoid mission creep, the United States should pursue these missions intentionally rather than unwittingly. That being said, one might ask what missions would contribute to developing a new world order, one that would fit within the framework of the evolving normative synthesis and would ultimately serve to advance human primacy.

I focus first on those missions that entail the application of force. True, other forms of intervention in the internal affairs of other nations also deserve scrutiny and prioritization,[2] such as imposing limited economic sanctions to foster changes in domestic policies.[3] But issues raised by these manifestations of power and influence are secondary to the ones that arise when one power uses its military force or clandestine agents to make another nation yield.

The question, as I see it, is for what purposes the United States, as the world's only superpower (or for that matter any other major power), may properly employ its might in the future. The criteria used in this assessment have been illustrated by the preceding discussion:

1. Actions should be based on a *convergence of interests* between those of the United States and those of other nations. I deliberately list this criterion first because so much has been made recently of the importance of legitimacy.[4] Legitimacy, while important, plays less of a role in international affairs than in domestic affairs; the convergence of interests is more important in the international arena. Moreover, convergence of interests is the reason some empires lasted longer than others and at lower costs to both those who governed and those who were governed.

2. Actions should be widely considered *legitimate* in terms of the goals they serve; the processes and institutions through which relevant decisions are being rendered; and the means employed. The term "legitimate" raises many complex issues as far as who defines what is legitimate, as well as its relations to moral pluralism. I explore these concerns elsewhere.[5] It suffices for my current purposes to indicate that the term is used here as it is typically used in political science literature and daily parlance, as action considered justified by whatever group or audience cited.

3. Actions should be constitutive for the evolving global regimes. Much has been made, especially by liberals, about the merit of proceeding in ways that strengthen rather than undermine evolving international institutions and laws.[6] I use the phrase *community building* to refer to actions that help lay the foundations for a new global architecture that includes much beyond formal institutions and laws, as we shall see.

From here on, I refer to these criteria as the triple test.

The answers to how the United States should conduct itself abroad depend on an elementary but often disregarded or deliberately overlooked recognition that the world is in a Hobbesian state and is not yet ready for a Lockean one. The first obligation of any state is to protect its citizens' lives and to provide safety, even if this entails the use of force.[7] Moreover, service to other goals presumes that at least a modicum of domestic order has been established.[8] Concerns for civil society, democracy, and human rights—other than the right to be safe—must be considered advanced causes. They are best attended to after the rudimentary duty to provide safety is discharged, however incompletely. Thus, in instances such as the Hutu genocide of the Tutsis in Rwanda in 1994, the ongoing bloodbaths in Congo, or the civil wars in Liberia and Burundi in 2003, the questions of whether human rights should be promoted before democracy, as Fareed Zakaria suggests, or democracy before human rights, or whether economic development should precede or be accompanied by political liberalization are all premature. (My reference to Hobbes over Locke should be taken as an analogy, and a limited one. I do not mean that given the demi-state of nature that the world is in, people everywhere should yield to some kind of a global dictatorship. My argument is that the best way to achieve a reasonable global governance is to *give safety the first priority*. Nor, we shall see, do I hold that Locke's concern with liberty and rights should be ignored.[9])

The recognition that the first duty of the state is to provide security to its people fully applies to the evolving international community. Much of the world is much closer to the raw, brutish, violent state of nature that Hobbes wrote about than all but the most unruly nation-states. The world first and foremost requires a higher level of security. As long as nations can threaten others with weapons of mass destruction or be threatened by massive terrorism, other considerations, however important, must take a backseat. The ultimate way to violate people's human rights is to terminate their ability to exercise any. Call it "survival ethics." According to Jewish tradition, he who saves one soul is as if he saves a whole world. Securing the lives of a whole people ranks even higher. I am, of course, aware of the sayings "Better dead than red" and "Give me liberty or give me death." I am not arguing that there are no higher values, nothing for which one should give one's life. But such heroics aside, day in and day out, the world would be a much better place if attention were first paid to making people safer. Nor can a regime that promises liberty and rights last long if it provides no safety.

I return here to the ethics of survival. It is one thing to take some lives to save many more from unprovoked and unjust attacks, and it is quite another to take lives in order to improve the lives of those who remain—by one's lights or even theirs. On the same grounds, we have seen that intervening in the internal affairs of another nation to stop massive violence inflicted on its own people or on others is justified—but not armed intervention to improve their political regime or to make it more democratic or more attentive to a whole slew of human rights. Nor is intervention justified to make people morally superior (or to secure them a better place in the afterlife) by bringing them one religion or ideology or another.

FROM CURBING TERRORISM TO
DEPROLIFERATION

Reflecting a healthy mission appetite, long before the American-led Global Antiterrorism Authority solidified its operations, it in effect undertook another mission: proactive deproliferation. Because the mission is security-related, it reflects an effort to shore up Hobbesian needs before turning to Lockean goals. Before the merits and defects of this mission expansion can be examined, I must clarify three matters, all concerning the nature of the dangers involved.

THE TRUE DANGER

First of all, I must state with as much emphasis as I can marshal that *small-scale* terrorism, of the kind the United States and other nations have faced so far (and which has been the focus of so much action, debate, and dedication of resources), is small potatoes compared to *massive* terrorism. Small-scale terrorism is the kind that Britain faced at the hands of the Irish Republican Army, Israel has faced during the intifada, and the United States faced overseas before the September 11 terrorist attack. Its victims include not merely the hundreds of individuals involved, but also people's basic sense of safety. These attacks truly terrorize. They often drive the nations involved to curtail their individual rights, to everyone's loss, and nations' economies pay a considerable price.

This kind of terrorism, though, is almost trivial compared to the effects of an attack with a WMD, whether by a state or a terrorist. Such an attack could obliterate Manhattan, Washington, D.C., or Tel Aviv. To give a sense of scale, the United States incinerated Hiroshima and Nagasaki with weapons available in 1945. Today, the number of victims, the human and economic costs, the resulting rage, and the demands to restore safety whatever the cost, even to democratic institutions, would be of a wholly different order of magnitude. The difference between small-scale and massive terrorism is as significant as the difference between a crime wave and genocide. The relevant distinction is not between terrorists and rogue states, but between small, garden-variety terrorism and the calamitous, massive terrorism that is most likely to be inflicted by the use of WMD—say, if Al Qaeda got its hands on a nuclear device—whether these weapons are used by terrorists or a rogue state.

Even when WMD are not actually used, the threat of such weapons is paralyzing. Take, for instance, the situation in Korea. In most deliberations, much attention is very properly paid to the fact that North Korea could use its chemical weapons and massive artillery equipped with special warheads to kill many hundreds of thousands of South Koreans. North Korea has openly blackmailed the United States by escalating its missile tests and accelerating the production of plutonium. Another major source of serious concern is that North Korea might sell "surplus" WMD, as it did with long-range missiles, to other nations and to terrorists.

Unfortunately, it is difficult for people to ponder the dangers posed by WMD, and they tend to focus on small potato terrorists. Princeton psychologist Daniel Kahneman was awarded a Nobel Prize for his findings in economics, which included the fact that people pay more attention to horror stories than to statistics.[10] Thus people tend to think that in the United States there are more murders than suicides, because murders are reported in great and vivid detail in the media while suicides typically are not. In the same vein, people pay more attention to September 11–like attacks—which received massive media coverage—than to the invisible danger of WMD, which are many thousands of times more dangerous but are not as well reported. It follows that *deproliferation is far more important to the national interest of many nations and to humanity, and it is even more legitimate than the drive against small-scale terrorism.*

Some say that differentiating between small-scale and massive terrorism is pointless because, in either case, terrorists must be curbed. For the same reason, in discussions of terrorism and rogue states armed with WMD, it is often assumed that there is no fundamental difference between the two since a rogue state could turn over WMD to terrorists. As a result, a major insight is lost: *If nuclear weapons and their means of production now held by rogue states could be eliminated—if we could deproliferate—the world would be much safer, even if there were no decline in the number or organizational competence of terrorists.* In contrast to the argument that the United States was being distracted from the key war against terrorism by its concern with North Korea and Iran, my contention is just the opposite: Without rogue states armed with nuclear weapons, the danger posed by terrorism would be greatly scaled back. From this viewpoint, the war against Iraq (to the extent that it truly sought to remove the threat of WMD) was the right war at the wrong time and in the wrong country. By the "wrong time" I am referring to the fact that not all peaceful options were exhausted before the war was launched; in that sense, it was "too early." And Iraq was the "wrong country" because other rogue states did have WMD. However, I do believe that once all options are exhausted, and there are many of them, forced deproliferation is necessary if all of us are to live in a reasonably safe world.[11] I join here with those who hold that an arms-control approach—allowing states to keep what are, in effect, the means for producing nuclear weapons while relying on inspections to ensure their peaceful use—is too risky. The new world order requires the removal of such capacities—through peaceful measures if possible and by force if necessary.

This is exactly the reason why Pakistan is the most dangerous place in the world at this stage—both because it exports the knowledge and technologies needed to make nuclear weapons (as well as the means to deliver them) and because there is a serious likelihood that a Taliban-like government will take over the reins and get hold of the country's nuclear weapons or that terrorists may acquire them from its poorly protected sites. (When the United States offered to help Pakistan protect these weapons, the government responded by saying that it was relying on its intelligence service to do so; it is this service that is most closely associated with the Taliban.) The fact that President Pervez Musharraf has survived two attacks on his life, which came rather close to succeeding, does not fill one with assurance about his longer-run prospects. And the widespread opposition to his policies further darkens the prospects of his government and raises the specter of a terrorist-allied coup, far from unknown in those parts.[12]

Massive terrorism would be further curtailed if other measures were undertaken to make it more difficult for terrorists to get their hands on WMD or the materials needed to produce them, such as neutralizing or purchasing old stockpiles of weapons and better protecting reprocessing plants.

My argument rests on two important facts. First, although terrorists can deliver a nuclear device—say in a container or speedboat—once they get their hands on one, or even build one once they have the needed material, for the most part production can be done only by a state because of the large-scale investments and activities that are required. Second, other weapons, such as chemical and biological agents, are not as easy to weaponize and deliver on mass targets, despite what is often suggested. So far, all such attacks—for instance, the Sarin nerve gas released in a Japanese subway by the cult Aum Shinrikyo in 1995— have been on a much smaller scale than the September 11 terrorist attack. And the use of the means of delivery of these weapons—for instance, crop dusters— can be regulated. True, a terrorist may one day feed such agents into a ventilation system with a spray can and cause considerable damage. However, under most conditions, the terrorist would be unable to wipe out an entire city, and certainly not as readily as a nuclear device could. (Dirty bombs, which are easier to make than nuclear ones, are held by experts to be much less dangerous.) If national stocks of chemical and biological weapons are destroyed at the same time that deproliferation takes place, the work of terrorists will be made much more difficult. Granted, small-scale terrorism will only be reduced, not eliminated. But a world without the danger of massive terrorism would allow us all to sleep much better.

MEETING THE TRIPLE TEST

Deproliferation passes the triple test. This mission engages the national interests of the United States and other major powers and those of many, albeit not all, other nations, and advances the construction of a new global architecture.

The major powers are keenly interested in such a rollback of nuclear arms and ensuring better control of the materials that might be used for their production, because it is the major powers who are most threatened by massive terrorism. America's concerns in this matter are all too obvious, but Russia also would greatly benefit. Although it helped Iran develop its nuclear facilities, supposedly to be used only for energy generation and research, an Iran without nuclear weapons would serve Russian interests well, given that these weapons could potentially be used by terrorists in former Soviet republics with large Muslim populations that border on Russia, and even in Chechnya.

China is concerned that it will be pushed into a major nuclear arms race, which will require a major diversion of resources from economic development and still not provide the same safety it now commands, if North Korea develops a nuclear arsenal. If North Korea and China proceed, Japan is likely to follow suit.[13] All other nations, with the exception of a few rogue states, have nothing to gain and much to lose if terrorists get their hands on nuclear weapons or rogue states threaten to use them.

In addition, if one could convince India and Pakistan to solve their dispute over Kashmir and give up their nuclear weapons in exchange for a guarantee of their borders, both nations would be the beneficiaries. I fully realize the complexities of the issues involved—the long history of animosity, the inevitable religious and ethnic confrontation, and the sense of prestige that nations claim to derive from being members of the "nuclear club."[14] However, none of these takes precedence over saving the lives of millions of their citizens and making nuclear war less likely. Religious and ethnic differences should not be allowed to simmer when nuclear weapons are involved, and should be tackled as they were in Northern Ireland. Arm-twisting for this purpose is justified and should take priority over other policy goals, even capturing bin Laden and his minions. Prestige, the legitimacy makers should help establish, comes with deproliferation, not with threatening others with massive devastation. There are few better tests for the evolving global community than finding ways, in a place that is very challenging, to avoid such a catastrophe.

The Indian-Pakistani conflict has gained a small fraction of the attention paid to the Israeli-Palestinian conflict, but if measured on a scale of potential danger it deserves much more.[15] I fully realize that misbegotten leaders on both sides cynically pursue great political gains by drumming up hate against the other nation instead of attending to problems at home.[16] However, if the notion of a world community is to mean anything, then the global and domestic abhorrence for such maneuvers must rise to a level at which such behavior will no longer be politically productive. Indeed, in 2004 pressure from China and the West led to a thaw in Pakistani-Indian relations and an attempt to resolve their differences. The United States, working with other powers, should encourage, offer incentives, and pressure Indian and Pakistani representatives to work out an agreed border in Kashmir, deploy an international force to guarantee the border (much needed if Pakistan, with its smaller conventional force, is even to consider giving up its nuclear arms), and seek deproliferation from both sides. Experts report that both the Indian and the Pakistani governments, far from being more cautious and circumspect since they acquired nuclear weapons, have actually become more avaricious and boastful.

Experts who have read the preceding lines have responded that "it is not that simple" and that Pakistan and India will "never agree to give up their nuclear weapons." Granted, it is complex. However, the same experts did not dream that Libya would abandon its WMD program. In my view, not enough has been made of the grand contribution to world peace that Libyan president Moammar Qaddafi has made by declaring that he would no longer seek to develop or acquire nuclear weapons; an accomplishment that, in my mind, has been the crowning success of Western diplomacy since the beginning of the twenty-first century: Deproliferating a country without killing anyone, without firing a shot. We have an odd tendency of showering billions of dollars on countries that threaten us while doing next to nothing for countries who disarm voluntarily. Libya should be awash in appreciation, and not just in fine words. Such recognition would encourage other countries to follow its lead, and it may even encourage Libya to take the next step: improving its dismal human rights record.

Even if their behavior threatened only their own people and no one else, the prospect of a nuclear war between Pakistan and India is so horrifying that deproliferating these nations should be granted a high priority among the endeavors of the evolving global authority strictly on humanitarian grounds. Deproliferation hence meets the second test on the face of it, by being highly legitimate in purpose, although there is room for debate about the ways deproliferation should be implemented.

Finally, deproliferation—which has been pursued in ways similar to the war against terrorism—is adding a whole wing to the Global Antiterrorism Authority, and thus providing another element for the formation a Global Safety Authority. That is, this added mission meets the criteria of transnational institution building and hence can serve as part of the development of a global community.

Without a particular announcement or extended deliberations, the U.S.-run Global Antiterrorism Authority has in effect already expanded its missions to include deproliferation. Often the same actors—CIA and FBI agents, Special Forces, troops, coalition partners—are used to advance deproliferation and fight terrorism, or these actors are switched back and forth between the two missions such that they often blur together. Most people consider both to be highly legitimate missions. And although the level of collaboration is not nearly as high as in the war against terrorism, China and Japan are working with the United States regarding North Korea, and Russia regarding Iran. In short, the Global Antiterrorism Authority is on its way to becoming a Global Safety Authority (GSA) that encompasses both missions.

Moreover, a distinct "department" has been added to the GSA for the purpose of deproliferation, although it is in a much earlier state of development than the antiterrorism one. Following a U.S. initiative, the Proliferation Security Initiative (PSI) is being forged, which involves more collaborations than typical intergovernmental efforts. In addition to the United States, the PSI has ten member nations and seven observers. The nations that are party to the PSI are fashioning military (largely naval) networks whose purpose is to intercept shipments of nuclear weapons and material that might be used in their production. To this end, the member nations share intelligence and have agreed to stop all such shipments that pass through their territory, ports, airspace or on ships flying their flags.[17] Training exercises take place in nine locations, including the seas around North Korea and Iran.

As of the summer of 2003, the countries involved, including Australia, France, Spain, Japan, and Portugal, began joint military exercises to prepare for a wider implementation of these powerful and unprecedented steps toward deproliferation. Some interceptions already have occurred, including the boarding of a ship deployed from a North Korean port and the seizure of a cargo ship traveling to Sudan.[18] In a similar effort, the United States has also forged an agreement with governments across Asia and the Pacific Rim to restrict the use and transfer of shoulder-fired missiles that could be used by terrorist groups to shoot down passenger planes.[19]

On the political side, it is noteworthy that the deproliferation wing of the GSA has a different directorate from that of the antiterrorism one. In effect, it is best to think about these new institutions as being run by floating directorates. The United States is a key and controlling member of them all. However, South Korea, Japan, and China are much more involved in seeking to bring North Korea into the new international order, as compared to their role in the management of the war against terrorism. In contrast, Britain is much more central for the antiterrorism drive. Russia and Australia are about evenly involved in both. As we shall see, other Global Authorities may have different—and changing—directorates.

Ways and Means

If deproliferation is to be accorded our top priority, it would follow that all means of persuasion—economic and ultimately military—should be applied to this purpose. That is, there is a global need to move from a basically voluntary system, which the non-proliferation treaties entail, to a system that has a coercive fall back, in which force would be used if all else fails. (The European Union acknowledged as much when it released the "Strategy Against Proliferation of Weapons of Mass Destruction," a document that calls for "coercive measures"—including force—to prevent proliferation when all other options have been exhausted.)[20] Given the dangers involved, coercive deproliferation is justified only if all other means have been exhausted. If Iran can be persuaded to cease developing nuclear weapons, we are all better for it, including the people of Iran. And if North Korea is willing to trade its nuclear-bomb-making facilities for economic aid, this is a fabulous bargain for all concerned, surely for its millions of starving citizens. But if all else fails, military action is justified. Deterrence will no longer do; we cannot assume that all actors will act rationally and in self-restraint, given the suicide bombers and the religious fanatics involved. Hence, those who might employ WMD or give them to terrorists— or employ them themselves—must be defanged one way or the other. A major reason is Pearl Harbor: If the Japanese could convince themselves then that they would bring the United States to its knees, there is no reason to assume that some future leader will not similarly misjudge a situation and attack.

The various ways in which deproliferation may be advanced more effectively deserve a major study by themselves. Several measures that might be promoted more actively once deproliferation becomes a more important goal include: vastly increasing programs (of the kind already introduced by the United States) that purchase both material out of which nuclear weapons can be made and small nuclear weapons that might be sold on the black market; providing other work to scientists and engineers working on WMD; converting the facilities for civilian use, which jointly might be called "plowshare projects";[21] trading nuclear weapons facilities for peaceful sources of energy and other products, such as the sort of deal worked out between the Clinton administration and North Korea.[22] (Much attention has recently been given to trying to curb the flow of funds that are used to finance the activities of small-scale terrorists. In my opinion, more effort should be dedicated to killing the market for nuclear material and technology. Even those governments who act favorably toward corporations, are keen to do business, or are simply easy to corrupt—allowing corporations to circumvent many rules, from those concerning taxation to those that ban piracy—should make it clear that trade in WMD and the materials needed to produce them is unacceptable. Severe penalties should be exacted and, above all, executives should be jailed when they help rogue states purchase what they need to make WMD.)

I very much agree with those who argue that deproliferation is so important that special measures should be take to advance it.[23] Nations that withdraw from international nuclear weapons treaties should be informed that they can no longer possess any of the nuclear technology that they received as a result of those agreements.[24] Any nation that ships WMD or their components across borders should be declared in egregious violation of international law, which must be modified to this effect. Such rogue nations—and they are rogue, whether their governments are stable or not—should be expelled from the World Trade Organization (WTO) and denied favorable trading status (after due warning). I agree with Robert Wright's suggestion that the WTO become the "fulcrum for ensuring compliance with international weapons-control law." In his words, "Refuse to admit nations to the WTO if they don't sign vital international treaties, and when WTO members violate a treaty—by, say, rebuffing inspectors—impose an automatically escalating set of penalties, in the form of rising tariffs, that culminate in expulsion."[25]

To the extent that such trade-offs cannot be worked out, it is fully appropriate, given the dangers involved, for the powers that be to pressure nations to give up their weapons. Pressure should be applied along the same lines that the United States and other nations employ for much less important goals, such as gaining a supportive vote in the United Nations or trade concessions.

Finally, as a last resort, with UN approval, military force should be used against nations like North Korea that command or are developing WMD, are governed by tyrants, and might turn the weapons over to terrorists. If the United Nations is unable to act, deproliferation and other measures needed to prevent the accumulation of WMD by rogue states and massive terrorism are still justified, although invasion and occupation are not necessarily the best way to proceed. Destroying nuclear facilities, as the Israelis did in Iraq in 1981, setting the Osiraq program near Baghdad back significantly, can give time for other processes to work. I realize that today's facilities are better sheltered, but bombing technology also has evolved and can be fine-tuned for this mission.

What about the United States and Russia? In a fair, just world, their WMD also would be removed. Nobody can question that foregoing nuclear weapons would greatly enhance the justness of their cause, their legitimacy as major GSA powers, and, of course, world safety. However, here idealism must be blended with a measure of realism. To demand that the United States and Russia submit to a deproliferation regime in order for deproliferation to take place in other countries amounts, in effect, to condoning leaving such weapons in the hands of much more dangerous states. Hence, at least for the near future, one will have to accept that these powers will retain their WMD. The good news is that the United States and Russia have agreed to curtail their stockpiles by two-thirds, following previous cuts, and to open inspections for each other to verify.[26] Not a bad start.

SOUND STARTERS

Deproliferation is not a pie-in-the-sky, peacenik idealist agenda. South Africa, which had long held out on joining the Nuclear Non-Proliferation Treaty (NPT), opened its facilities to IAEA inspectors in 1991 and dismantled its nuclear program.[27] After signing the treaty, Egypt, Sweden, Italy, and Switzerland canceled their nuclear weapons programs.[28] Under the 1991 Guadalajara Agreement, Brazil and Argentina agreed "to use their nuclear materials and facilities exclusively for peaceful purposes and to prohibit the receipt, storage, installation, deployment, or any other form of possession of any nuclear weapon."[29] The agreement requires both countries to file reports with the IAEA and submit to inspections, a commitment that has been roundly honored.[30]

The cooperative threat reduction and disarmament programs of the United States are credited mainly to Senators Sam Nunn (D-GA) and Richard Lugar (R-IN). These programs, known as Nunn-Lugar, have been responsible for the elimination of significant numbers of weapons from the territories of the former Soviet Union. In 1994, all nuclear warheads and six hundred kilograms of weapons-grade uranium were removed from Kazakhstan.[31] In 1996 nuclear warheads were removed from the Ukraine, a number of missile launchers were destroyed in Russia and the Ukraine (witnessed by U.S. officials), and all intercontinental ballistic missiles were removed from Belarus.[32] In total, by the beginning of 2002, Nunn-Lugar had eliminated 5,809 nuclear warheads, 1,212 ballistic and cruise missiles, 795 missile launchers, 92 long-range bombers, and 21 ballistic missile submarines.[33] Kazakhstan, Ukraine, and Belarus were declared free of nuclear weapons.[34] This deproliferation is of particular interest because after the breakup of the Soviet Union in 1991, these countries had emerged as the third-, fourth-, and eighth-largest nuclear powers in the world.[35] Other beneficial but all-too-rare actions include the purchase of weapons-grade material from Yugoslavia and its safe shipment to Russia,[36] as well as a secret deal with Romania that led to the removal of uranium from an insecure site.[37]

Many details remain to be worked out. Which actions should be taken to deal with countries merely suspected of having nuclear weapons, such as Iran? And what if their governments are solidly democratic and not considered to be dangerous, as in the case of Israel? Is it even practical to talk about removing biological and chemical weapons, as these can be produced in small laboratories on the sly? These are all fair questions that should be addressed, but they should not be used to delay the urgent mission of removing nuclear weapons from rogue nations and ensuring that terrorists are unable to acquire them.

AN ANTAGONISTIC PARTNERSHIP

A critic may well argue that, despite all of these dangers, the United States should not be the one to lead the drive to save the world from massive terrorism and WMD. Would this mission not be best suited for the United Nations, which can draw on the IAEA and base its actions on treaties that various parties have agreed to and properly endorsed? Like all contracts, once voluntarily entered, these treaties must be honored. Agreeing to inspections is part of a contract, and hence enforcing them does not constitute interfering in the internal affairs of the nations involved. The last thing the world needs is some kind of a new authority, a critic might conclude, controlled by a superpower.

The next part of this volume discusses at some length the relationship between force and legitimacy, might and sweet. However, the issue at hand is too pertinent to ignore. The fact is that although the IAEA is a source of legitimacy, it has little enforcement power unless a national power backs it up. It is all soft in a world that requires a combination of soft and hard. With rare exceptions, without threats, economic pressures, and other forms of arm-twisting proliferating nations would not have agreed to disarm or even be inspected, and even if inspectors would have been allowed into such nations they would have been much more limited in what they were allowed to examine. The scope of the inspections that Saddam allowed prior to the invasion coincided almost perfectly with the variable pressure that big powers applied on him.

In 2003 North Korea withdrew from the NPT, which it is legally entitled to do. Initially it refused to engage in multilateral discussions on the matter, insisting rather on bilateral negotiations with the United States on its own terms. However, after the swift victory of the United States over Saddam's troops, which sent Kim Jong Il into weeks of hiding, North Korea dramatically changed its position, declared its willingness to engage into multilateral negotiations, and somewhat moderated its terms.

In short, for deproliferation to progress, a vital part of the new world order, the IAEA, needs a collaborator with significant "hard power."[38] Before 2001 hard power was often provided by either a single power or a group of nations on an ad hoc basis, which was wholly inadequate. Since 2001 the United States, working with China, Japan, and South Korea in the case of North Korea and Russia in the case of Iran, has provided some of the needed muscle. It is thus best to view the GSA as working with the United Nations, despite their often-contentious relationship, but it is incorrect to assume that the United Nations could make a dent in the problem on its own—or that big powers do best when they ignore it.

PACIFICATION AND HUMANITARIAN INTERVENTIONS

Next I examine three other global missions that concern basic security, the Hobbesian mission. In the past, these missions were pursued with less vigor (I am reporting, not advocating) because they engage less directly the interests of the superpower and other powers than do antiterrorism and deproliferation. This situation is likely to change somewhat for reasons to be discussed. My exploration is both empirical and normative in the sense that I ask both in which direction the trends are unfolding and whether these trends are justified.

PACIFICATION

Pacification occurs when an international intervention stops a war between two nations or prevents it from occurring in the first place—for instance, between Greece and Turkey over Cyprus. Or it may occur when such interventions employ force to curb a civil war or an armed ethnic conflict, as in Northern Ireland. The term "pacification" may bring to mind brutal oppression. This is not what I have in mind. The intervention need not be brutal, but by definition it must use force (or at least the threat of its application) to stop armed conflicts. (I find no other term that serves better. "Peacekeeping" refers to maintaining a peace after it has been established, but not to halting the conflict.)

Pacification is often, albeit not always, and surely not in earlier colonial periods, highly legitimate precisely because it passes the Hobbesian survival test. True, the various powers promote pacification only in part out of humanitarian concerns, although these should not be dismissed. Pacification often engages nonessential national interests of the big powers, such as the U.S. desire to keep NATO countries from fighting each other or satisfying particular, often ethnic, groups of voters. But given that these are not hard-core interests, pacification has often been pursued listlessly.

Now that the United States has in effect assumed the role of a global cop, it finds it more difficult to look the other way when local conflicts brew or explode. When Pakistan and India edged toward war in 2002, it undermined the U.S. war against terrorism because Pakistan removed troops and attention from its northwestern border and refocused them on its southeastern one. If the United States stands by as the Palestinians and Israelis fight it out, this inaction hinders its antiterror efforts in the Arab world, and so on. Moreover, like a national government that loses its credibility if there are warring factions on its turf, to the extent that the United States has accepted its role as the leader and main force that makes the GSA work, large-scale bloodshed undermines its credibility. Other powers have also dedicated troops to pacification due to a similar mixture of self-interest and humanitarian concerns. Hence we have witnessed an increased commitment to pacification in recent years and we should expect more in the foreseeable future. In 2003 the United Nations voted to increase the size of the peacekeeping force in Congo; the United States was brokering a peace agreement between the warring parties in Sudan; and the UN Security Council authorized the deployment of a multinational peacekeeping force in Liberia. In 2003, 36,000 UN peacekeeping troops were engaged in fourteen operations in countries such as Cyprus, Ethiopia and Eritrea, Ivory Coast, Lebanon (observers on the border with Israel), Sierra Leone, and Western Sahara. The budget for fiscal year 2003 was more than $2.5. billion.[39]

The combined result of all these actions is a pacification "department" of the new global architecture that is much less streamlined and less active than the antiterrorism drive, but it is nevertheless recognized implicitly as part of the new world order, and is gaining in importance.

HUMANITARIAN INTERVENTIONS

A highly legitimate role for the evolving GSA is to prevent genocide, even if this entails armed interventions in sovereign nations. Such interventions are legitimate on the same grounds as deproliferation: They entail the protection of a large number of lives from a clear and present danger, therefore discharging the elementary duty of the state on a transnational level when intrastate security fails or the forces that are supposed to provide for it are themselves the source of the danger. The fact that the value of humanitarian interventions trumps that of national sovereignty is widely recognized, more so as the years pass. The cause of humanitarian intervention has been particularly advanced since Kofi Annan assumed leadership of the United Nations, to the point that it is sometimes referred to as the Kofi Annan doctrine.

As I see it, there is a level of normative commitment that might be called "a moral minimum." If people stand by and allow masses to be slaughtered, a massacre that they could have prevented—the way the Dutch troops stood by in Srebrenica in 1995[40]—they (and those who order them to stand down) fall well below this minimal level of morality. Because of the large number of lives involved and the violence that accompanies these interethnic slaughters, preventing a genocide or ethnic cleansing is a higher moral command than avoiding other crimes or even doing good deeds such as giving to charity, helping the sick, and feeding the homeless. People who see themselves as moral creatures should need no other reasons. Preventing mass killing is one of those few causes that speaks to us directly, in unmistakable and compelling terms, and should command our attention and commitment.[41] (I realize that numerous volumes have been written about the moral considerations involved, volumes in which the issue is discussed in much more complex and nuanced terms than I can do here.[42] Among the many issues that must be sorted out is under what conditions humanitarian interventions are to be undertaken, whose troops should be used, how they are to be paid for, what the scope of their mission ought to be, and how they are going to extricate themselves.[43] To address these would take a volume larger than this one.)

Humanitarian interventions are best carried out with UN authorization, but they are highly legitimate even if advanced without it when the United Nations acts slowly or disapproves. The United Nations is not the only arbiter of that which is legitimate. The European Union and the United States should never have stood by as more than half a million people in Rwanda were slaughtered; they should have intervened much earlier in East Timor; and they were right to stop the ethnic cleansing in Kosovo.[44] The respect for all human rights presumes first of all that the right to live is not violated and masses are not slaughtered merely because of their racial, ethnic, religious, or political identities, or any other affiliation.[45]

Humanitarian interventions in the past were overdue, slow, and reluctantly pursued, if they took place at all, largely because they directly engaged even fewer national interests of the big powers than pacification. Two factors will make it somewhat more likely that the GSA will take on more than the big powers have in the past: one is the growing power of global public opinion, which tends to favor stopping genocides; the other is the sense that whoever accepts the responsibility for introducing order into the world cannot ignore such atrocities, any more than, say, a new police chief can ignore gang warfare, even if gang members kill only one another and battles take place only in the inner city.

Humanitarian intervention (and pacification) would benefit from the positioning of GSA forces in unstable regions as well as from the development of lighter, more rapid response forces than the United States and other big powers have had in the past. This "forward" positioning entails placing troops and military hardware close to a potential front line or, as the Pentagon refers to them, "hot spots."

Humanitarian interventions (and pacification) should involve regional forces, although these may need the assistance of big-power forces. A major reason to favor regional forces is that they often enhance the legitimacy of interventions, as opposed to those carried out by former colonial powers or the new big powers—United States, Russia, and China—and they reduce the costs involved. Moreover, further developing regional forces, especially preparing them to act quickly—standby and nearby—can also serve the primary missions of the GSA: to fight terrorism and encourage deproliferation. In several cases such forces engaged in looting, sexual abuse, and other conduct unbecoming a peacekeeping force. Making them standby provides an opportunity to turn them into a more professional transnational police force.[46]

Humanitarian interventions also illustrate the peculiar and troubled relationship between the United Nations and the various national powers, especially the United States, which is best referred to as an antagonistic partnership. The United Nations often acts as a key legitimator, but—to reiterate—it does not and cannot command the hard power required to back up its resolutions and declarations. If the United States (in Haiti, Somalia, and Liberia), France (in Ivory Coast), Russia and NATO (in Kosovo), or Australia (in East Timor) did not provide the muscle, UN resolutions would have been of little consequence. The United States did not provide adequate security for the UN headquarters in Baghdad (or the UN staff did not feel that they needed such protection); when terrorists attacked the building in August 2003, the resulting damage and loss of life forced the United Nations to greatly scale back its operations in Iraq. Very often in the past, the United Nations did not act until a national power was willing to or had already committed its forces to a cause. Those who confuse the ought-to-be UN with the as-is UN tend to ignore this unpleasant truth. Thus, despite UN resolutions dating back to 1975, East Timor was ravaged for years by Indonesia until 1999, when Australia finally decided to support the East Timorese claim of self-determination and began to exert the necessary pressure and force to change the situation. With Australia providing leadership, infrastructure, and troops, the United Nations finally was able to address the East Timor humanitarian crisis.[47]

In 2000 the Revolutionary United Front of Sierra Leone captured UN peacekeepers who had been stationed there to stop the civil war. The United Kingdom sent troops to free its citizens and stayed in the country in order to secure the capital and restore some semblance of order. The British then sponsored a UN resolution to ban the sale of diamonds from Sierra Leone, the revenues from which were believed to be fueling the war.[48] British involvement was crucial in restoring order and to augmenting the UN peacekeeping efforts. After Iraq overran Kuwait, UN resolutions were of little consequence until the United States and Russia acted in unison to combat the aggression.[49] When no power came forward in Rwanda, the United Nations was useless.

Michael Ignatieff has observed wryly that "[m]ultilateral solutions to the world's problems are all very well, but they have no teeth unless America [or some other power] bares its fangs."[50] Though history is his ally, such statements underestimate the role of legitimacy in developing a new world order. In humanitarian interventions, as in the other safety missions I have reviewed, both the big powers and the United Nations have a role to play.

PLOWSHARES

Farther down the road, in a place where reality fades and visions loom, is the mission of ratcheting down the manufacturing and trade in all arms. The dream of—and the argument for—turning swords into plowshares is as old as history; still, the world that this dream envisions commands attention. When people are killed en masse with conventional weapons, they are just as dead as if they are killed with WMD, only it takes longer, and we have become inured to this form of slaughter. We also have grown accustomed to the absurd situation in which nations demand and receive foreign aid, loan forgiveness, and massive credit because they are poor, while they use their own resources—or those granted them by taxpayers of richer nations—to purchase weapons and fight their neighbors or kill their own people.

The billions of dollars spent each year on conventional weapons and other military expenses vastly exceeds all that is available in foreign aid. In 2002, $794 billion was consumed by military expenditures.[51] If even half of these funds could be used for peaceful purposes, deserts all over the world could indeed blossom.

One of the evolving norms that could lead to the formation of a potential disarmament regime can be seen in the kind of deal that the Clinton administration was pursuing with North Korea: trading the forfeiture of arms (in this case nuclear weapons) for foreign aid. The nations of the world ought to treat making and selling arms as they are beginning to treat tobacco. Governments are slowly moving from subsidizing its growth to paying farmers to plant something else. Public opinion is souring on those who produce, sell, promote, or use the product. If smoking can be curbed, can't we dream that one day conventional weapons will be treated with as much concern as cigarettes?

Some sophisticated political scientists may well argue that the issue is not arms, but rather conflicts that are not settled by peaceful means. Fair enough. Hence we cannot expect large-scale arms reduction until global political institutions are advanced. Meanwhile, scaling back the trade rather than promoting it is a mission that belongs on the GSA's task list.

MISSION APPETITE REVISITED

To briefly sum up the argument to this point: The United States, its allies, and other big powers already have taken one giant step in moving from fighting terrorism on a global scale, in what amounts to a Global Safety Authority, to greatly expanding previous efforts to deproliferate. Although the United States received precious little support for its hunt for WMD in Iraq, it received considerable assistance in its drive to deproliferate Iran and North Korea. There is much less doubt that these nations possess WMD and pose a danger to others.

Further expansion of the work of the Global Safety Authority, which involves taking on still other safety missions—pacification and humanitarian interventions—has been much slower (although both are legitimate), largely because they do not engage the interests of the big powers as directly as do fighting terrorism and eliminating WMD. Still, there have been increased efforts, especially to end civil wars and armed conflicts, and more are expected in the future. The GSA and the United Nations currently function (although the GSA is still evolving and the United Nations may be reformed one day) in an uneasy, tense relationship, and still frequently as antagonistic partners.

For now it is safe to state that the world has a new security agency, formed in the wake of the 2001 attack on the United States. Like other police forces, and indeed like any application of force, the actions of the new global cop raise numerous questions, but none of them will make him go away or obviate the need to attend to safety on a global level. I turn shortly to examine non-safety-related transnational missions, such as advancing human rights and democracy, protecting the global environment, and advancing welfare.

THE WILSONIAN DAYDREAM

The notion that introducing human rights and democracy is an advanced goal that cannot proceed unless a nation or group of nations provides rudimentary safety may seem self-evident. Anybody who considers the situation in the streets of Baghdad in the first months after the American occupation—when looting was common, crime exploded, assaults on Americans became a daily affair, shopkeepers who sold alcohol were killed, and interethnic violence escalated—will realize that the conditions for holding elections were not ripe. The same was true in the streets of many Russian cities after the collapse of the communist regime in 1989. Moreover, such domestic turmoil courts international instability, because it invites other powers to interfere, as Iran and Turkey tried to do in Iraq in 2003.

The main counterargument, so often repeated that it has become a kind of mantra, is that the best way to ensure international safety and peace is to promote domestic democracy. The reason? "Democracies do not fight each other."[52] It is an idea at the core of the Wilsonian daydream, a long embraced, political science cliché, of a world peace cobbled together by democratic polities.[53] Recently it has even been asserted that "the 'promotion of democracy worldwide' should be put at the center of America's national security strategy."[54]

Whether a world composed of wall-to-wall democracies would be peaceful is not at issue because the incontrovertible fact is that democracy can advance only very slowly, if at all, in countries that lack the necessary social, cultural, and economic foundations. Most of these nations have not yet democratized. We cannot wait to prevent a nuclear attack by North Korea—say, if Kim Jong Il has a paranoia attack—until his nation is democratized. We should not wait to take measures to prevent a nuclear war between India and Pakistan until Pakistan becomes democratic. We cannot rely on the reformers in Iran to usher in democracy, nor presume that they would give up their country's nuclear weapons. Even for countries that have no WMD, when they are sliding toward war or genocide, as in the case of Congo and Liberia, democratization *cannot* be relied on.

Thus, one can be fully committed to promoting democracy on a worldwide scale (albeit with democratic means and not at the point of a tank, bayonets, or cruise missiles) and still realize that, in the short run, security is needed first. I cannot stress enough that I am not opposed to the promotion of democracy (and other elements of autonomy) across national borders; on the contrary, I am all in favor. However, I argue that democratic developments *cannot* be rushed, while rudimentary safety cannot wait.

Aside from short-order democratization being unable to deliver on a strategy that seeks to establish world peace, it also provides a poor source of legitimacy. When other rationales lost their credibility overseas and with considerable segments of the American public, the Bush administration claimed that it sought to democratize Iraq, as well as the rest of the Middle East. However, critics correctly point out that the United States supports many authoritarian governments elsewhere. In contrast, arguing that force must be used against those tyrants armed with WMD—assuming that they truly are—is much more compelling. This is the case because, just as a policy setting out to liberalize societies is bound to be very inconsistent, and hence difficult to defend, so can a policy seeking to deproliferate be applied consistently, although that does not necessarily mean that all those involved will be treated in exactly the same manner. In short, pacifying the world is a goal that is much easier to legitimate than regime change. (Note that with the exception of France, other members of the Security Council were willing to support a military invasion of Iraq to remove WMD, but sought to give more time to inspectors—which shows that the international community is willing in principle to disarm failed states. There is, however, little support for coercive democratization.)

Non-safety missions—democratization included—must wait until there is basic security. To try to build democratic institutions in short order in a newly freed nation that lacks sociological elements of modernity is a violation of the principle of self-restraint. More importantly, such a policy flies in the face of major social forces, and it is as likely to succeed as pilots who pay no mind to gravity.

CHAPTER EIGHT

CURTAILING NATIONAL SOVEREIGNTY: FOR WHAT?

TREATING NATIONAL SOVEREIGNTY OR SELF-DETERMINATION as in-fallible, as Americans often treat the First Amendment, is an attitude that was developed under specific historical conditions that no longer apply in most parts of the world. Neither God nor nature created national sovereignty. It was barely known before the 1648 Treaty of Westphalia. That treaty brought an end to the Thirty Years War (1618–1648), which erupted after the Reformation broke the Catholic religious hegemony over Europe. This conflict entailed what in post-Westphalia terms would be called interfering in the internal affairs of another nation, seeking to determine the religion to which the citizens of another nation would adhere.

The architecture of this treaty provided the basic premises of international relations ever since.[1] Politically, the treaty recognized the "sovereign state" (wherein there is a monopoly on the legitimate use of means of violence within a defined territory) as the basic unit of world politics and the highest authority of civil society. Militarily, it accepted war as an instrument of policy only in conflicts between sovereign states; in other words, it was acceptable for one state to fight another for its own interests, but not because of some internal affair within the other country. Finally, the treaty separated religion and politics, thus removing religion as an acceptable cause of war.

The high level of respect for national sovereignty that followed was heightened further after the horrors of World War I and World War II, as well as other wars between nations. These events lent strong support to the idea first ensconced in the League of Nations and then the United Nations: No nation should invade the territory of another. Another key historical reason why national sovereignty is so dearly held is that, during the era of empires, numerous ethnic groups around the world were dominated by world powers. Their members had little influence on those who governed them (although details differ between the somewhat more benign British empire and the more brutal Belgian and French ones) and, as a rule, no say in metropolitan politics, in which key decisions about their fate were rendered. Beginning with the independence of most Latin American countries between 1810 and 1825 there followed almost 180 years of wars of national liberation, in which ethnic groups succeeded in dismembering the empires and achieving self-government. These movements first flourished in Latin America and in Europe—liberating the Balkan countries from the Austro-Hungarian empire—and then spread into Asia and Africa until no empire was left standing. In the process, national self-determination became a key normative claim. By this light, one nation had to thoroughly justify its dominance over or invasion of another.

This architecture has been challenged in two ways. In the last decade, states have disintegrated into ethnonationalist and religious elements, especially since the breakup of the Soviet Union. Also, transnational concerns about economics, environmentalism, and human rights have presented moral challenges to the notion of sovereignty. In this limited sense, the world is returning to a pre-Westphalia stage. This is a trend not without human costs, especially in the form of religious and ethnic conflicts in states in which the national community never flourished or has been undermined. Hence the reasons to favor curtailing national sovereignty and granting more legitimacy to transnational forces need to be clearly articulated, their limits stated, and their legitimacy more widely established.

The most important reason, which alone justifies respecting national sovereignty much less than in recent generations, is the threat of wholesale terrorism, the use of weapons of mass destruction (WMD) directly by rogue states or by rogue states providing such weapons to terrorists. The value of deproliferation, of protecting the world from nuclear devastation, trumps the respect for the national sovereignty of nations that insist on clinging to WMD.

There are several additional reasons to favor diminished national sovereignty.[2] Wars of national liberation basically have exhausted their mission. There are few ethnic groups that still seek self-expression and are held back by imperial forces. Members of a number of groups such as the Basques, Quebecois, Corsicans, and Scots favor independence, but these ethnic groups differ from the people of India, Ghana, and Congo fighting for their independence from colonial powers; these current groups live under democratic representative governments. Moreover, there are good reasons to hold that if these ethnic groups seceded, the people involved would live under less, not more, democratic governments than those that now govern them, as was the case when Slovakia seceded from Czechoslovakia. In these situations, increasing the autonomy of various parts of a country—or of ethnic groups within existing nation-states—is much more justified than granting them full-scale self-government or nationhood. For those who live in free societies, self-determination—gaining national sovereignty for distinct groups—no longer should have the moral cachet it had in earlier colonial days.

In short, a key source of legitimation for the new global architecture is that it will not tolerate mass killing, whether by WMD or by genocide, thus providing the very first element of a state on the global level—a measure of security. The new global architecture thus will draw on replacing respect for national sovereignty with a growing respect for a human good—the right to live, whatever one's nationality. This is a much more compelling standard for action than the enforcement of a whole slew of human rights. The list of these rights is too long (and yet some argue not long enough) and too unclear to justify forceful intervention in the internal affairs of other countries at this stage in the development of the Global Safety Authority and the United Nations. This standard does apply, however, for fighting terrorism and deproliferation, and increasingly to pacification and humanitarian interventions, and—one day—to general arms reduction.

Nonetheless, however demanding this list of missions, one clearly senses that it is not good enough.

PART III

BEYOND GLOBAL SAFETY

CHAPTER NINE

THE OLD SYSTEM IS OVERLOADED

WILL THE UNITED STATES BE ONLY THE WORLD'S COP AND REFUSE to be of service as a gardener, healer, or nanny? In less metaphorical terms, will the formation of the Global Safety Authority be followed by a Global Environmental Protection Authority, a Worldwide Health Department, and a Worldwide Welfare Department?[1] Or will the new global architecture look more like the American national one, in which the federal government (the analog of the Global Authority) deals only with some crimes, especially terrorism, while many others are left to the local police departments of the fifty states (the analog of the nations), as are welfare, education, and health?

The need for expanded Global Authorities to attend to additional missions is clear. What I shall refer to as the "Old System"—the national governments *and* intergovernmental organizations, composed of representatives of the same nation-states—cannot cope with numerous rising transnational problems, some concerning garden-variety crimes (transnational mafias and cybercrime) and many concerning non-security related issues (environmental degradation and pandemics that know no borders).

The Old System cannot handle a high volume of significant activities because decision makers must consult with their respective governments on most matters before they can proceed (or else they are instructed in great detail ahead of time, which limits their maneuverability). Also, when it comes to global or even semi-global policies, so many different nations with divergent interests and values are involved that decisions are hard to reach. Although some matters are worked out, often after a great deal of effort, when it comes to numerous other matters, progress is slow compared to the pace of the increase in problems, and it is much more common for nations to agree on declarations than to actually implement them. In short, the Old System is too formal, too cumbersome, and too slow.

Once upon a time, in the long gone age of the 1980s, national governments could ban hate speech, require patients to be guided by a physician when seeking to purchase a whole slew of medications, curb gambling, and prohibit trade in Nazi paraphernalia.[2] I am not arguing that these were all sound public policies, only that national governments could more or less effectively implement them in their respective countries.

The Internet greatly undermined these national policies. People in Canada, Great Britain, and Germany—where hate speech is banned—now can freely make such speech, as long as they do it in cyberspace, cloaked by its anonymity; patients now can order medications from other nations that demand no prescriptions or settle for phony ones; and so on. The Internet is both a major causal factor and a convenient symbol for the decline in the capacity of individual nation-states to manage their affairs, one at a time, domestically. I am not arguing that the nation-state is dead, that national governments have lost all their power, merely that their capacity to guide matters has diminished greatly.

For instance, the World Health Organization (WHO) reportedly was concerned that due to the Internet people have access to a host of websites that represent themselves as medical sources but are highly misleading, if not dangerous. It wanted to formulate standards that websites would have to follow worldwide. However, WHO soon realized that, given the highly different notions of what constitutes health and medical treatment, such a task was impossible to carry out. This seemingly limited issue, medical advice websites, goes to the heart of the question—how can the international community, with its diverse and complex array of voices and perspectives, agree on standards and regulations?

Moreover, when agreements finally are reached, they often are not honored or are openly breached. The mechanisms for enforcement usually either do not exist or are themselves cumbersome, slow, weak, and able to carry only a small volume of traffic. The argument may be made that intergovernmental efforts to promote trade have worked quite well.[3] However, trade is different in character from most other transnational issues,[4] and it would be a grave mistake to generalize from the experience of trade treaties to other international organizations.*

---

* The European Union also had the fewest difficulties, although far from none, when it was largely a free trade association.

As a result, more and more problems call for transnational treatment. In earlier eras efforts were made to deal with such matters by forming scores of intergovernmental organizations; these worked in the past and continue to do so reasonably effectively on matters that are relatively unimportant or of limited scope, such as arranging for mail service and assigning radio frequencies. However, the fact that many transnational problems remain largely untreated or poorly handled is prima facie evidence that the Old System—intergovernmental organizations included—is not meeting the need. The problem is not the decline of the nation-state per se, but rather the fact that so far precious little has been provided to fill the authority void caused by this decline.

The result is a growing sense of ennui, a sense that we are governed by forces that we neither understand nor control, which push the establishment of human primacy farther beyond the horizon. This sense is a major source of legitimacy for new transnational solutions. It is paralleled by a growing convergence of interests that would benefit from more effective ways of doing the public's business that the Old System no longer can handle. Hence we should expect, and there is some evidence that follows to show that this is not an idle thought, that any new global architecture, whether it initially will takes the shape of the Global Safety Authority or some other form, will be under pressure to expand to include other missions.

In the following chapters, the analysis of the need for new transnational structures, and the ways that the nations of the world may provide for them, draws on existing developments rather than on designers' dearest wishes and dreams. In the process the discussion moves further from recent events and deeper into the future.

TRANSNATIONAL PROBLEMS: A QUICK OVERVIEW

TRANSNATIONAL ORGANIZED CRIME

Although crime organized across national borders—by the mafia, for instance—has long posed a problem for governments due to globalization, this form of criminality has exploded recently. James H. Mittelman and Robert Johnston explain: "The move toward opening markets, liberalizing trade, lifting regulations, and privatizing formerly public holdings has presented criminal groups with unprecedented opportunities."[5] A report by the National Security Council notes that "international criminal networks [particularly in Russia, Nigeria, China, Italy, and Japan] . . . have taken advantage of the dramatic changes in technology, world politics, and the global economy to become more sophisticated and flexible in their operations."[6] The Bank of Credit and Commerce International, which secretly channeled funds to terrorists and bribed public officials until the early 1990s, managed to link up the financial systems of thirty-two separate countries.[7] Since the 1970s, globalization has enabled organized crime groups to cooperate with each other in a "global division of labor and power." Thus:

> Russians specialize in business scams and frauds; Chinese triads, in credit-card counterfeiting and human smuggling; Colombians, in narcotics and money laundering; Nigerians, in bank and credit-card fraud; and so on. The Colombian cartels work with Russian organized crime groups to open heroin and cocaine markets in Eastern Europe, with Colombians supplying the product and Russians attending to distribution. Taking collusion one step further, the Russian groups in New Jersey even pay so-called license fees to the Cosa Nostra for permission to operate fuel tax scams in their territory.[8]

Global organized crime groups are estimated to earn nearly $1.5 trillion in revenues per year.[9]

Such crime has been found to have a "disintegrative effect on the world political, economic and social order [that] *transcends the enforcement ability of the nation-state.* . . . In many countries, the infiltration of organized crime into political structures has *paralyzed law enforcement from within.*"[10]

The future of combating organized crime looks even bleaker. The U.S. National Intelligence Council has concluded that:

> Over the next 15 years, transnational criminal organizations will become increasingly adept at exploiting the global diffusion of sophisticated information, financial, and transportation networks. . . . They will corrupt leaders of unstable, economically fragile or failing states, insinuate themselves into troubled banks and businesses, and cooperate with insurgent political movements to control substantial geographic areas.[11]

TRAFFICKING IN PEOPLE

Unlike illegal immigrants, most of whom are smuggled into a country they wish to enter, many victims of trafficking are abducted against their will and forced into labor in a foreign country, often of a sexual nature. Interpol has called sex trafficking "the fastest growing type of crime" in the world; it exploded in Europe following the dissolution of the Soviet Union.[12] The United

Nations estimates that trafficking in people across national borders involves about 4 million individuals worldwide each year. According to U.S. Deputy Secretary of State Richard Armitage, it nets about $7 billion each year for traffickers. Armitage predicts that this global slave trade "will outstrip trade in guns and narcotics within a decade."[13]

Sex tourism typically consists of citizens of developed countries vacationing in less developed nations and engaging in sexual relations with prostitutes, many of whom are children. More than 1 million children worldwide are involved in sex tourism, and the numbers are increasing.[14]

Trafficking in people and sex tourism strains the traditional state system because combating these activities involves multiple investigative agencies in multiple countries.[15] Australia's experience illustrates the resulting difficulties. Australia passed a law penalizing its citizens who engage in sex tourism. However, "[o]verseas corruption, cultural differences, inexperience among police and problems with witnesses are preventing prosecutions among people who encourage child sex tourism." Additionally, police in Australia have "warned it is nearly impossible to use the laws successfully because of difficulties dealing with foreign authorities, getting child victims' evidence to stand up in court, and because of a lack of police officers with specialist skills."[16] The absence of international coordination on this issue has been damaging even within European Union, as Britain has become a staging post for the trafficking in children to other European nations, which tend to have much stricter anti-trafficking laws.[17]

ENVIRONMENTAL DEGRADATION

The global environment seems to continue to deteriorate.* The 2001 edition of the annual *State of the World*, published annually by the World Resources Institute, reports: "Despite abundant information about our environmental impact, human activities continue to scalp whole forests, drain rivers dry, prune the Tree of Evolution, raise the level of the seven seas, and reshape climate patterns. And the toll on people and the natural environment is growing as stressed environmental and social systems feed on each other."[18] Other reports suggest that water is imperiled: "Today thirty-one countries and over 1 billion people completely lack access to clean water." The problem is so severe that

---

* I write "seems" because there are so many aspects of the environment that it is difficult to find a reliable overview. The following information provides a sense of the findings that are available.

"unless we dramatically change our ways, between one-half and two-thirds of humanity will be living with severe freshwater shortages within the next quarter-century."[19] It is estimated that, in the 1990s, 9.4 million hectares of forest area worldwide were lost annually.[20] Worldwide, nearly half of all fisheries are fully depleted and another crudely estimated 25 percent are overfished.[21]

Environmental degradation poses particular problems for national governments because most environmental damage is not limited by borders, as pollution from one country invades another, overfishing by one country affects another country's ability to maintain its catch, and so on. Attempting to manage the global commons goes beyond the capabilities of any one country, hence the large number of environmental treaties that have been concluded in the last thirty years. Nonetheless, the environment continues to fall behind as governments flout the restrictions they agreed to in those treaties, which were to begin with often symbolic rather than substantive commitments. The struggle that preceded reaching an agreement on the text of the Kyoto Protocol highlights the difficulties in reaching agreements that often are more rhetorical than realistic.

Spread of Infectious Diseases

More than 25 million people in Sub-Saharan Africa had HIV/AIDS in 2001, five times more than those infected a mere twelve years earlier. Based on current trends, affected African countries will lose between 10 and 30 percent of their workforce by 2020.[22] Asia also has been heavily affected, with an estimated 7.2 million people infected by the end of 2002. India and China have significant populations with the virus. The Joint United Nations Programme on HIV/AIDS (UNAIDS) estimates that nearly 4 million people in India were infected at the end of 2001. Estimates for China are around 1 million. The number of cases in China alone is expected to grow to 10 million by 2010 if prevention measures are not put in place. Eastern Europe and Central Asia have 1.2 million cases of HIV/AIDS, due particularly to high infection rates in the Russian Federation. UNAIDS and WHO find that "in the Russian Federation, the total number of reported HIV infections climbed to over 200,000 by mid-2002—a huge increase over the 10,993 reported less than four years ago, at the end of 1998." These organizations see a strong impact on Russia's future growth, as almost 80 percent of new cases are reported in those under age 29. Worldwide, as of December 2002, 42 million people were living with HIV/AIDS.[23]

The Old System is unable to halt the spread of infectious diseases. Writing about the difficulties that WHO faced while combating severe acute respiratory syndrome (SARS), Dr. Andy Ho notes: "Without enforcement powers, the agency can do little to stop a country from trying to hide an outbreak that it finds embarrassing—until it's spread so much that it's no longer a secret. And even when a threat has been recognized, conflicting national policies hamper the WHO's ability to control the response to it."[24]

Epidemiologist Jack Woodall adds:

> It's just not practical. UN bodies are made up of member states and they are sovereign states and they will do what they want regardless of international regulations. All that the WHO could do is say, 'You know, it really is in your own interest to invite us in to help us solve this disease problem for you.' But they certainly can't enforce it [25]

SARS, the avian flu, and God only knows what else will jump across national borders, evading our attempts to contain them.

PIRACY

Intellectual property theft, through counterfeiting or piracy, is a growing transnational problem, particularly with the rise of the Internet and the improvements in technology that make copying products easy and cheap. The U.S. Trade Representative estimates that businesses lose between $200 and $250 billion per year due to counterfeiting.[26] Businesses with major concerns about piracy include the motion picture industry (estimated losses of $3 billion each year), the music industry (also estimated to lose $3 billion each year), and software companies (losing an estimated $12 billion every year).[27] Twenty-three percent of all business software installed in the United States are illegal copies, as are 35 percent in Western Europe and 55 percent in Latin America and Asia.[28]

Combating these problems within a country's borders is difficult enough, but preventing counterfeiting and piracy outside the country in which a product is manufactured is much more difficult. Typically, Bilal Khan, a Pakistani national accused of selling counterfeit computer software online in Britain, fled the country and simply continued his pirating operation in Pakistan.[29]

Moreover, as the *Economist* puts it:

> [P]olice or customs officers are often more interested in fighting what they consider to be more serious offences, such as homicide or drug smuggling. There is also the problem of job protection: in many poor places, counterfeiting is the biggest business in town, and local police would rather not be responsible for putting local people, and even their own relatives, out of work. . . . In America, convicted counterfeiters face fines of up to $2m and 10 years in prison for a first offence. In China, counterfeiters can still get away with a $1,000 fine, which even there provides little deterrence.[30]

CYBERCRIME

Worldwide, reported security violations (computer break-ins or network attacks) increased from around 1,000 in 1992 to 81,000 in 2002.[31] Nearly 20 million people command the skills needed for "malicious hacking."[32] Discovering the perpetrators of these crimes and stopping them is difficult, since 65 percent of computer break-ins on U.S. companies—the main target of hackers—originate abroad.[33] Computer crimes are likely to increase in the future as more people gain knowledge of hacking techniques and the infrastructure upon which computer networks are built.[34] Computer crimes are a growing and serious transnational problem because not only personal information is stored on computers but so are governments' classified documents, nuclear information, and businesses' product development strategies.[35] In addition, computer crimes result in financial losses due to the costs of cleanup and lost productivity. In 2000, businesses lost $17.1 billion worldwide due to computer virus attacks.[36]

The Old System is unable to deal with cybercrimes. "International law is often ill-suited to deal with the problem [of hacking], with conflicting views on what constitutes cybercrime, how—or if—perpetrators should be punished and how national borders can be applied to a medium that is essentially borderless."[37] When the person suspected of creating the "Love Bug" virus was identified, a virus which affected governments and businesses around the world and caused billions of dollars in damage in 2000, he was charged with a minor crime because the Philippines had no national law in place under which he could have been prosecuted.[38] As Dan Larkin of the Internet Fraud Complaint Center stated, "[i]t's difficult to dust for fingerprints in a digital world."[39] So far there have been no major interruptions of services, for instance of airline traffic, but they must be expected.

The thesis advanced here—that new regimes are called for to cope with rising transnational problems because the Old System can no longer carry the rising load by itself—may not be much contested. International treaties have been drafted to address most, if not all, of the aforementioned issues since 1950 (the year in which the United Nations passed the Convention for the Suppression of the Traffic in Persons and of the Exploitation of the Prostitution of Others), but these treaties often are not implemented, as reflected in the continued increase in these problems—and the number of treaties that are supposed to deal with them—over the years.[40] However, there is much less agreement about the nature of the required new global architecture. Some people focus on transnational regimes that do not entail any new governmental authority , while others assume that supranational authorities are essential (e.g., the International Criminal Court). I turn next to examine to what extent the global civil society can provide the treatments that are lacking and whether some true new global authorities are needed and feasible.

CHAPTER TEN

GLOBAL CIVIL SOCIETY:
ITS SCOPE AND LIMITATIONS

A MAJOR SOURCE OF BUILDING BLOCKS OF THE NEW GLOBAL architecture are "nonstate" actors, in particular international *non*governmental organizations (INGOs),[1] transnational informal networks, and social movements. These groups are said to provide "governance without government"[2]—that is, to perform the kind of jobs governments used to by drawing on other forms of organization, especially transnational voluntary associations. The term "global civil society"[3] sometimes is used to refer to the evolving social fabric that these bodies engender, as well as to transnational social norms, in contrast to a world state or government that relies on laws. In a few extreme cases, the phrase "governance without government" is associated with the old dream of abolishing all states and replacing them with local communitarian bonds and bodies. Most of the time, when governance includes both the organizing bodies of the global civil society and state governments,[4] nonstate actors are expected to carry an important part of the load, but not to replace the Old System.

There is a considerable measure of optimism about the capabilities of nonstate actors.[5] This position is so well captured by Lester M. Salamon that his quote can stand for all others:

> A striking upsurge is under way around the globe in organized voluntary activity and the creation of private, nonprofit or non-governmental organizations. . . . The scope and scale of this phenomenon are immense. Indeed, we

are in the midst of a global "associational revolution" that may prove to be as significant to the latter twentieth century as the rise of the nation-state was to the latter nineteenth.

Salamon adds that there is a

> crisis of confidence in the capability of the state. Broad historical changes have thus opened the way for alternative institutions that can respond more effectively to human needs. With their small scale, flexibility and capacity to engage grassroots energies, private nonprofit organizations have been ideally suited to fill the resulting gap. The consequence is a sweeping process of change.... [6]

To what extent can nonstate actors actually fill the gap? In trying to answer this question, I am focusing on *transnational communitarian bodies* (TCBs), those groups that have a set of shared beliefs and bonds between their leaders, their staffs, as well as some of their members across national borders. That is, these bodies have some of the attributes of real, or at least imagined, communities.[7] Although I am reluctant to add to the terminological clutter, a term is needed to distinguish these bodies—which include most INGOs, informal transnational networks, and transnational social movements—from narrowly based transnational interest groups, transnational corporations, and trade associations. I do not discuss these latter entities here; if the goal is to find ways for moral and political measures to control the use of technological and economic means, then such entities are largely part of that which needs to be treated rather than a source of treatment.

Since the end of the Cold War the number of TCBs has exploded. They have been particularly effective in setting transnational agendas; in mobilizing public opinion in general and that of concerned groups in particular; in acting as public interest groups that lobby various national governments and international organizations to spur them to a higher level of performance; as well as acting as important counterweights to private interest lobbies. (Wolfgang Reinicke and Francis Deng provide a fuller list of the functions of these bodies, which include contributing to establishing global policy agendas, facilitating processes for negotiations, disseminating knowledge, creating and deepening markets, and creating processes that build trust and social capital.[8])

In addition, TCBs play a key role in developing transnational values and norms through transnational moral dialogues. These norms[9] (or what have been called soft laws) both help to define the global normative synthesis and provide moral foundations on which people of different nations can agree, such as the need to curb child pornography. Ethan A. Nadelmann studies in detail the ways norms turn into effective laws through five stages and shows their effects in matters that range from curbing "white slavery" to commercial whaling.[10] (In some of the writings on the subject, the differences between transnational norms and international law are blurred or both ideas are folded into the term "regimes." However, only norms are part of the global civil society; laws are tools of a state, even if they are ultimately an expression and institutionalization of these norms.)[11]

TCBs' effects can been seen in matters concerning the environment (pressure on the United States to join the Kyoto Protocol), the curbing of land mines (encouraging various governments to endorse a treaty that bans the production and use of antipersonnel land mines), and advances in women's rights (as reflected in reports delivered during the 1995 Fourth World Conference on Women in Beijing).[12]

In several areas, the work of TCBs is so well known that it suffices to list their names to evoke an image of the nature and scope of their endeavors. These include Amnesty International, Friends of the Earth, Greenpeace, and the International Committee of the Red Cross.

There is a considerable literature on the specific outcomes of these efforts. One of the most important studies concerns human rights. The authors point out that the UN Universal Declaration of Human Rights was not a treaty, but a declaration of principles, which in effect set moral claims that called on the international community to respect national sovereignty less and to act to foster human rights in various countries, even if such action entailed interfering in states' internal affairs. The study then examines the ways these norms moved from mere statements to become important social forces in a large variety of countries, including Kenya, Chile, Indonesia, and South Africa.[13] Another major study shows the effects of transnational advocacy groups and social movements both in developing norms and fostering attention to them.[14]

To illustrate briefly the ways TCBs are reported to work, two examples, culled from the many hundreds available, follow. In the 1990s several INGOs joined together to pressure the World Bank, the International Monetary Fund, and the G–7 countries to forgive the debt of poor nations. With the impending calendar change to the year 2000, the INGOs connected their campaign with the urgency of forgiving debt before the start of the new century, hence the name "Jubilee 2000." This network of groups focused their campaign particularly on Sweden, Denmark, and Britain. These governments were, in turn, the first to raise the issue in intergovernmental meetings. Since then, some debt relief has been provided to 26 countries, including nearly half a billion dollars of debt relief granted by the United States.[15] Although Jubilee 2000 cannot be credited with all this success, the vocal presence of this network played a key role in pressuring governments and international organizations to address this issue.

Another case in point concerns the Narmada Valley Dam Projects in India, which stirred up considerable controversy. One proposal in particular, the Sardar Sarovar Project (SSP), gained international notoriety due in no small part to the efforts of INGOs. Funded by the World Bank and other large donors, the SSP was the centerpiece of India's projects to dam the Narmada river so the water could be put to use. However, the SSP would have displaced many thousands of residents. When local grassroots efforts to halt dam construction failed, a transnational coalition emerged. Drawing on shared environmental norms developed in the decades since the 1972 Stockholm conference, the coalition pressured the World Bank and the Indian government to halt construction. The coalition was successful in gaining the attention of the World Bank, which began to doubt its decision to fund the project and required a more comprehensive study by the Indian government. In 1993, the World Bank withdrew its financial support for the dam projects and attributed the changes in its policies to pressure from INGOs. Also, opponents of the dam took their case to the Supreme Court of India and were able to have construction halted until the social and environmental issues created by the building of the dam were resolved.[16] However, in 2000, the Indian Supreme Court ruled that construction of the dam could begin. Construction on the dam has started, but activists are still trying to stop it or slow it down by arguing that further construction violates the Supreme Court ruling because new homes for displaced people have not yet been found.[17]

TCBs do handle some problems on their own, or at least make significant contributions to solutions. Benjamin Barber points to a movement to affix "Good Housekeeping seals" to food (dolphin-safe tuna) and rugs (made without child labor).[18] And when a natural disaster strikes, INGOs (working with local organizations) such as CARE International and the International Committee of the Red Cross can take care of victims and their families. Doctors Without Borders has some 2,500 volunteers who have helped individuals in as many as eighty countries. Habitat for Humanity International has built some 150,000 houses around the world.

The great strengths of TCBs are that they can employ new social techniques, they are more flexible and less hierarchical, and they are arguably more transparent than many national and international governmental bodies.[19]

TCBs are particularly effective community builders. By spawning millions of transnational interpersonal bonds, by creating transnational loyalties to bodies that are regional or global in nature, and by developing ideas that legitimate sharing sovereignty for the sake of global agendas, they are making significant contributions to the global community.

Increasingly, public intellectuals, specialists, activists, and leaders of various associations form informal transnational networks. They meet each other in conferences, stay in touch via email, or share a listserv. This easy communication leads them to collaborate above and beyond what they would have if they merely followed their national loyalties.

Also, although TCBs as a rule cannot engage directly in transnational activities relating to safety, they do make significant indirect contributions. Mediation (of the kind provided by former president Jimmy Carter and his associates), informal meetings of opponents arranged by INGOs (e.g., a camp for Israeli and Palestinian youths in the United States), and education for peace are all of value, although what they accomplish is far from being commensurate with the problems at hand.

In short, if the question is whether TCBs can help deal with the transnational problem overload, the answer is clearly a strong affirmative. However, another key question still stands: How much weight can TCBs carry and to what extent can they operate truly on their own?

The Limits of Civil Society

Since World War II, much has been made of the role of the civil society within each nation in protecting citizens from excessive intrusion by the state and in ensuring that the state will not weaken communities, voluntary associations, and families by preempting their functions. Thus, civil society—and the communitarian bodies that are an important part of that society—has been viewed largely as a counterweight to a potentially overpowering state. Less has been made recently (in contrast to the work of earlier social philosophers) of the benefits that civil society derives from the state. For example, the civil society derives a major benefit when states curb intergroup and interpersonal violence. The civil society also relies on the state to enforce its norms when they are strongly challenged and informal social controls do not suffice. Even in the many situations in which the state is not called in for support, the very fact that such support is available strengthens the hand of the civil society. However, given the world's bitter experience with totalitarianism and authoritarianism during the last century and before, much more attention has been paid to protecting society from the state than to the state's nurturing of civil society.[20]

As attention now turns to undergirding the evolving global civil society, and the TCBs within it, it is important to keep in mind the considerable extent to which a thriving domestic civil society relies on the state. This observation suggests that there are considerable limitations on how far global civil society can evolve without a global state.

Although TCBs can and do help handle several transnational problems, often they rely on getting more mileage out of the Old System, which limits what they can deliver. Many of their activities are aimed at changing public policies—that is, policies of nation-states and of intergovernmental organizations. Often TCBs seek to activate the state where it is neglectful, redirect its efforts, and monitor its work, rather than carry out the necessary tasks themselves. The targets of TCBs are nation-states (pushing them to endorse a treaty banning the use of children in armed conflicts) and international organizations (pushing WHO to pay more attention to AIDS). Frequently, the effectiveness of TCBs requires that there be states that can act effectively, which is precisely the problem.

Thus, TCBs that seek to protect the environment largely focus on what they hold governments ought to do or ought to prevent others from doing (issuing more regulations limiting the private sector) and less on acts people themselves can undertake (e.g., voluntary recycling).[21] Or, these groups argue for legal restrictions on the use of cars or for government-sponsored bicycle paths and focus less on encouraging people to walk more. TCBs concerned with the protection of endangered species and wildlife do raise donations and provide educational materials to many people, but their main focus is on government regulations, set-asides, and subsidies. The same holds, of course, for those TCBs that seek more foreign aid for alleviating poverty and fighting disease. To return to the two examples chosen at random and presented above: In one case a TCB pressured governments and international organizations to forgo the collection of debt, and in the other governments and the World Bank were halted from acting, at least for a time. But here we come full circle: States and intergovernmental organizations are elements of the Old System, unable to cope with rising transnational problems. There are limits to how much one can flog an old horse. I am not suggesting that spurring governments to better apply their resources—or stopping their ill doings—is not of import, only that it speaks less to what can be done above and beyond making the Old System work somewhat more effectively or serve a truer purpose.

A similar issue arises for the various TCBs that raise public consciousness and change people's norms, a task at which they can be quite effective. The development of these transnational norms is essential for the development of a global civil society and eventually a global community. However, it is widely recognized that the work of TCBs is more consequential if and when it results in institutionalization, the enactment of new laws or court rulings, or action by government agencies. Domestic institutionalization has been the key to success for several TCBs on the national level in areas such as the environment, civil rights, and women's rights. However, to the extent that no transnational institutions can enact and enforce the needed laws and no new agencies of this sort can be created—that is, when these movements try to work transnationally without some form of transnational government—TCBs longer-run effectiveness is limited. None of this is said to denigrate the importance of social action and the formation of transnational norms. Norms are an essential basis for institution building and shared bonds, and can lay the foundation for efforts by people for themselves and for each other, such as when people in one country make donations to help people in another, arrange for student exchanges, or visit each other's home. But just as communitarian bodies within each society cannot carry the needed load without the government doing its share, so the global civil society cannot take on much of what must be done without new transnational bodies. The evidence in support of this statement is the size of the untreated transnational problems.

As long as we look at saving even one child from starvation or abuse as a fully worthy act, as long as we look at curing even one ill person in a corner of the world that lacks medical facilities as a good deed, we cannot but be full of admiration for the likes of CARE and Doctors without Borders. However, if we ask these TCBs to provide necessary services, we find that to the extent that these groups must draw on governments funds, transportation, communication, and above all law enforcement and security, they can provide only part—albeit an important part—of the solution. The proportion differs from area to area and can range from a small fraction to a significant share, but the global civil society cannot provide governance without government.

Nadelmann, after an exhaustive study, concludes that "[t]ransnational moral consensus regarding the evil of a particular activity is not, however, sufficient to ensure the creation of a global prohibition regime, much less its success in effectively suppressing a proscribed activity, even when it complements the political and economic interests of hegemonic and other states." Moreover, the scope of possible action depends greatly on the states involved: "the ultimate success of global prohibition regimes depends greatly on the vulnerability of an activity to global suppression efforts by states."[22]

To reiterate, I do not mean to denigrate the work of INGOs, networks, and social movements. Acts that save human lives or acts that provide relief are worthy and commendable. But they also serve to highlight—if we examine the totality of the need in whatever issue is at hand—how much remains uncovered, unregulated, and unserved. And the question stands: How can we better attend to these transnational issues?

It might be said that even well-formed nation-states have been unable to solve many domestic problems, from drug abuse to curbing the spread of HIV. Indeed, for this reason I systematically avoid the phrase "solving social problems." They are almost never solved. However, well-formed nation-states— which often do a rather poor job on numerous social fronts—have been much more effective in dealing with most national problems than transnational communitarian bodies. Reallocation of wealth, for instance, which is meager domestically in all democratic societies, is minuscule on the international level. Efforts of national public health authorities to curb HIV in well-formed nation-states have not been fully effective, but they have been much more effective than attempts to prevent its flow from nation to nation and to provide international help to countries that cannot cope with the disease on their own. Most important, a point to which I return in the next chapter, a major reason for the woefully insufficient capacities of nation-states is that problems are handled nation by nation rather than globally. Thus, although no system may be able to banish social problems, the Old System, even when augmented by various nonstate actors, is especially inadequate and is falling ever more behind what is needed.

Social scientists often hold that one should not argue from need, that needs do not per se generate responses, as Arnold Toynbee and many before and since have had it (in other words, if needs would be horses, then beggars could ride). The fact is that in the current international situation needs do drive progress. People and governments have become increasing aware of what they are lacking. As a direct result, additional new bodies are beginning to grow to close the gap between need and response above and beyond whatever service is provided by both the Old System and the global civil society (including transnational communitarian bodies).

CHAPTER ELEVEN

NEW GLOBAL AUTHORITIES

IF ONE GRANTS THAT THE OLD SYSTEM IS WOEFULLY INADEQUATE and will continue to become even less effective in the foreseeable future, and if one agrees that although transnational communitarian bodies (TCBs), and more generally, the global civil society, can carry part of the load much still remains to be carried, then the mind turns to seek new transnational *governmental* organizations.[1] In this quest it is natural to look for a magic bullet solution in which one new institution that could cope with most, if not all, that must be attended to would be created in short order. Historically, many hoped for a world government that would, for all intents and purposes, act like a national one; it would be the only governing body on a global scale. Many World Federalist groups envisioned the future in this way, at least initially.[2] More recently, visionaries have evoked the specter of a much reformed and restructured United Nations to become such a body.[3]

The enormous obstacles and opposition faced by the formation of a global government are so familiar that they need not be rehashed here. Various developments on the ground already point to the formation of a mixture of various new elements that together may lay the groundwork for a *sui generis global architecture*, unlike any currently existing national or international one (although it might have some similarities to the evolving European Union structure).

Sketching the design of this architecture must be delayed until the building blocks from which it is expected to be composed—and that are already in sight—are introduced.

MONOFUNCTIONAL, TRANSNATIONAL
GOVERNMENTAL NETWORKS

There are some limited signs that several transnational governmental networks might develop, each dedicated to one mission. Such an architecture has been called functionalist.[4] (Transnational governmental networks should not be confused with transnational informal social networks).

As described by Anne-Marie Slaughter, citing earlier work by Robert O. Keohane and Joseph S. Nye, Jr., as well as Samuel Huntington, transnational governmental networks are composed of government officials who are working on the same missions in their respective countries.[5] The merits of these networks are said to be that they do not require the formal consultation typically involved when representatives of governments are laboring together; participants get to know each other personally; they are concerned about the same issues; they care about the ways that they are regarded by their cross-border colleagues; and hence they are keen to cooperate above and beyond their instructions.[6] "They are fast, flexible and decentralized,"[7] and also apolitical, technocratic, and efficient.

As examples of transnational governmental networks, Slaughter and others cite the Basle Committee of Central Bankers, the International Organization of Securities Commissioners, the International Association of Insurance Supervisors, the Financial Stability Forum, the Organization of the Supreme Courts of the Americas, and the International Accounting Standards Committee.[8]

Although most of these examples are from the world of trade and finance—networks that, because of the high convergence of interests in collaborations in these fields, might be easier to come by than in other areas—in principle there is no reason that such governmental networks could not be formed to cover more issues, to include civil servants concerned about higher education, human rights, immigration, or other areas.[9]

In assessing the potential effectiveness of transnational networks, one should not ignore the fact that they face several obstacles. As I already mentioned, but cannot stress enough, as long as nations maintain their sovereignty they generally will refuse to allow their representatives to work out significant transnational agreements and arrangements without elaborate prior instructions, continuous consultation, and a priori approvals. Otherwise, the results may be well outside the consensus worked out in domestic politics and in the institutions to which the executive branches of national governments are accountable, especially legislatures. And as long as the officials involved receive only limited license, there are clear limits to what such transnational agencies can accomplish above and beyond the work of traditional intergovernmental committees and organizations, many thousands of which are part of the Old System. To the extent that these transnational intergovernmental networks gain a life of their own, each becoming something of a transnational authority that marches to its own drummer rather than acting as a collection of national agents, they are loose cannons that are not accountable to anyone.

Comparing these governmental transnational networks to the Global Safety Authority (GSA) and other transnational authorities is illuminating. The GSA is more hierarchal, because to a large extent the representatives of one country are setting the basic policy, albeit after some consultations with some others, or taking into account, within limits, the interests and values of others (e.g., American commanders ban women soldiers from wearing shorts on Saudi streets). And the more the GSA and other such Global Authorities seek legitimacy, which I expect that they will tend to do, the more they will act less unilaterally, abide by international laws, and work with global institutions, such as the United Nations. As a result, the differences between the GSA and the much "flatter" networks will diminish.

At the same time, Global Authorities have two advantages over networks. The superpower behind the GSA, the main Global Authority in place, provides many of the needed assets and, above all, force; and it strongly encourages the other powers involved to provide their share, as the United States did for the members of their coalition during the 1991 Gulf War. Also, the GSA is accountable to a legislature of at least one country, while networks (and INGOs in general) are not accountable to any elected official or democratically formed legislature.[10] (This limited accountability by itself does not make the GSA into a legitimate global authority, but merely makes it somewhat more legitimate than it would be otherwise, at least by traditional standards of accountability.)

OTHER AUTHORITIES?

I have already shown that the ad hoc antiterrorism coalition is on its way to becoming, or at least might be converted into, a standing Global Safety Authority, and that it is expanding the scope of its missions to include deproliferation and, to a much lesser but growing extent, pacification and humanitarian interventions. So far the evolving GSA has been limited largely to missions that engage the national interests of many countries, and its basic purposes (albeit not all the means that it employs) are legitimate. As long as one superpower in conjunction with other powers is willing to undergird the evolving GSA with military and economic means, as well as with more soft power than in the past, it might well last and solidify. After all, there is little reason to believe that it will accomplish its goals in the foreseeable future. The war against terrorism is unlike any other; there is no V-day, especially as domestic terrorist groups, such as the Chechens in Russia and the Basques in Spain, are included on the enemy list.

But what other missions might the expanding Global Authority take on, or what other authorities might be developed to tackle the long list of other transnational problems that plague the world?

Other safety issues seem good candidates for further expansion of the missions of the Global Safety Authority, such as dealing more effectively with transnational mafias, drug dealers, illegal traffic in people, and crime in cyberspace. (Whether divisions of the GSA are created or separate transnational authorities develop to deal with these issues is of secondary importance and not explored here.)

The main challenges to mission buildup will arise if and when the GSA (or some other Global Authority) takes on missions concerning non-safety-related transnational problems, such as environmental protection, preventing pandemics, and addressing other health issues; fighting illiteracy and poverty; and any other problems whose serious treatment would require a considerable reallocation of wealth between the have and the have-not countries. Welfare and educational agencies tend to provide direct payoffs to some and large costs to others despite some valiant attempts to make them seem enriching to all concerned. Hence, realistically, one must expect that they will be slower to expand than safety-related authorities. Modest beginnings in this area already exist, including the United Nations Development Programme (UNDP) and the World Bank, but most of what might be done remains uncovered.

I am not arguing that advancing safety is an easy task, not by a long shot. However, the difficulties entailed pale in comparison to those faced by other, more "advanced" social missions, mainly because instead of generating a convergence of interests and clearly legitimate goals, they pit the interests of some nations against those of others more than security missions do, and their legitimacy is less self-evident. The future development of the much needed global governance will face a profound dilemma in dealing with these advanced issues. Those in power have much less interest in many, if not all, non-safety-related issues; yet if the Global Authority does not expand its missions to serve needs that have top priority for those with less or little power, it will not be considered widely legitimate, nor will the worldwide moral and political gap be much narrowed. To put it more concisely, to move from a semi-empire toward a community requires expanding the missions that the evolving Global Authority will serve beyond law and order.

Up to a point, moral appeals by representatives of the have-not countries and people of goodwill everywhere have led—and can lead—to some more global efforts in these areas. Appeals have led to some debt forgiveness, increases in development aid (as announced at the Monterrey Summit in 2002), and contributions to the Global Fund to Fight AIDS, Tuberculosis, and Malaria. Critics argue that these measures are woefully inadequate, are done with mixed motives, and that limitations on imports from developing nations or farm subsidies in the West cause more harm to have-not counties than all of the help that the donations could ever provide.[11] This may be true, but it is also true that moral appeals can carry only so much water.

To further expand the advanced missions of the Global Authorities (or to create additional ones) will require finding ways to engage the interests of the have nations, most of which are in the West. Advocates of such an expansion, mostly liberals, are increasingly recognizing the need to broaden the basis of their appeal beyond humanitarian concerns and producing guilt. They have argued that large-scale economic development throughout the world will "drain the swamps in which terrorists breed" and will ensure stable democratic governments overseas, which would be committed to peace.[12] They have asserted that greatly increasing the resources that the United States sets aside for fighting HIV overseas would directly serve American national security.[13]

So far these arguments are not compelling to most of the public in the United States and in many other free countries. The notion that HIV will undermine African armies or regional social order is of great humanitarian concern, but it does not seem like a realistic security threat to many Americans and others.[14] (Arguably, it has the opposite effect, as in the case of China.) The claim that terrorism can be prevented by economic growth disregards the facts that there are only a few thousand terrorists among the billions of people who live in "have-not" countries and that many terrorists are well off and well educated (bin Laden is a billionaire, and several leading terrorists who participated in the September 11 terrorist attack were middle-class students in Hamburg). A study by Alan Kruger and Jitka Maleckova has found that local terrorist supporters are, in fact, likely to be more affluent and better educated than average.[15]

The champions of the poor, the ill, children, and other vulnerable members of the world had best formulate stronger arguments rather than preach to their choirs. A person would have to be heartless and have ice flowing in his veins not to be sympathetic to the millions of children and adults who suffer throughout the world and who could be helped with a relatively small amount of funds, as people like Jeffrey Sachs, George Soros, Gene Sperling, and Joseph Stiglitz keep reminding us.[16] However, to leave no stone unturned in the quest to find ways to address people's misery all over the world requires new, hard-headed thinking. John Rawls, widely held to be the greatest liberal thinker of this age (however liberalism is defined), held that one should embrace policies that make the rich richer if they also help the poor, even if not to the same extent. It is not a theme many liberals have adopted yet, either on the domestic front or in international relations.

Some economic incentives would lead more Western corporations to invest in "have-not" countries, especially if a safer environment and greater respect for the law are created. Many large and small countries have successfully followed this course to one extent or another, including China, India, Thailand, and to a lesser extent Argentina and Tunisia.

As simplistic as this might sound, let me attest, based on my experience during a year in the White House, that it would do some good if aid recipients and their champions once in a while took a break from criticizing the United States and instead acknowledged whatever good it did do. It is difficult to sell Congress and the electorate on giving more if they are chastised for not having done more and earlier rather than occasionally also lauded for what they did provide.

Many of my students and some of my more progressive colleagues keep pointing out how unfair the world is, reminding us that the United States consumes a great share of total world consumption (although they do not always remember that it is also producing a similar proportion of the total global product); that "the richest nation in the world" gives so little foreign aid, is unmindful of the poor and the ill of the world. They wish that somehow one could make the United States (they rarely mention other affluent nations) engage in massive transfers of wealth from its coffers to the pockets of other people, if not to create global equality then at least to vastly reduce worldwide inequality. Asked how such transfers may come about, in view of the fact that the affluent nations are also the most powerful ones—and leaving aside the question whether such a massive reallocation of wealth is justified, especially in light of the ways funds already given are used—they often are much less articulate. A few still subscribe to a pseudo-Marxist notion that the downtrodden of the earth will unite and make those in power yield. Others implicitly assume that guilt-provoking rhetoric will do the trick, ignoring that we have had so much of it that it has more or less exhausted its effectiveness. Indeed, such rhetoric may well have helped propel conservative forces to gain the upper hand in American—and in other affluent nations'—politics. I hence stand by my point that those who favor more reallocation will have to find new briefs, forces, and agents to advance their cause if significantly more progress is to be made on this front.

It is far from clear which liberal argument or political formula will be effective. I am fairly certain, however, that the social wing of the new Global Authority will develop much more slowly than the safety one, and the authority's pace and scope will depend on finding new interests and arguments in support of such an expansion. I digress here to briefly discuss a domestic development pattern that I suggest will, with the expected time lag, occur on the global level, as part of my general thesis that on many fronts the world will proceed along the same path as a developing nation. The domestic pattern might be called Marshall's March of History, which I named after T. H. Marshall, the social scientist who first described it.[17]

The hypothesis that eventually there will be a global state and community, that the global civil society will acquire many of the features of a single nation, may seem as outlandish as they come, even from someone who spent most of his life in academia. It is difficult enough to build one nation in one country such as Afghanistan, but tomorrow we'll encompass the world? My counter to this position is that I am referring to a naturally occurring process and not to an imposed one, which is many times more difficult to engender, and that I am not referring to a process that will take years or decades but a generation or more. Also, if one asks what purpose states and communities serve, one can see why people would favor a Global Nation (i.e., a global community invested in a global state). It goes without saying that today no single state or group of states can guarantee safety. Economic interests favor global markets that increasingly function the way that domestic ones did. People can communicate from one end of the earth to the other with greater speed and ease than they communicated in one village before the advent of the telephone and a growing number of local leaders can converse with each other in the same tongue—English. A core of shared values is beginning to develop and cultures are converging. Progress toward a Global Nation, however, will not have the same pace in all of the sectors involved. It is here that Marshall's March enters the picture.

Marshall's March of History

According to sociologist T. H. Marshall, social history in the modern age progressed along a set pattern. His starting point is the European feudal society, in which no rule applied equally to all. In a typical feudal society, individuals were located within a hierarchy. They were either superlords, sublords, or vassals of varying degrees, all the way down to serfs. Lords specified duties and rewards, which their subordinates could not refuse, as, by and large, there was no alternative way to make a living. Moreover, a person's position in any one of life's hierarchies was "meshed" with similar statuses in the other hierarchies. If one was subjugated economically, one was sure to be subjugated politically, in the eyes of the law, and so on.

Marshall found a gradual evolution over centuries from feudal, authoritarian regimes to modern democratic governments; in this sense, his idea can be viewed as an early prediction of the end of the history. Humans achieved progress through the separation of statuses. With this evolution, one's position in one of life's hierarchies—say, economic—no longer dictated one's social or political standing. Instead of people being inferior or superior in most, if not all, areas of life, they became equal first in one, then in another, while remaining unequal in still others. Marshall's main historical finding is that progress was uneven. People were not simultaneously granted the same rights and the same measure of equal status in political, economic, and social realms. Marshall traced the gains people made during this gradual process by dividing them into three historical phases: civil (legal), political, and social (socioeconomic).

Specifically, in analyzing British history, Marshall found that civil or legal equity arose first. In earlier ages the same crime would lead to very different sentences, according to the status of the person. For example, a lord slaying a serf would be treated much more leniently than the other way around. By the eighteenth century, however, the socioeconomic status of a person gradually mattered less and less in the eyes of the law. Next, people gained political equality—one person, one vote. In other words, legal equality preceded political democracy.

Marshall thought that the next step in the historical march toward equality would take place within the social or socioeconomic arena. Among the steps that were taken in this direction in Britain were the introduction of a progressive income tax, the inheritance tax, and various welfare programs, which amounted to "transfer payments," that is, moving resources from those better off to those less well off, all steps toward socioeconomic equality. Marshall's belief in the intractable march toward progress was widely shared.

Actually, in the decades that followed Marshall's 1950 prediction, it has turned out that the cumulative effect of all the policies seeking to reduce socioeconomic inequality has been quite limited. In the United Kingdom, for example, income distribution was not rendered significantly more equal.[18] Attempts to push more strongly in this direction undermined or were perceived to undermine the economy, and they led to a conservative backlash, in the form of Thatcherism in Britain (and Reaganism in the United States). Public support for socioeconomic equalization has largely been lost. It sometimes seems as if the classes have struck a deal: Those with economic advantages agree to accord to those without it a large measure of political and legal equality; in exchange, the disadvantaged accept a lower socioeconomic status and refrain from revolting to change the regime by the use of force.

The breakdown of Marshall's March is an empirical observation, not a judgment about the moral appropriateness of this sociological phenomenon. As I see it, discussions about whether economic equality is just, whether it conflicts with liberty and economic productivity, or whether all can be reconciled, are important but, given the power realities, also highly academic. Moreover, the argument that one cannot have a strong measure of political equality (a basis of democratic government) without socioeconomic equality is incompatible with the evidence: None of the nations considered democratic exhibits socioeconomic equality. (It is true that economic development helps democratic development, but it does not enhance equality.)

In contrast, it is possible to make a compelling normative case that every human being, just by virtue of being human, is entitled to a certain basic minimum. As we grant even serial killers and captured terrorists three meals a day, clothing, shelter, and health care, we recognize that no one should be denied these basics. At a minimum, the evolving global architecture should commit itself to ensuring that all people are so treated, not as a reflection of some socialist conception of equality but because of the basic moral worth of all human beings.[19] And, as political forces and economic conditions allow, the bare minimum should be increased.

Hence, as I see it, the measurements that determine to what extent various segments of the world's population have fulfilled basic needs such as food, shelter, literacy, work, and health care—and whether these basic needs are better fulfilled as time passes—are much more to the point than measures of socioeconomic inequality. *A world in which basic supplies are securely available to one and all is vastly preferable to one in which whatever meager resources are available are more equally distributed.* To highlight the point: A world in which everyone is paid the same X and has control over identical Y assets—one of full economic equality—is vastly inferior to a world in which everyone has at least 2 X and 2 Y, and these amounts are rising, even if some others have many more Xs and Ys and their supply is growing more rapidly than those of the less endowed. Moreover, given that equality is unattainable, and given that promoting it often squanders the political appeal of those who care about the vulnerable members of society, equality is a notion best avoided.

GLOBAL SOCIAL AUTHORITIES

A good candidate to lead the march on the socioeconomic front toward a shared and rising basic minimum is a Global Health Authority, to evolve out of the World Health Organization (WHO). For most of its existence, WHO was a cumbersome, bureaucratic, intergovernmental organization. In 2003, when SARS jumped across the world from China to Toronto, penetrating thirty-two other countries as if they were a spit away and borders were thinner than face masks, suddenly much attention was paid to the WHO's limitations. As a typical international organization, it had to rely on the cooperation of the governments involved. To a large extent the whole problem of SARS arose because Chinese authorities concealed for months that it was spreading.

To battle the threatened epidemic, WHO was accorded considerable new powers. Its members were allowed to deal directly with medical staff and local groups within various countries. WHO also was given the authority to intervene in countries afflicted by a health crisis, even one unacknowledged by the government of that country, and further was permitted to enter countries to investigate whether they were dealing effectively with a crisis, thus giving the agency "the authority to begin ground inspections without a formal invitation."[20] True, one may wonder: How strong has WHO really become? Could it march into a country without the consent of the government? However, the direction of the change, unlike its extent, is clear: WHO has moved to become somewhat less of an intergovernmental agency and a bit more of a global authority, even when dealing with relatively small-scale health threats. It is easy to foresee that if a future illness were thousands of times more devastating than SARS or the avian flu has been so far, more akin to a true pandemic, WHO would be given many more resources and even greater authority, especially if the pandemics afflicted affluent societies in full measure (the way the 1918 influenza epidemic did)—unlike AIDS, which largely spares them.

In facing a global pandemic, WHO would be given still more resources and the authority to close borders, quarantine large numbers of people, force vaccination, and much more. Such increases in resources and authority are even more likely to come about if the pandemic were the result of biological terrorism and not a naturally occurring disease, because then it would involve security and not merely health.

One may be quick to assume that future Global Authorities would be led and financed largely by the United States, although other, probably Western, nations will participate and contribute resources. In principle, there is no reason why other powers could not develop such an authority (as long as the direction it takes does not confront the key interests of the big powers). Thus, there is no reason why Canada, Norway, and Singapore could not promote a strong WHO. Or China, Russia, and India could not formulate and lead a powerful anti-HIV authority. The reasons some of these countries have been reluctant to proceed so far are numerous and complex. They include shortage of resources, cultures of denial, a fatalistic approach to life, and the fact that curbing HIV requires major social and behavior changes that are difficult to come by. However, in principle, a variety of powers can form Global Authorities.

The prospects for the formation of a Global Environmental Protection Authority has some similarities to those of a Global Welfare Authority and some to a Global Health Authority. The parallel with welfare is derived from the fact that many of the environmental measures that most nations seek adversely affect the interests of affluent nations more than their own. Hence, although numerous governments pay lip service to environmental protection and are willing to undertake some limited steps, major expenditures and adaptations cannot be realistically expected. All this would change if the environmental crisis equivalent of a pandemic arose. When there was a sense that the depletion of the ozone layer would cause irreparable harm to life on Earth, national governments worked together to develop an international framework that resulted in the conclusion of the Montreal Protocol on Substances that Deplete the Ozone Layer. This measure, which aims for the elimination of ozone-depleting substances, was developed only thirteen years after the problem was discovered, and just one year after negotiations began.[21]

Similarly, if the world were to face what would be a clear and present danger due to sizeable global warming, it likely would act. (Some may well argue that once warming becomes a clear and present danger, it will be much more difficult to deal with it than it is now. However, the attentive publics must be convinced that the current and anticipated level of warming poses a serious threat before they will agree to burdensome measures that must be undertaken to reverse this trend.) Meanwhile, the global environment, which has a wider appeal than welfare, will draw some resources—but not enough to prevent further degradation. As with welfare, those who wish for more action are better off finding new interests to further engage the nations of the world and stronger normative arguments to present than berating the rich.

An Agency for Rights and Responsibilities might find its place in the new institutional map, as well. The agency could serve to give expression to the idea that members of the global community have not merely rights but also responsibility for the welfare of others and the common good. Liberals have been much too reluctant to add responsibilities to the language of rights. It is not enough to preach to the rich nations what they must do, without at the same time encouraging those mired in poverty and illness to change their cultures and behaviors. Such changes are the only way truly to slow down the HIV pandemic (as Uganda and Senegal have done[22]), prevent the siphoning off of large parts of international aid and loans to Swiss (and other) bank accounts, increase transparency and reduce corruption, and lay the foundations for the rule of law in places where it is largely missing.

This agency would serve as a sort of combination between Human Rights Watch or Amnesty International and a Global Agency for Community and Civic Service. It could initiate the formation of a UN Peace Corps, in which youths of different nations would work together to help those most in need or to shore up the environment. Such global volunteer programs already exist on a small scale. The UNDP currently administers a multi-issue volunteer program that operates in developing countries around the world and annually recruits close to 5,000 volunteers representing over 150 different nationalities. A major symbolic step in this direction would be to augment the UN Universal Declaration of Human Rights with a Declaration of Responsibilities and fashion a global agency for the promotion of rights and the fostering of responsibilities.

The idea that rights entail responsibilities—and a global authority created to promote this idea—would benefit if from here on aid-granting nations would demand that those who benefit from such assistance would commit themselves, as they reached a given level of economic development (say a per capita gross domestic product of $10,000, measured in 2000 dollars, a level that South Korea reached in 1993),[23] to gradually repaying the funds donated to them into a revolving account. The funds could then be used for countries that have not yet reached the given level of income per capita. Also, most nations should be expected to send some troops to serve as part of standby regional peacekeeping forces.

The point that I made regarding who can launch a Global Health Authority applies to all such authorities. There is no principled reason why such authorities cannot be promoted by powers other than the United States and its allies, as long as these other powers tax themselves as they seek to increase the resources that they ask of others and do not proceed in ways that would confront directly the basic interests of the big powers.

THE "CROWNING" ISSUE

With every expansion of mission, the evolving Global Authorities will face more and more opposition due to the inadequacy of their mechanisms for working out differences among the values as well as the interests of governments involved. Additional problems will arise out of the lack of mechanisms to coordinate the activities of the different authorities. It would be like a bunch of domestic agencies cut loose, without a head of state, cabinet, or legislature to pull them together—without "crowning." A semi-empire can get away, for extended periods of time, with making short shrift of the building of consensus, legitimacy, and coordination because its various agencies can fall back on their ability to enforce the policy. However, the legitimacy of the added missions that are not related to safety is particularly thin; various governments and peoples view cyberpiracy, the illegal trade in people, and other such missions very differently. Hence it is safe to suggest that the more transnational problems the Global Authorities take on, the more resistance they will provoke, the higher the costs they will incur, the less cooperation they will find, and the more they will tax the funds and patience of the citizens of the participating countries if these authorities continue to act without crowning institutions. Hence, if a Vietnamesque effect in many parts of the world is to be avoided, the Global Authorities will be pushed to introduce at least some crowning.

Transnational governmental networks face the same challenge. Their success entails removing themselves from the oversight and control of national democratic legislatures, and there exists no supranational democratic authority to oversee them.[24] Such exemption from accountability may not unduly trouble those who are eager for the treatment of specific transnational problems to proceed, but there is no assurance that these networks will attend to those problems. Some of these bodies could dedicate themselves to setting up Swiss bank accounts for their members, fooling the World Bank, or smuggling immigrants. This danger is best allayed not by curbing the scope and license of such evolving networks and keeping them under close national rein, but by providing new transnational forms of oversight.

To recapture the argument made so far: Mission expansion of Global Authorities is likely to occur, to encompass additional security issues, as well as some social ones. However, the more missions that are added, the more problems resulting from lack of legitimacy and interest convergence will exacerbate, due to highly divergent values and interests of those involved and, above all, the absence of mechanisms for working out disagreements, differences, and conflicts. The question hence becomes: Which architectures, if any, could both deal effectively with a broad array of transnational problems and generate much more legitimacy and interest convergence than a multifunctional GSA or a whole slew of Global Authorities—and how might this come about?

The implied thesis is that a semi-empire will be under pressure to become more legitimate and engage the interests of more people (share more power, become less unipolar, become more "democratic"). That is, although sweet may not come out of might, it may at least become less bitter. This is more than merely an expression of optimism. To reiterate, historically, ever since the advent of mass education and the development of popular media, it has become increasingly difficult to lock people out of politics. Empires have been dismantled and there have been movements in numerous parts of the world toward less authoritarian governments. In earlier eras, nations that were formed initially through the exercise of power by one state eventually democratized. As the nineteenth century shows, military force has been key to the formation of modern nations. For instance, the modern German state was created through three military conflicts, the Second Hollstein War, the Seven Weeks War, and the Franco-Prussian War. Italy's "wars of unification" included more than a dozen armed conflicts that occurred over more than a decade. The United States, kept together by force during the Civil War, by many measures became one society only in the 1870s.[25]

Various levels of democratization followed in all these countries, sometimes as a direct result of the unification wars (e.g., the liberation of the slaves), while in others it took social movements. For example, in the United States it took considerable time for women to gain the right to vote and for African Americans to be granted de jure and de facto voting rights—but in all cases democratization eventually took place. I do not mean to advocate the use of force in forging a country or global community, but to suggest that the use of force does not necessarily mean that the resulting polity will be authoritarian or totalitarian in the longer run.

All this is not to suggest that democratization of any one country, and surely not of any global organization, is ever nearly complete or that power differences have disappeared. I merely mean to say that when empires are formed, over time they generate pressures that render them less hierarchical and more accountable, and when they are slow to respond to those pressures, they are destroyed. So far, the main difference has been how fast and how much the empires responded, and hence how long they were able to maintain dominance. None made a community, although the British Commonwealth tried. However, all these empires took place in the age before mass politics. Given contemporary accelerated politics, empires that do not accommodate are likely to have a much shorter life span than earlier ones. Indeed, as I suggested in chapter 6, the American semi-empire is already both straining and transforming.

Crowning encompasses two related issues: The need for a body to help legitimate the work of the transnational authorities, especially in all matters in which their acts are not controlled by nor accountable to nation-states (I assume that in the new design, nations would not disappear but be subsumed by the new system), and to the need for transnational institutions in which differences of interests can be worked out in a way that is functionally equivalent to the way that they are worked out in national legislative bodies and cabinets—even if the scope of issues to be tackled is considerably narrower than those addressed on the national level. That is, there is a need for one or more bodies in which a large-scale convergence of interests can be generated. This convergence is achieved by familiar political devices such as log rolling (splitting the difference) and compromises. It presumes a body in which such work can be facilitated by shared procedures, norms, tradition, and mutuality of interest. This kind of work often takes place in legislatures and cabinets. (I should add in those that function, if not well, at least adequately, because in some countries legislatures are so deadlocked, and cabinets—especially of coalition governments—are so divided, that they hardly provide a good model for working out interest convergence.)

Such crowning presumes a measure of parallel development of consensus within the public, which in turn entails some sharing of values and the development of an imagined transnational community, that is, community building. Otherwise the establishment of human primacy will recede ever further.

There are major differences of opinion among scholars about the way in which national polities work. Some see them as the coming together of special interest groups, which work out policies that serve them. The legislature—and more generally the government—serves as a sort of clearinghouse. The arrangements are voluntary, and basically no sharing of values and affective bonds is required. This model suits the existing intergovernmental system well because, in principle, there is no reason that in this system the coalescing of interests needed to create a global policy cannot be worked out.

In contrast, my analysis relies on the Durkheimian model (for reasons that cannot and need not be explored in this volume), which assumes that collective decision making often entails imposing on various participants sacrifices for the common good. If these sacrifices are not backed up by shared values and bonds, they will not be treated as legitimate, and hence they will either have to be effected through force or they will not be enforced. It follows that new crowning entities, in order to encompass groups of nations, will have to possess some Durkheimian qualities: A measure of shared values and bonds, a measure of commitment and loyalty.

Because most people, especially scholars and experts, find it next to impossible to believe in the possibility of a global parliament (and, more generally, a world government) and community, one that commands such Durkheimian qualities, the impossibility of developing these global governing bodies has long been taken more or less for granted. The strongly held belief that such institutions are extremely unlikely to be realized is grounded in experience, as centuries of grand schemes to form world governments[26] to ensure global peace, law and order, or social justice have yielded only disappointment. Hence, for the last several decades, practically all serious international relations literature has focused on any architecture other than anything resembling a global polity, especially one that would be multifunctional.[27]

In the same period, however, three major developments unfolded suggesting that it is time to reexamine the subject.

1. Nation-states and the Old System that relies on them have proven more inadequate for coping with transnational problems.
2. New technological developments have vastly increased the potential for worldwide communication and concerted action and hence governance.
3. As has long been argued, the world might unite if it faced a global threat, a threat that massive terrorism and weapons of mass destruction clearly constitute.

Thus, oddly, as international relations theory has increasingly taken it for granted that even thin forms of world government and a global community are utopian, conditions have arisen that make movement in this direction less inconceivable. This is especially true if one presumes, as I do, that such a Global Nation will have unique features rather than duplicate all of the national features on a larger scale—that is, a sui generis global architecture.

I turn next to explore other building blocks in addition to the Old System, transnational networks, and Global Authorities, including some that might provide a measure of crowning. All of these bodies already have been constructed; and although they are still in the early stages of development, they are slowly gaining power and legitimacy. The primary way in which their development differs from that imagined by visionaries is that scope of the functions the bodies embrace and the authority they claim is limited. They are evolving gradually rather than being fashioned in one fell swoop—as, for instance, the League of Nations was created at the end of World War I and the United Nations at the end of World War II, or the way that United Federalists used to think a world government would come about. In the next chapter I discuss these supranational authorities and in the following one I examine the relationship of these building blocks to what should be a much restructured United Nations.

By now I have used the term "global" or "international community" several times. I agree with Kofi Annan, who states that this community is "hardly more than embryonic."[28] However, its elements are the same as those of much more robust communities: the sense of a shared fate, a moral culture, and a whole slew of transnational communitarian bodies. It is a sociological embryo, to use Annan's metaphor, but one that is growing.

CHAPTER TWELVE

SUPRANATIONAL BODIES

SUPRANATIONAL BODIES ARE MAJOR BUILDING BLOCKS OF A NEW global architecture, a breakthrough in post-nation building. They are, as we shall see, particularly important for crowning. These bodies are constructed, in part or in whole, on a fundamentally different set of principles from those of both the Old System and the transnational communitarian bodies. Once defined, I briefly introduce several existing, albeit limited, supranational bodies. Then I explore whether an intermediary level of supranationality can be stabilized, especially in light of the experience of the most advanced supranational body, the European Union. The analysis closes with an examination of questions concerning democratization of global bodies, an important element of crowning.

SUPRANATIONALITY DEFINED

I use the term "supranationality" to characterize a political body that has acquired some of the attributes usually associated with a nation, such as political loyalty and decision-making power—based not on an aggregate of national decisions or those made by representatives of the member states, but rather on those made by the supranational bodies themselves. It is useful to think about supranationality as a composite of several elements.

As I already mentioned, one such supranational element is decision making carried out by a transnational governing body that is not composed of national representatives—a body that follows its own rules, policies, and values rather than being "instructed" by national governments. For an institution to qualify as supranational, its decisions must concern significant matters, as all international organizations can make some minor decisions on their own but most must fall within the boundaries and limits set by the governments represented. The much greater capacity to make decisions on their own terms to allows supranational bodies to move with much greater agility and speed than international organizations.

Another element of supranationality is that the nations that compose these entities, as well as their citizens and member units, including corporations and labor unions, are expected to follow the rulings of these supranational bodies without requiring separate decisions from their respective national governments. In addition, supranational bodies tend to have some kind of effective enforcement capacity of their own, such as the ability to directly fine corporate bodies and individuals within the member states or to order them to desist from some action rather than to fine the national governments or to ask governments to rein in corporate bodies in their respective state. That is, supranational bodies have more power than networks or TCBs. To put it differently, supranationality presumes some surrender of sovereignty by the member nations.

MONOFUNCTIONAL SUPRANATIONAL INSTITUTIONS

Key examples of supranational institutions are the International Criminal Tribunal for the former Yugoslavia at The Hague, the International Criminal Tribunal for Rwanda at Arusha, and, most important, the more recently established International Criminal Court. The judges for all of these courts are elected by the General Assembly of the United Nations. Once elected, they are not accountable to any nation-state or intergovernmental body. (I am not suggesting that the court is fully neutral; it may reflect Western values and powers or those of other democratic societies. To be supranational does not mean to be without a normative or political profile; rather, it means not to have a profile that is tied to the specific values and instructions of the nations involved.)[1] The rulings of these courts do not draw on specific or general instructions from individual nations, but are based on international law.[2] Rulings do not require approval from individual nations. Moreover, these courts have enforcement powers, including the ability to imprison those convicted of crimes against humanity.[3] These powers are achieved at least in theory because all the signatories of the treaty that formed the ICC—most nations—obligated themselves to carry out its judgments.

Some scholars characterize the World Trade Organization (WTO) as a supranational body. For instance, Alec Stone Sweet concludes his examination of the WTO with the statement: "More generally, it can be argued that the WTO is a supranational constitutional polity and that the SAB [Standing Appellate Body] is nothing less than a [supranational] constitutional court. . . . The SAB['s] . . . function is to interpret and apply fixed norms of reference. These norms are supranational, and they take precedence in any conflict with national norms."[4]

Others view the WTO as only partially supranational, suggesting that it often acts like a traditional intergovernmental body. For instance, Mary L. Volcansek argues that the WTO judicial structure has only some of the characteristics of a supranational court.[5] She concludes that it is sitting "at the margins" of supranationality.[6] In addition, the WTO General Council and Ministerial Conferences are less supranational than WTO judicial bodies because the former are composed of national representatives. However, these bodies are supranational in that their decisions are binding on national governments.

Many characterize ICANN (the Internet Corporation for Assigned Names and Numbers) as a supranational body and hold that it has been quite effective in regulating the Internet in select matters.[7] Transnational business associations, such as the International Chamber of Commerce, are somewhat supranational in that the commercial codes they formulate and commercial arbitration they provide, while voluntarily agreed to by industry, have become, through international laws or norms, somewhat authoritative.[8] The EU supranational authorities are multifunctional and command more power than any of those mentioned so far. Hence they require a separate treatment, provided shortly.

There are two basic ways to view these monofunctional supranational bodies. One is to see them as self-standing attempts to supplement the Old System. If viewed in this way, the question of their legitimacy arises, primarily because they are not accountable to anyone. To the extent that they are supranational, by definition they are not accountable to national representatives (and hence to their parliaments and electorates), nor is there a supranational electorate that might hold them accountable.[9] Moreover, these bodies directly challenge national sovereignty and democracy on the national level. Finally, they lack crowning, which is essential for their legitimation and for the generation of a convergence of interests.

Another view is to see these supranational bodies as temporarily not accountable to anyone, but to expect that as a new global architecture is constructed, these bodies (and others like them) will become accountable to some kind of a global legislature, such as a greatly reformed United Nations.

The Extraordinary Prerequisites
for Full Supranationality

At this point, one cannot avoid the question of whether there could be a true global government. In light of the new global conditions, the fact that all attempts to move in this direction in earlier generations did not take off is an insufficient reason not to reconsider the question. The fact that such deliberations had an aura of daydreaming in the past should not stop a serious analysis, given the pressing global problems and the inadequate responses by existing governmental and nonstate actors. Moreover, even if global community building is a pipe dream, could several nations fully unify and form a United States of Europe or a Latin American community? Such regional supranationalities would significantly enhance the treatment of regional and even global problems.

The following analysis of the prerequisites of supranationality draws on my study of four attempts to absorb nations into encompassing supranational polities (the Nordic Council, the Federation of the West Indies, the United Arab Republic, and the European Union)[10] as well as other case studies and analyses. To put it briefly, I found that forming full-fledged supranational unions (a combination of a supranational government and a community) requires three capabilities on the supranational level:

1. Legitimate control of the means of violence, which must exceed that of the member units;
2. The capacity to allocate resources among the member units (essential for generating a high level of interest convergence); and
3. The ability to command political loyalties that exceed those accorded to member units (an essential part of community building).

These three elements are complementary in the sense that each benefits from the other two and that all three are required to form a stable supranational union.

Weak enforcement capability or an anemic ability to provide resources undermines loyalty, which in turn further limits the ability to enforce and reallocate. Unless the rulings of supranational bodies can be enforced without being first endorsed by national governments—if a supranational body cannot implement its policies independently of national governments or cannot command sufficient resources to produce significant outcomes—it will be unable to deal with transnational problems much more effectively than the Old System. The same holds for loyalties; if the people of various nations regularly side with their nation when a conflict arises between it and the supranational body, what that body can accomplish will be greatly hindered and its stability undermined.

According to this analysis, what is required to attain full supranationality is not merely split sovereignty, but also for the supranational layer to crown the encompassed national entities. In a case of conflict between the layers, the supranational authority must trump the national ones, although only on those issues encompassed by its functional domain. My study of four unions indicates that a full-fledged supranational union must take the form of some kind of federation (or even tougher, a unitary state) rather than a confederation or some still looser form of constitutional relations.[11] Finally, the commitments to the supranational community must exceed those to the national communities of the member states.

There are a considerable number of sociological assumptions behind the preceding statements that need not be spelled out here in full. Basically, they assume that intra-community processes deeply affect political loyalties.[12] Hence, when communities consider a government illegitimate or when they are loyal to other political authorities that conflict with the government in question—whether this loyalty is to a foreign government, to a local level of government, or to some other body, whether religious or ideological (which may vary as much as the Catholic Church does from what used to be the Communist International controlled by Moscow)—the government in question will be unable to command the three capabilities that a supranational union requires. In short, there must be considerable overlap between the scope of the political community and that of the government to make for a stable supranational polity.

A lower level of bonding did not suffice to contain divisive centrifugal forces in three of the four cases that I studied. Since that study, other examples have arisen that support the same conclusion. The Soviet Union long controlled the means of violence and economic resources of its fifteen member republics with much more force than any of the supranational governments I studied, but its inability to command the loyalty of the people of these republics became one major reason why they chose to break away from the USSR when its government weakened.

Also, the lack of such loyalty destroyed Yugoslavia despite the fact that, even after the death of Marshal Josip Tito, the national government was in control of the military, the police, and the courts, and it had a very considerable ability to reallocate resources. The main reason Quebec considered pulling out of Canada was not Canada's lack of control of the means of violence or an inability to reallocate resources, but because Anglo-dominated Canada does not command sufficient loyalty from many of the people in Franco-dominated Quebec. Hence, as demanding as the upward layering of loyalties is, the main conclusion of my study is that *without forming at least some measure of a supranational community, rather than merely a supranational government, it is impossible to sustain full-fledged supranational unions,* which might be better able to cope as nations once were able to.

In short, the bar that must be cleared to form a viable supranational bodies is indeed a high one. We have come full circle here. This discussion started by suggesting that we should not avoid the question of creating full-fledged supranational communities just because such ideas are so visionary; it concludes by affirming that building such communities is very taxing indeed. The question hence becomes: Will less do?

Ernst B. Haas raised a closely related issue in his book *The Uniting of Europe,* published in 1968.[13] Haas asked how a supranational unit might come about in Europe. He argued that as specific interests are "lifted" from the national to the regional level (which occurred as the European Commission in Brussels dealt with more and more specific "functional" issues that were of interest to various groups, such as farmers and labor unions), politics and loyalties also would be shifted upward, from the national to the regional level.[14] Haas's approach has been widely criticized in the following decades.[15] I shared his view in my book published in 1965.[16] Recent developments, especially the European Union's intensive search for a new constitution and increased supranationality by planning to rely more on majority votes than has been the case until now, reopens the question of whether Haas (and I) were on the right track. As I write these lines, the jury is still out.

THE EUROPEAN UNION AS A TEST CASE OF HALFWAY SUPRANATIONALITY

Given that full supranational integration of even two nations, let alone a larger group, is at best very difficult to achieve, and limited supranationality is woefully insufficient and above all difficult to stabilize, we must wonder: Can what might be called "halfway integration" suffice for coping with transnational problems, and is such a level of integration sustainable? I define "halfway integration" as taking place when the nations involved maintain full or nearly full autonomy in some important matters while providing full or nearly full authority to a supranational body on other important matters.

From the viewpoint of the thesis advanced here, and for all who are interested in the development of supranational states, the European Union provides the most telling experiment. For the first decades of its existence, the European Union tried mainly to integrate the economies of the member nations, while maintaining each country's political independence.[17] If such a halfway integration could be stabilized, it might be preferable not to take on the much more onerous task of forming a full-fledged supranational European Union.

To put it metaphorically, the question is: Can the European Union, as a developing, supranational authority, stand between two steps? Can it maintain a level of integration that falls between a low level limited to a few sectors (e.g., trade and cultural exchanges) and full union (as the term "United States of Europe" implies)? Obviously nations can sustain a low level of integration; there are no apparent internal contradictions in such a limited cross-national bonding, say, the way the Nordic countries or the Benelux ones related to one another before the formation of the European Union. Also, if a group of nations manages to merge into one encompassing community (as the colonies did in forming the United States and cities and regional states did in the formation of Germany and Italy),[18] clearly such a high level of integration can be sustained. The question that the European Union faces is whether it is possible to supranationalize several important sectors (especially those related to the free flow of goods and services, capital and labor, and financial policy), while keeping political integration at a low level.

As I see it, halfway integration cannot be stabilized, and the process of fuller integration must involve open and inclusive consensus building. The basic reason halfway, mainly economic, integration is not sustainable is that the libertarian model is erroneous. Society is not composed of individuals seeking to maximize their pleasure or profit, and society will not, as libertarians suggest, naturally gravitate toward a system that, by rationalizing the allocation of economic resources, will enhance those individuals' income and wealth. Nor are markets self-controlling (guided by an invisible hand). People are not merely traders and consumers, but also citizens whose sense of self is defined partly by their nationality. Hence, when economic integration that benefits their pocketbook threatens their national identity, people will tend to balk. (The exact level of economic integration at which nationalist opposition rises to a level sufficient to undermine economic integration depends on numerous factors, including how strong national identity is to begin with and when people realize that higher levels of economic integration undermine their nation's ability to guide its own policies.)

Moreover, halfway integration—high economic integration combined with low political integration—cannot be sustained because markets and, more generally, economies are not freestanding systems with their own distinct dynamics;

rather, they are integrally tied to the polity and to the society of which they are a part. Moreover, in free societies, major economic policy decisions must be made in line with a nation's values and politically negotiated consensus. Otherwise, the sense of alienation will increase to a level that will endanger the sustainability of the regime. This happened in Argentina, Turkey, and Indonesia when their governments heeded the instructions of the International Monetary Fund, even though those instructions were outside of the political and popular consensus.

It may be argued that, despite various delays and setbacks, the economic integration of the European Union has proceeded to ever higher levels with little political integration and even less formation of a shared creed and a sense of community. European bodies are largely intergovernmental, not supranational. The Council of Ministers is composed of national representatives. Although theoretically the transnational parties of the European Parliament represent like-minded Europeans across national lines regarding European issues, in reality these transnational parties are largely combinations of national parties. They are reported to "exploit" European elections for "immediate, domestic purposes" rather than to promote Europe-wide platforms.[19] (This is not to deny that these transnational parties have made some strides in organizing parties at the European level and in adapting to the structure of the European Union.)[20] Although the European Parliament may be a bit more supranational than the Commission and the Council of Ministers, it is not strongly so and it is by far the weakest of the three bodies. As for community building, for a while it was fashionable to claim a "European" identity rather than a national one, especially among the young, sometimes referred to as the E-generation (especially in Germany).[21] However, most people still identify more strongly with their own nation than with Europe, and Germans are once again becoming more, not less, nation-oriented.[22] True, the European Commission tends to speak more often for Europe rather than a combination of various national interests. However, in doing so, it has fueled an ever growing opposition rather than support.

Recently, however, it has become clear that because of the pains that pan-European economic policies inflict on many members, supranational policies will not be sustainable without a greater transfer of political power and citizen loyalty from the member nations to the European Union and without the EU Commission becoming more accountable. Above all, it is clear that the intergovernmental composition, in which each nation has de facto veto power, is too cumbersome for the high and rising volume of EU transactions. Hence the need for a majority rule—a hallmark of supranationality. The 2003 Constitutional Convention was supposed to lead to such higher levels of political integration. If this and other such polity- and loyalty-enhancing measures fail, the European Union will be unable to move to a high supranational level. I predict that the EU experiment will show that standing between two steps is impossible; one needs to move to either a higher or a lower level of integration, and a higher level means supranationality. This, I suggest, holds true not merely for the European Union.

Many of those who study the development of the European Union focus on what is called the democratic deficit. It refers to the fact that the European Commission, that is, the European Union's executive branch, is not effectively accountable to anyone, although theoretically—and to some extent in reality—it is accountable to the European Parliament (as well as to the national governments that make up the European Union). This democratic deficit not only undermines the legitimacy of "Brussels" but also works against expanding the scope of unification. There is, however, a whole other deficit, much less often studied, and that is the *community deficit*. Without strong bonds among the EU members and strong loyalties to the European Union, Europeans have shown little willingness to make the kind of major sacrifices that members of a national community are willing to make for one another. West Germans have been shelling out hundreds of billions of dollars for the reconstruction of East Germany—because the former East Germans are members of their national community. They would not make anything remotely approaching such contributions to others. Similarly, Americans regularly put up with the fact that some states (especially in the South) pay much less in federal taxes but gain much more of the expended federal dollars than other states, but surely Americans would not tolerate such transfer payments to Mexico and Canada, not to mention nations farther away.

The European Union faces painful decisions as it seeks to harmonize its welfare, tax, immigration, and law enforcement policies. Either it will move to narrow the community deficit, or it will have to ratchet it down. The same holds for other communities in the making, especially the weak and thin global one. And, we shall see, without such a community, there is no "self" that can seek a democratic expression. On important issues, people rarely are willing to subject themselves to votes by others whom they do not consider members of their community.[23] For the democratic deficit to be diminished, the community deficit needs to be narrowed.

FACILITATING FACTORS

A FAMILIAR LIST

Although the task of building supranational authorities on a regional or even more encompassing level is daunting at best, several developments facilitate such constructions. As these have been depicted often, I merely list them here for the completeness of the record and for balance. They include:

- The development of English as a de facto lingua franca (approximately 1.6 billion people, almost one-third of the world's population, use English in some form).[24]
- The rise of worldwide communication systems.
- Great increases in international trade and travel.
- The development of worldwide media (e.g., CNN and BBC).
- The development of transnational civil and legal institutions and norms, part of the evolving global normative synthesis.

All of these factors make the development of a Global Authority and community somewhat less implausible.

A Special Kind of Subsidiarity

Applying the concept of subsidiarity can ease the formation of supranational communities. Although a supranational community must possess the three crowning capabilities described earlier (control of means of violence, ability to reallocate assets, and command superior loyalty in select matters), it need not command full control of any of them. Indeed, in each of these areas considerable control can be left in the hands lower-level entities, including national and local governments, communities, and voluntary associations. Supranational communities can provide a context for a group of nations, but they need not seek to replace these states or to abolish their autonomy. Crowning, though, refers not to any and all kinds of subsidiarity, nor to any division of control or functions within a state, but to the capacity of the encompassing entity to have the final say in cases of conflict, no matter how much power and resources are delegated to the smaller member entities.

The United States provides a major case in point. Many powers and rights are reserved, by the Constitution, for the member states. The Federal Bureau of Investigation has not replaced the local and state police, and the U.S. military has not replaced the National Guard, which is state controlled. However, in the rare occasions in which national and local priorities clash, the nation has taken precedence.[25] The "supremacy" of the federation over the states, in select matters of foreign policy and defense and several others, often has been tested not merely in courts of law but also most dramatically (since the Civil War) during the desegregation of the schools in Little Rock, Arkansas, which required a crowning show of force. Also, it is well known that local and state courts dispose of numerous issues, but the U.S. Supreme Court is the forum for the final appeal (both for matters concerning federal law and for state-federal relationships). It rules on matters that concern conflicts between the fifty states and the national government.

Moreover, although in the United States and several other nations, states and local governments and communities can collect some taxes and allocate the revenue according to their preferences, a major source of revenues are taxes collected by the national government and then allocated to the states, localities, and communities. The federal government, though, maintains the ability to set rules that affect the use of these funds; in other words, it maintains federal crowning in this area.

Loyalties, too, are divided between the states (and regions such as the South) and the nation. However, following the Civil War, commitments to the nation have tended to prevail when in conflict with commitments to states and regions on political matters.

In addition, numerous other matters are handled by nongovernmental nationwide bodies that cut across state lines. These bodies include many thousands of nonresidential communities, ethnic and racial groups, as well as a large number of voluntary associations. But, again, these social entities are contextualized by the federal government and by society-wide values. For instance, none of these bodies is free to violate the Constitution, which reflects both the ultimate legal crowning authority and the shared values of national society. The U.S. political architecture proves that the difficulties involved in building supranational community can be eased by crowning subsidiarity, a form of federalism.

THE ADVANTAGE OF BEING GLOBAL

Why expect supranational bodies to be able to handle transnational problems that national governments have been unable to address at the national level? For instance, national governments have had difficulty stemming the flow of controlled substances across their borders, at least without resorting to extreme, undemocratic measures of the kind employed by Singapore and Malaysia, because drug dealers have well-heeled and strong transnational organizations. When pollution flows from country A into country B, often there is little that country B can do to stop it. If one nation (e.g., China) produces 10 million additional highly polluting cars, other countries cannot stop the effect on their climate. When there is a nuclear meltdown in one country, as there was in Russia, there is little other countries downwind can do to protect their citizens. The same holds for most transnational problems.

True, nations can try to make offenders desist by imposing sanctions, offering incentives, or appealing to their better nature. Sometimes, for some matters, after much give-and-take, such moves may generate some measure of success. However, if the world is to move significantly toward establishing human primacy, then we need to narrow the vast gap between what is achieved in this way and what is needed to cope with the problems at hand. Dealing with these problems cannot be done until the scope of the remedial action encompasses all the main sources of the malaise.

Under a Global Authority, whether it is one limited to safety or one that takes on additional missions, none of the transnational problems will disappear, but they all will be easier to manage—without the national governments or the new supranational authority having to spend a penny or hire an additional cop. The basic reason is that once the systems of control include everyone, they become more effective. To highlight this point, it might be useful to examine the trade in cigarettes. This mental experiment can be applied to numerous other public policy issues.

When the United States tried to discourage smoking, several states raised their taxes on cigarettes—but they were greatly hindered by the fact that neighboring states had lower cigarette taxes. If all fifty states raised taxes to the same level, it would enhance tax enforcement, although cigarettes still could be smuggled in from Mexico (as they already are on a large-scale from the United States to Canada where taxes are higher still).[26] However, if a North American body or, better, one that encompasses all nations in the Western Hemisphere or, best, worldwide, would levy a similar level of taxation on cigarettes, it would greatly enhance the ability to collect these taxes without any increase in policing. True, the problem of tax avoidance would not disappear. Nations would differ in the level of law enforcement, and if taxes were high, local contraband would be produced. However, the ability to cope with this and numerous other problems would be increased significantly by fashioning regional or, best, worldwide policies and enforcement.

With worldwide enforcement there would be no place to hide, no place beyond the reach of the government wherein nuclear bombs, missiles, submarines, and other banned arms could be safely bought or sold; where factories could legally and openly cause radiation or acid rain that spills across state lines; where sex slaves could be traded; or where tax evaders could find a haven. I am not claiming that curbing national and transnational problems would become easy; I am only suggesting that our ability to deal with them would be significantly enhanced.

REGIONAL COMMUNITIES AS BUILDING BLOCKS

Some argue that forming supranational trade blocs, which have served as stepping-stones to regional communities, will hinder the formation of a world community. For instance, it is feared that the development of regional trade blocs will undermine worldwide free trade.[27] This could happen, especially if regional communities are anticommunities, centered around an antagonism toward other communities rather than positive identification and purpose. Thus, at the high point of the 2003 conflict between the United States and Germany and France, a good part of the European rhetoric acquired such an "anti" flavor; public officials made numerous suggestions—especially to form a strong European defense force—in order to be freed from dependence on America and be able to act to counter American influence throughout the world. However, expressions of these sentiments have been an exception to the rule. For a long period, no more than mundane tensions existed between the European Union and North America, nor is there a principled reason why regions cannot live as civilly with one another as nations do—after all, this is not a particularly high bar. Thus, while the growth of the European Union has caused some minor tensions, it has caused no serious difficulties for the United States, for its dealings with other worldwide organizations, or for the United Nations. The same holds for Mercosur, a trade bloc of six South American nations, in its dealings with other blocs, and for the Association of Southeast Asian Nations. In effect, the opposite seems to be the case. Instead of having to negotiate with fifteen European countries (soon to be twenty-five) on issues such as the reduction of farm subsidies, other countries and regional associations will be able to deal with just one representative.

The way that the United States, as a superpower, treats regional bodies in general (and the European Union in particular) reflects which global architecture the United States is seeking to advance. If its purpose is to maintain a semi-empire, led and governed by one nation, with all other actors kept as weak as possible, it is tempting to follow the colonial policy of divide and conquer that was employed by many, if not all, imperial powers. (In this case it might be more precise to talk about divide and control.) However, if the United States is keen to advance global community building on the assumption that however considerable its power advantage is, in the longer run it cannot ride roughshod over 200 nations, then the United States should favor most regional building drives.

Moreover, to reiterate, numerous problems—from fighting terrorism to preventing genocide—are easier to deal with when working with a handful of regional bodies than with scores of nations. These regional organizations can take care of some matters internally and make collaboration much easier because there are fewer interests for which to find a point of convergence. In short, regionalization eases the international digestion of treatments of transnational problems and makes them easier to swallow.

I am not denying that such a community-building orientation might exact some short-term costs. The United States may have to delay its intervention in the next Iraq or make some other such accommodations (which are acceptable as long as these sacrifices do not involve vital interests, which no nation, let alone a superpower, would allow). However, assuming that the basic merit of community building is seen, these are costs worth absorbing.

A world organized into a dozen or so regions, which will continue to contain semi-independent nations, instead of 200-odd nations (and counting) offers considerable benefits. To highlight one, a basic social science observation is worth repeating: When dealing with a large number of people, it is useful to break the crowd into subgroups. Doing this involves letting each subgroup build an internal consensus and then send a representative to the next level, in which an encompassing consensus is worked out among the representatives (i.e., the merit of representative versus direct democracy).

To illustrate the point further, imagine that there are 200 people in a room (a greatly simpler situation than representatives of 200 nations) and that they are asked to agree on any matter of some complexity, about which they have some vested interest or emotion, or both. They would have difficulty reaching a consensus. Instead, consensus building will become much easier if those involved were divided into, say, ten smaller groups of twenty each; after each develops a consensus and then sends a representative to the next level, one would end up with a much more manageable group of ten. (For the two levels—or more if there is larger number of participants—of consensus building to work, each group must accord its representatives some leeway, a point that Edmund Burke made about elected representatives and consensus formation in the legislature.) Also, the final resolution can be subject to an up or down vote by all the members to ensure that the representatives did not stray too far from their instructions. The analogy to nations is obvious: Regionalism could vastly ease consensus building on the transnational level.

It is difficult to imagine that a world community could evolve out of bonding among some 200 nations. True, after years of complicated negotiations, even such a large number of nations might be able to reach some limited, narrowly crafted, poorly enforced agreements. However, if these nations first formed a number of regional bodies—a United States of Europe, a Union of Latin American States, a Union of Southeast Asia, and so on—it would be easier for the regional communities to develop shared policies, and it would make possible the formation of a more encompassing community, a global community of communities. After all, the formation of the European Union is based on the coming together of two previously functioning regional bodies (the inner six and the outer seven), which benefited from preexisting bonds among the Benelux countries. Moreover, it is widely recognized that until the U.S. Civil War, the South and the North were rather separate societies and that American society coalesced mainly after the 1870s out of two regional "blocs." The Association of Southeast Asian Nations (ASEAN) was similarly constructed from a base of countries that shared historical ties. Later it added other countries to become ASEAN Plus Three.[28] In Latin America Mercosur promotes economic cooperation; likewise ECOWAS joins countries in West Africa with shared bonds. (So far, all three of these associations are much weaker than the European Union.)

Elements of such a two-level consolidation already exist in the World Bank. On many issues, instead of having nearly 200 representatives negotiating with one another, representatives of groups of nations deal with one another. For instance, in the World Bank, while some countries have their own "executive directors" (of the Bank), others stand in for groups such as the Middle East and Central America. Thus, in total, there are 24 executive directors, not 200.[29]

If we accept the regional building blocks approach to global community building, rather than a hasty jump from the many to the one, it is possible to imagine the formation of an additional supraregional level (e.g., North and South America, or the United States and the European Union in the form of a revived Atlantic Alliance). In this way, the road toward a Global Nation might be significantly eased.

CHAPTER THIRTEEN

A GLOBAL GOVERNMENT *AND* COMMUNITY?

TOWARD A GLOBAL COMMUNITY

PERHAPS IT IS POSSIBLE TO IMAGINE SOME KIND OF A DE FACTO global government, limited in scope and authority, a scion of the semi-empire; but the notion that we might have a global community truly challenges the imagination. People often associate community with local residential social entities in which members know one another personally. It is further assumed that for informal social controls to work, which is important for establishing social order, people must both bond with one another and share a moral culture. However, it has been long known that nations can acquire some features of community.[1] But what about a worldwide "we"? Are not communities typically defined by their separation from some other people? Can there be a "we" without a "they"?

My response is that the new "they" are weapons of mass destruction and pandemics; they fully qualify as enemies of humanity. We have long seen people unite to fight a runaway fire or flooding rivers; people do not just fight other people. Tragically, the world has gotten used to WMDs as they have been rarely employed and because the United States and the Soviet Union were able to work out rules and strategies that reduced the danger of a nuclear tragedy. Fear of WMD, especially nuclear weapons, has greatly subsided from the days people built shelters and participated in evacuation drills to protect themselves from "the bomb."[2] Now Pollyannas believe that other countries with much less stable governments might be able to do the same. For instance, it has been suggested that North Korea could be allowed to maintain and develop its nuclear arsenal because of the countervailing force offered by American, Chinese, and Russian nuclear weapons and by those to be acquired sooner or later by other nations.

This is a dangerous way of thinking, reminiscent of military strategist Herman Kahn—of making a world with nuclear powers thinkable rather than impossible. Suffice it to note that even the relatively stable United States and Soviet Union came close to nuclear Armageddon on several occasions. Newly released documents reveal that Nikita Khrushchev's threats to invade West Berlin prompted the Kennedy administration to seriously consider a first-strike nuclear attack against the USSR.[3] The United States also considered using nuclear arms in Vietnam.[4] Fearing that Israel was about to be overrun as it lost the first rounds in the October War of 1973, its defense minister, Moshe Dayan, ordered Israeli missiles to be armed with nuclear warheads.[5]

Even more dangerous is that the governments that now labor to develop or that already command WMD are much less reliable world citizens than even the United States and the Soviet Union. The ruler of North Korea, Kim Jong Il, is widely held to march to a different drummer, to put it kindly. And there is always the danger that one of these countries will sell WMD to a billionaire like Osama bin Laden or to other terrorists. In short, WMD have in the past and still do constitute a clear and present danger for one and all.

The world is facing another common enemy. The outbreak of SARS in 2003 showed that the phrase "global village" is much more than a cliché. Imagine a much more fatal illness, one that could spread even more easily than SARS, and one that is fatal to many more people. A drug-resistant bug, even a flu, could readily generate such a pandemic. Aside from a naturally caused pandemic, terrorists could unleash one. We are unprepared for an anthrax or a botulinum toxin attack, the likes of which could cause the kind of global disasters the flu did in 1918, when more than 20 million people died worldwide. HIV could become even more devastating if it were to produce a stronger mutant strain.

These scenarios share one attribute: The people of the world face a clear and present danger that requires urgent handling and cannot be treated effectively by the Old System and its old-fashioned ways. The gravity of these situations justifies global action, which is likely to be viewed as legitimate, much like the formation of the antiterrorism coalition in reaction to terrorism. The convergence of interests is obvious and a major side-effect of such concerted action would be community building.

One of the reasons to walk through the steps involved in forming effective and legitimate Global Authorities, as I have attempted to do, is to capture the imagination of public intellectuals, leaders, and citizens in favor of preventive rather than reactive action. At the very least, having a design on the shelves (to be taken down when a crisis erupts) may help to guide policy makers once panic or anger makes people eager to proceed. Experience suggests that if no thought-out designs are available the mobilizing effects of the catastrophes dissipate, or people embrace less effective or unsustainable designs.

There are a few harbingers of the development of a global community, including rising personal ties across national borders, as well as a rapid increase in what has been called transnational citizenship: people who hold passports of more than one country; people who have a blurred national identity; or people who consider themselves to be global citizens.[6] Above all, as outlined in the discussion of the global normative synthesis, current worldwide moral dialogues already are leading to the formation of some global norms and values and the beginnings of a shared political culture, which are important building blocks for community formation, however slow and distant such a development may seem.[7]

Communities, it is important to stress, do not come in digital switches, on or off; they come in varying degrees of thickness. The evolving consensus, however meager it might be, is already reflected in specific attitudes and not just in shared generalities. Examples of such specific attitudes include shared opposition to land mines, sex slaves, whale hunting, trade in ivory, the degradation of the environment, and much else. Not everyone shares such attitudes, though the same is true for values within each national or even local community: Not everyone adheres to values that are shared, but this is an inevitable quality of human nature. There is, however, a wide and thickening consensus that has some nontrivial consequences, as explained in some detail in the first part of this book.

Lawrence Lessig, a major legal scholar, not a dewy-eyed visionary, wrote recently: "We stand today just a few years before where Webster stood in 1850. We stand on the brink of being able to say, 'I speak as a citizen of the world,' without the ordinary person thinking, 'What a nut.'"[8] He may be well ahead of the curve, but so was Webster in 1850. The development of the global community may have only reached the equivalent of America in 1750, or even 1700, when the colonies were part of an empire and not yet ready to form one united political community, but still had communal bonds and several elements of a shared moral culture.

In time, measured in generations rather than years, I can envision a world of perhaps twenty regional communities, further grouped into a smaller number of supraregional ones, crowned by a Global Authority and a global civil society. It would have many of the features of a nation, often defined as a community ensconced in a state. That is, it would not merely have the powers of a state but also a core of shared values, and it would command a measure of loyalty from the world's citizens. These features are essential if what may be called a Global Nation is to be able to contain conflict and legitimately impose burdens on some parts of the citizenry for the benefit of others.

Francis Fukuyama disagrees. He writes:

> Some Europeans may believe that the steady accumulation of smaller international institutions like the ICC or the various agencies of the United Nations will some day result in something resembling democratic world government. In my view, the chance of this happening is as close to zero as you ever get in political life. What will be practically possible to construct in terms of international institutions will not be legitimate or democratic, and what will be legitimate and democratic will not be possible to construct. For better or worse, such international institutions as we possess will have to be partial solutions existing in the vacuum of international legitimacy above the level of the nation-state. Or to put it differently, whatever legitimacy they possess will have to be based on the underlying legitimacy of nation-states and the contractual relationships they negotiate.[9]

Let the reader—and the future—be the judge.

A NATION-LIKE GLOBAL STATE OR A SUI GENERIS DESIGN?

How will the various new Global Authorities be "crowned," made accountable, their actions legitimated, and their underlying divergence of interests worked out? If these authorities are not accountable to the nation-states but do command the power to act directly on behalf of their citizens, then how are these agencies to be subjected to oversight, and by whom?

The mind favors parsimony over complexity, neatness over fuzzy arrangements. Hence projecting on the world the image of the government of a unitary state is very seductive. For those who hold to such a vision, a reformed United Nations would be the World Parliament (with two "houses": a reconstituted Security Council and a restructured General Assembly); the Secretariat would serve as the world's cabinet, and so on. Some even envision a constitutional assembly, of the kind that formed the United States, convened on a global level, to form a "seamless global legal system" under a Global People's Assembly.[10]

As I see it, it is more likely that a new global architecture is going to be cobbled together out of several different elements, which, at least for the foreseeable future, will not make up one streamlined global government. It is also likely that the new architecture will not result from a top-down approach (of a constitutional assembly) or a bottom-up one (the expression of some kind of global social movement), but rather constitute a Rube Goldberg-like combination of different preexisting pieces learning to work with one another.

In one limited but important sense the new structure is likely to resemble the pre-Westphalia world in which no one authority had a monopoly of control in any one territory; no one power had full sovereignty.[11] It was a world in which the church and feudal lords and kings all had a legitimate and effective claim over some aspects of life, and worked out the relationship with each other.[12] Similarly, in this new global architecture—the Global Nation—a radically restructured United Nations would provide partial crowning, but so would various supranational bodies (e.g., the International Criminal Court), and meetings of the heads of various Global Authorities.

Here, the developments of the European Union may turn out to be instructive. Several changes in the formation of its various bodies have already occurred. The details are complicated and they will change again, depending on which of the various constitutional drafts under consideration is finally adopted and how it will be implemented. (Polities often diverge significantly from their founding designs. For example, the American Constitution makes no reference to political parties.) Under one proposal, some decisions would still be made by each national government domestically and by intergovernmental bodies via negotiations (e.g., justice and home affairs, particularly immigration), in accordance with the Old System. Other issues would be governed by a structure in which each nation would have veto power because, although votes will be taken, unanimity would be required (e.g., deciding on an EU-wide corporate tax). Still other policies would be formed as if the region were more or less one democratic nation, in which the people of Europe would vote directly (e.g., to elect one or two presidents) or for parties of their choice (e.g., as they do in the European Parliament). And, in a feature rarely used before that fits neither the old nor the national model, the EU member nations would be increasingly bound by the decisions made by a majority of the *nations* involved—by a weighted, not a normal, majority, which gives votes of smaller nations more weight.

I am not suggesting that the EU model (which itself is changing) is going to be the political structure of the evolving global architecture, or that it cannot be improved upon. My example serves merely to illustrate how a supranational system can be formed out of various elements without necessarily following any particular existing design. Over time these various bodies are likely to pull together into a more coherent and comprehensive Global Nation. However, a preference for a highly streamlined government should not cause us to overlook the promise of more complex new global architectures.

What might such a global design include? I provide here a composite picture of all the pieces so far introduced. Its lowest layer is going to be the nation-states, although their sovereignty will be less sacred in general, particularly because they will be absorbed into regional bodies. It also will include the common, garden-variety intergovernmental (and increasing interregional) agencies. That is, the new global architecture will include the Old System adapted to greater regionalism.

Whatever problems (or segments of problems) the Old System will be able to handle presumably will be subject to intranational accountability, as national representatives report to their governments and are instructed by them, in the traditional ways of constitutional democracy. Increasingly, though, regional bodies (such as the European Court of Justice) and supranational ones (such as the ICC) will begin to affect the way the Old System works. To provide but one example: When the European Court of Human Rights ruled that it was unlawful to ban gays from the military, the United Kingdom had to change its domestic policies in order to comply with the ruling.[13]

Around the nations there will continue to develop a rich fabric of international nongovernmental organizations, informal networks, and social movements—transnational communitarian bodies—the elements of a global civil society in which participation is voluntary. Hence the actions of these bodies do not require the same level of accountability as an agency with governmental powers, although their actions must of course stay within the confines of the law.

One major new governmental layer, superimposed on the Old System and to a significant extent overruling or replacing it, will be a whole slew of Global Authorities (or one Global Authority with multiple functions and divisions). Here accountability will be provided in part by supranational courts of which the ICC (which itself needs to be somewhat redesigned) is a forerunner. These courts would draw on the evolving international law[14] and the UN Universal Declaration of Human Rights, which—especially if augmented to include responsibilities—can serve as a major element of an evolving global constitution.

If the EU model is followed in one way or the other, still other matters will be decided by a weighted vote of the representatives of the nations (or regions) involved (rather than requiring consensus, as NATO demands). Decisions will also involve a close and continuous consultation of various deliberative bodies, especially the United Nations, with the superpower or big powers, the leaders of various Global Authorities, the sources of hard power. Also, a greatly restructured United Nations will be the major source of legitimation and an important place convergence of interests will be worked out.

The sui generis formation of the evolving Global Nation stands out in comparison to a streamlined nation-state. Most important is the fact that Global Authorities will not be directly accountable to the United Nations; they will likely act more like heads of agencies that take into account in their deliberations and decisions the guidelines set by the United Nations. However, their appointment will most likely not be subject to UN advice and consent nor will the United Nations be able to replace them by a vote of no confidence in the foreseeable future. The much restructured United Nations will be able to invite the head of these authorities to report on their activities to the General Assembly or its committees, and the United Nations may issue statements, either supportive or critical, regarding an agency's actions. (Note that even in well-formed nation-states, parliaments' control of various government agencies is hardly as cut and dried as some political science textbooks suggest or as simple as the public's popular notion of the way democracies work.)[15] To put it differently, I expect that as the new Global Nation develops, it will entail a significantly higher level of crowning than currently exists in the international system, but not nearly the same level that exists in a well-developed nation (see figure 13.1).

A Reconstituted United Nations

An important piece of any new global architecture is the United Nations, though it will have to be restructured. Many champions of the United Nations, who are numerous in Western Europe and among progressive people in the United States and elsewhere, treat the organization as if it already were some kind of a democratic world government. Hence they attribute enormous importance to whether the United Nations approves of a course of action, as most recently seen in the 2003 U.S. invasion of Iraq. They confuse what the United Nations one day can be with the way it is, the *ought-to-be* UN vision with the *as-is* UN reality.

The as-is UN, fashioned by the United States at the end of World War II, is a deeply flawed institution. The Security Council's composition reflects the way that the world was composed in the 1940s and ignores major changes in the world since that time.[16] Today, for instance, it would make much more

Figure 13.1

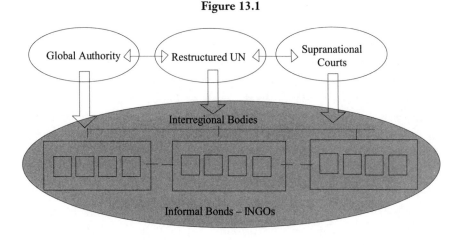

     ☐   Nations

    ▭   Regions

   – –   International Governmental Committees

sense to include India rather than France in the Council. There is nothing representative or democratic in the fact that, in effect, five nations, because of their veto power, control the only body in the United Nations that has a serious enforcement capability. In the past the United Nations often rubberstamped actions that the Western superpowers favored, for instance, during the Korean War. (President Truman already had committed U.S. troops to this war before Security Council authorized the use of force in this arena.)[17]

The legitimacy of the United Nations has been long corroded because the General Assembly, not just the Security Council, has passed scores of resolutions that have been widely ignored, with little if any consequences for those who flouted them. As of the end of 2002, countries in violation of Security Council resolutions included Croatia, India, Indonesia, Pakistan, Russia, and Sudan.[18] Turkey and Morocco have been among the worst offenders, with Turkey in violation of at least twenty-four Security Council resolutions dating back to 1974 regarding Cyprus, and Morocco in violation of sixteen Security Council resolutions from 1979 to 2001 concerning Western Sahara.[19] At one point or another various members of the UN Security Council went to war without the Council's approval. The United States invaded Grenada; the Soviet Union attacked Czechoslovakia and Hungary; and the French and British invaded Egypt. The main credit the as-is United Nations deserves is that it serves as a forum where representatives of many nations meet and can commune with one another.

Even a dedicated friend to the United Nations allows: "[The General Assembly] was not a parliament to which the Security Council was a cabinet in need of continuous support. Nor was the relationship structured to provide the separation of powers that is a feature of some democratic systems. The General Assembly was, from the outset, only a deliberative forum; it had power to discuss and recommend, to debate and pass resolutions, but no real authority, certainly no power to take decisions binding on member-states."[20]

References to UN peacekeeping forces, the "Blue Helmets," invite idealism, but the troops are in effect provided at the will of those member nations involved in a particular action.[21] Thus, when Richard Butler writes that the nonproliferation treaties require "a reliable means of enforcement" that only the Security Council can provide, he of course must mean the military forces that are controlled by national governments, especially the United States.[22]

Moreover, the United Nations cannot collect taxes or generate other revenues. Hence its budget is dependent on what are, in effect, voluntary donations from the nations involved.

The legitimacy of many resolutions of the General Assembly and of various UN committees is profoundly tainted by the fact that its members include many tyrannies and highly authoritarian governments, such as Burma, Cambodia, the Central African Republic, Eritrea, Libya, Laos, Singapore, Saudi Arabia, Syria, Sudan, Turkmenistan, Uzbekistan, and Vietnam, among others. In the General Assembly, the votes of tiny nations such as Tuvalu and Liechtenstein have the same weight as votes of China and the United States. (In 2003 the United States failed to garner a majority in the Security Council for a second resolution in its quest for approval of military action against Iraq because France essentially bribed Guinea, Angola, and Cameroon more effectively than the United States did.)[23] The fact that the UN Commission on Human Rights members include Armenia, Cuba, Saudi Arabia, and Sudan, and that Libya was its chair in 2003, does not add to the organization's credibility.

The notorious UN bureaucracy puts many other ones to shame. And because of the organization's intergovernmental structure, any work done through it has many, if not all, of the failings of the Old System. Also, the United Nations has taken on so many missions that it is vastly overextended. In effect, many of those who relied on the United Nations to criticize the U.S. invasion of Iraq in 2003 have severely criticized the United Nations itself in many other cases.

Numerous suggestions have been made to reform the United Nations.[24] Some seek to keep the United Nations basically as it is, merely to "update" it by, say, including Japan and Germany as members of the UN Security Council in recognition of the fact that they have been restored to prominent membership in the community of nations. Others seek to increase the inclusion of Third World countries and favor inviting India and Brazil to the Security Council. I am far from sure that these suggestions are realistic or would suffice even if introduced; however, few would disagree that the United Nations must be greatly reformed if it is to play a key role in the evolving Global Nation.[25]

Rarely discussed, but of special importance if the preceding analysis is considered to have some merit, is the value of greatly increasing the role of regional bodies in the United Nations to make consensus formation much easier and to encourage the development of such regional supranational communities. Proceeding in this way, France would not be replaced in the UN Security Council by Germany, as some suggest, but it would be replaced by an EU representative. Other regions, for instance, Latin America, would get a seat once they solidify. Because such changes are, to put it mildly, very unlikely in the foreseeable future, it might be more practical to create a new body.

In view of the importance that I attribute to regionalism as a stepping-stone to Global Authority and community building, it would make sense for the United Nations to form a third body, a Council of Regions, composed of the representatives of various regions. Such regional groupings already exist, although considerable regrouping is possible. (The United Nations already has several regional economic commissions: one each for Europe; Latin America and the Caribbean; Asia and the Pacific; and Africa.) A UN Council of Regions would likely be able to form shared views and express them much more effectively than the General Assembly is able to. Hence a Council of Regions would be more likely to command the attention of the global attentive publics and the heads of the Global Authorities. The Council of Regions could, for a time, absorb both some of the work the General Assembly is supposed to carry out and some of the missions undertaken by the much less representative Security Council. Often, fashioning a new body to take over the tasks of those more resistant to change works better than insisting on modifying the obsolescent ones.

None of these reforms, however, speaks to the major issue: The desire to make the United Nations into a sort of global parliament that will speak for the people of the world to those who govern them on the transnational level and hold them accountable. A document from the Campaign for a More Democratic United Nations expresses the sentiments well:

> [A] more solid and structurally sound means must be developed for the enfranchisement of 'we the peoples.'
>
> Popular representation must be taken much more seriously in the United Nations of the future.
>
> Greater representation of people interests in global decision making through, for example, a UN People's Assembly.
>
> A two-chamber General Assembly could be considered, one with government representatives as at present, and the other representing national civil society organizations . . . [This] is only a vision for the future at this stage. . . . As a first step in this direction, the Commission recommends that representatives of nongovernmental bodies accredited to the General Assembly as Civil Society organizations be grouped into a World Forum. . . . [26]

Such suggestions do not take into account the fact that a political architecture cannot deviate too far from political reality. In a global one-person one-vote system, a few countries, say China, India, and Indonesia, would have a global majority, and the rest of the world would be expected to heed to their will. Not merely the have countries, but numerous smaller and less endowed nations are sure to quit any such polity even if it contained constitutional protections for minorities—which may well encompass the people of scores, if not most, nations.

Aside from being impractical, one profound issue is almost always ignored when the role of the United Nations in the world is discussed or its future is contemplated: Democracy makes sense only when there is a community to be governed. This is a topic I explored in the last chapter, but is of such pivotal importance for a communitarian theory of international relations—and the future of the United Nations—that I return to it here and expand it some.

Just as we cannot expect someone boarding a bus to get to his place of work to yield to majority rule—the passengers voting to decide where the bus should travel—so UN members cannot be expected to submit to majority rulings until and unless a much stronger global community exists. Being subject to majority rule entails a willingness to make considerable sacrifices when one loses, not merely because one believes in the process but also because it expresses the will of the community of which one is a member. And it entails a significant measure of caring for the other members, a sense of commitment not typically extended to nonmembers.

Charles Taylor, the communitarian philosopher, writes, "a modern democratic state demands a 'people' with a strong collective identity. Democracy obliges us to show much more solidarity and much more commitment to one another in our joint political project than was demanded by the hierarchical and authoritarian societies of yesteryear."[27] Democracy, as the voice of a majority, tends to alienate subgroups, and it fails to truly embody the will of all citizens. If a state has no community, if it is not enough of a nation, it is hard to introduce or sustain democracy.

The same holds many times over for groups of nations whose shared bonds and culture and identity typically are insignificant compared to those of nations. It follows that the United Nations' ability to function one day as a democratic regime for all nations—in which the majority can impose policies on minorities—can come about only as a global sense of community develops a great deal more. In the process of getting there, the United Nations is going to benefit not only from increased transnational bonds and networks but also from the evolving normative synthesis that was explored in the first part of this volume. Communities are not merely places in which people care about one another; they are also social bodies that share a moral culture.[28] However, the global community has a long way to go; hence the democratization of the United Nations will be well beyond the sociological horizon of even those who are willing to look far into the future.

While the as-is United Nations will not even remotely resemble a global democratic parliament for the foreseeable future,[29] since the end of the Cold War it has become the major source of broad-band global legitimation. By providing a global forum—the only one of its kind that is also permanent and inclusive—it is a place where people of different parts of the world come together to voice what they consider to be morally appropriate. Their motives vary a great deal; posturing is common; and many of the speakers do not voice the views of their free citizens because none of them are free. Still, jointly—when they speak in relative unison—they articulate and help form and mobilize a global public opinion.

Other bodies provide legitimation, ranging from the Catholic Church to Amnesty International, but their voices are heeded by much smaller publics and their agendas are composed of a much smaller array of international issues than that of the United Nations, which has a near monopoly on speaking for the admittedly fuzzy and vague voice of the world's populations. Thus, when the United Nations expresses concern for the status of women or the warming of the Earth, its voice is heard not because 51 percent or more members of the General Assembly have voted in favor of a given position, and surely not because it actually holds nations accountable if they refuse to heed its resolutions. General Assembly debates give voice to a vague consensus of the global attentive public—if and when there is such a consensus—and, on quite a few occasions, the debates help to form and articulate such a consensus.[30] That is, democratic procedures are not the only way to legitimate a course of action. Hence the United Nations, without being democratic, has a major legitimizing role to play in the evolution of the Global Nation.

The notion that an institution can provide legitimacy but not be democratic should not be surprising. For instance, the Catholic Church proffers legitimacy to millions of Catholics, but no one ever claimed that it is democratic. Groups of intellectuals—not elected by anyone—issue statements, say on what is considered a just war, because it is known that their public voice bestows some legitimacy.

When treaties are concluded, the United Nations creates secretariats and committees that oversee the work of treaty parties and issue reports on the progress being made. In this way, the United Nations calls attention to countries that are not complying with these conventions, even though it has few enforcement powers. This behavior falls under the communitarian idea of "gentle prodding," prodding countries to change their direction through public shaming when they fail to live up to what the consensus called for and, conversely, praising them when they live up to their commitments. That is, the United Nations can, aside from giving voice to a desired direction, also mobilize public opinion to support those who heed it and censor those who do not.

By far the best way for the United Nations to gain more credibility in the future is for its members to become more democratic themselves. In other words, the best way to reform the United Nations is to reform its members. I do not mean to create one more UN committee to issue verbose and vacuous reports reflecting member posturing. I mean that as members are going to become better societies, more attentive to autonomy and social order in line with the communitarian conception, the United Nations also would be a major beneficiary. Assuming that the crablike walk of global progress toward democratization will continue, it will increase the global attentive public that has access to free media and is able to express itself morally and politically. As the national representatives to the United Nations will speak for their people—rather than for their autocrats—it will have more of a voice.

If, at the same time, there is a growing sense of commitment to the common good, UN members may feel more obliged to heed more of the organization's resolutions and pay their dues. One day the United Nations might even be able to collect some kind of tax and control the ways the resulting revenues are dispensed—a hallmark of parliaments. A report of the Commission on Global Governance reviews several methods of taxation or user charges that could be used to fund the United Nations, including a tax on foreign exchange transactions (the Tobin tax), a surcharge on airline tickets, user fees for non-coastal ocean fishing, and user fees for activities in Antarctica, among others.[31] As long as the United Nations is dependent on national appropriations, its general capacity to act, especially in contravention of national preferences of the major sources of its income, will continue to be limited. If and when the United Nations is able to generate a serious flow of revenues, it will have made a giant step toward being a major element of the evolving Global Nation.

In short, the United Nations already brings a major source of legitimation to the global nation. Theoretically other organizations could do so, but the United Nations has largely cornered this role. Indeed, it often speaks in terms of the normative synthesis introduced earlier. A critic may point out that often the United Nations is sharply divided on the issues. This, however, is no different from the public in one nation being divided on issues concerning, say, the legitimacy of abortion. (I use the term "legitimacy" rather than "morality" because I am referring to the ways that public policy and not personal conduct is judged.) That is, on those issues in which there is no broad-based consensus, the United Nations cannot and does not act as a legitimator. However, there are issues on which it does carry clout, ranging from human rights to environmental protection (as one can glean from the fact that those who violate various resolutions try to hide their violations, make some amends, promise to do better, or otherwise pay homage to the values involved). Thus, as various Global Authorities evolve, a reconstituted United Nations could credibly address the question of whether their actions are legitimate, which would turn them from mainly power based into more genuine authorities, bodies that draw largely on legitimate rather than raw power.

Even a visionary cannot peer so deeply into the future to know when such restructuring will occur, or when the various Global Authorities will submit to full UN oversight. However, in line with the EU model, these agencies are likely to draw on the restructured United Nations as the major source of legitimation of their actions. The fact that their antagonistic partnership will continue to be tense should neither surprise nor unduly trouble anyone. After all, even within what are considered well-established democracies, there is considerable tension between the legislature and the executive agencies. And there is no reason to expect that the Global Nation will look like the best nation, whatever that is. Turkey and Chile, for instance, have reasonably effective and stable governments and domestic peace, although their militaries are not fully accountable to their parliaments, just the way the GSA is not accountable to the United Nations, but would be expected to seek the legitimating blessings of the United Nations.

Soft and hard power rarely mesh neatly, but enhanced legitimation can slow down and redirect the application of hard power, and those who wield hard power can provide the kind of backup without which soft power cannot carry the day. In short, the political gap will not be closed, but it can be much narrowed, which will bring us closer to the establishment of human primacy.

In Conclusion

THE OBSERVATION THAT MORE AND MORE NATIONS THROUGHOUT the world are moving, some very slowly, some more rapidly, toward incorporating some elements of autonomy into their regimes (including respect for rights, a democratic form of government, and freer markets) should not be considered as proof positive that they are moving toward a Western model of polity, economy, and society. Because the East has started from such a high level of social order (albeit often a forced one), and a low level of autonomy, Eastern nations may well be moving toward a balanced model of both autonomy and order rather than seeking to make autonomy their central value. The fact that the United States—the most westernized society—is moving to shore up its social order provides further support for the thesis that East and West will meet in some middle ground, although their autonomy and social order may well not be balanced in exactly the same way.

It is important to keep in mind that East and West are not merely bringing their respective values to the evolving global normative synthesis, but that these values are being modified in the process. There are three highly important areas in which values are being modified.

1. Social order is being altered to rely more on soft power and less on coercion.
2. Building up the moral foundations of order can draw on both *moderate* religious sources as well as secular ones rather than merely relying on the latter.
3. Autonomy must be contained, rather than accorded unlimited range, especially when dealing with the market, just as social order must be limited.

The evolving global normative synthesis is taking place now. Further advancements should be encouraged, as such synthesis leads, at least from a communitarian viewpoint, toward a normative characterization of the good so-ciety.[1] Beyond the general contours of such a society—a careful balance between autonomy and social order and an order based largely on moral suasion and in-formal normative controls—such a synthesis favors several specific principles: The accommodation of particularism within the context of universalism; the promotion of soft power; a thick, but far from all-inclusive, range of normative controls; a sense of self-restraint; and appropriate restrictions on the market.

Finally, the evolving synthesis has several specific implications for foreign policy, including the adoption of a service leaning approach; opening societies rather than making democratization the first priority; engagement rather than isolation; and support for not only secular groups, but moderate religious ones as well. It favors multilateralism and institution building and, above all, com-munity building—a new form of global architecture.

At the end of the Cold War, many wondered what the composition of the new global architecture would be. After the September 11 terrorist attack, both friends and foes of the United States held that it was fostering a new global empire, albeit a rather unique one. The U.S. led invasion of Iraq in March 2003—without UN legitimation; without the collaboration of most al-lies and other nations; and as a preemptive attack without a clear and present danger—was the high point of the short season of the American empire. But a few months later, the United States was seeking the United Nations' blessing; courting allies and others to share the burden of the occupation; turning to multilateral approaches in dealing with North Korea and Iran; and beginning to realize that transforming Iraq and Afghanistan, not to mention the whole Middle East, into a "shining and prosperous democracy" was way beyond its reach. The American people, typically highly ambivalent about the U.S. role in the world and accustomed to quick and easy military victories (as well as low casualties and costs), showed growing impatience with shouldering the burden of the empire.

I expect that in the near future, while the United States will not give up its role as the superpower, it will invest more of its power in multilateral and le-gitimate endeavors—the war against terrorism and deproliferation—which provide a foundation for a Global Security Authority. That authority is laying the groundwork for a global state, whose first duty—like that of all states—is to protect the safety of the people living in its territory. The relationship be-tween this authority (and others that I see beginning to form) and the United Nations is a complex one. I called it an antagonistic partnership. Essentially, the United Nations acts as a legitimator, a major source of soft power, and it will be able to generate even more soft power as it is restructured. We should, however, not overlook the fact that the United Nations, without the hard power of the United States and others, is often ineffectual. By itself, the United Nations is not even a beginning of a global government. However, in conjunction with the powers that be, it can be. There is much evidence to suggest that an increased measure of global governance is not only badly needed, but also slowly evolving.

This entire book, as an attempt to contribute to a communitarian theory of international relations, is deliberately both positive and normative. I identify trends and I judge whether they are making the world better than it would be otherwise or whether they are pushing the world in the wrong direction.

For a book that is dedicated to international relations, I pay a great deal of attention to moral issues. This approach is in sharp contrast with that of the realists, who see public affairs in general, and international affairs especially, as governed by military and economic factors. My thesis is that as a global society is evolving, as global governance is expanding (albeit it from a low base), as more and more people in more and more parts of the world enter politics—in short, as a global community is beginning to form—normative factors are growing in importance.

Moreover, the existence of a widespread spiritual hunger reveals that as people in many parts of the world are left in a moral vacuum resulting from the collapse of secular or religious totalitarian regimes, they are likely to embrace belief systems that are incompatible with a good society. Hence the special and urgent need to provide "soft" moral answers.

I asked in this book what makes for a good society (a much richer concept than the civil society). I suggested, to repeat my communitarian mantra one more time, that it is one in which there is a carefully crafted balance between autonomy (rights, liberty) and social order, and one in which the social order is based largely on persuasion rather than coercion. Some straws blowing in the wind indicate that the new global architecture is moving in this direction, paying mind first and foremost to what I call survival ethics, and then attending— though regrettably slowly—to other transnational challenges with which neither nations nor intergovernmental organizations can cope.

The new Global Nation is cobbled together from a variety of building blocks. It is far from a neat, streamlined design. Nations and intergovernmental organizations (the Old System) continue to play a role. Transnational communitarian bodies—INGOs, networks, and social movements—help some, although less than their champions like to believe. Evolving shared transnational mores, laws, and moral dialogues are another piece of the global puzzle that help establish a global civil society. Above all, the still rare supranational bodies—those that do not depend on national governments or intergovernmental organizations—are an important addition. These include regional bodies (especially those of the European Union), the ICC, ICANN, and some parts of the WTO. As far as regional bodies are concerned, there is no denying that they could become each others' enemies, as was the case in earlier eras—indeed, we already hear that Europeans are from Venus and Americans are from Mars.[2] There are, however, some reasons to hold that these bodies may well serve as elements of a global architecture that strains under the burden of having to process new policies and institutional arrangements with scores of nations, if not with 200 of them. The new global authorities are a very different kind of building block, on which the evolving global architecture draws. The most developed one, the Global Antiterrorism Authority, is a sort of worldwide police department, run by the United States and its allies. It has already opened a second wing, working on deproliferation of weapons of mass destruction. It is further expanding, albeit much more slowly, to deal with pandemics and prevent genocides through humanitarian interventions. I hence predict that the global government, to the extent that it will be fashioned, will follow the pattern in which nation-states developed: First and foremost nation-states focused on providing safety. Legal and political rights followed; social and economic rights lagged.

With considerable regret, because I fully realize the great difficulties involved, I conclude that in the longer run a global government cannot be stabilized without evolving some measure of an imagined global community. I am somewhat comforted by the fact that various developments make such a community less inconceivable than it long has been. This is especially the case as there is no shortage of enemies humankind jointly faces.

The stakes are high as access to and production of weapons of mass destruction are becoming easier and terrorism more popular, and scores of other transnational problems—from environmental degradation to traffic in people—simply cannot be treated effectively by nations in the old-fashioned way.

There is no doubt in my mind that in order for humanity to govern, rather than being the subject of history, the world needs a new set of shared core values and political institutions, indeed eventually a true global community. Only then, in Samson's terms, will might turn into sweet. Meanwhile, I hope, we can make the mix sweeter.

NOTES

INTRODUCTION

1. Judges, Chapter 14 of the King James Version of the Bible. According to the King James' translation, the quote is "from strong came sweet." "Might" is my translation.
2. The terminology is taken from the following: "lite empire" from Michael Ignatieff, "The Burden," *New York Times Magazine*, January 5, 2003, 24; "virtual empire" from Martin Walker, "America's Virtual Empire," *World Policy Journal* 19, no. 2 (2002): 13–20; "neo empire" from G. John Ikenberry, "America's Imperial Ambition," *Foreign Affairs* 81, no. 5 (2002): 44–60; and "liberal empire" from Jedediah Purdy, "Liberal Empire: Assessing the Arguments," *Ethics and International Affairs* 17, no. 12 (2003): 35.
3. A Newsweek poll found that 66 percent of Americans oppose the current spending levels for rebuilding Iraq and 69 percent are "concerned that the U.S. will be bogged down in Iraq for many years without making much progress in achieving its goals there." See "Newsweek Poll" *Newsweek*, August 25, 2003.
4. See Amitai Etzioni, *My Brother's Keeper: A Memoir and a Message* (Lanham, Md.: Rowman & Littlefield, 2003), 319–363.
5. For my views on communitarian thinking see *New Golden Rule: Community and Morality in a Democratic Society* (New York: Basic Books, 1996). For the text of the communitarian platform, those who endorse it, and information about the Communitarian Network, see http://www.communitariannetwork.org. Articles from a communitarian perspective can be found in *The Responsive Community*, the only journal of communitarian thought. For other major communitarian texts by sociologists, see especially Philip Selznick, *The Communitarian Persuasion* (Washington, D.C.: Woodrow Wilson Center Press, 2002) and *The Moral Commonwealth: Social Theory and the Promise of Community* (Berkeley: University of California Press, 1992); Robert N. Bellah, Richard Madsen, William M. Sullivan, Ann Swidler, and Steven M. Tipton, *Habits of the Heart: Individualism and Commitment in American Life* (Berkeley: University of California Press, 1985); as well as previous works by Martin Buber, Emile Durkheim, Robert Nisbet, and Ferdinand Tonnies. Political theorists writing about communitarianism include Michael Sandel, Charles Taylor, and Michael Walzer. A particularly well-written and well-documented book is Alan Ehrenhalt's *The Lost City: Discovering the Forgotten Virtues of Community in the Chicago of the 1950s* (New York: Basic Books, 1995). Other good books include Daniel A. Bell, *Communitarianism and Its Critics*

(Oxford: Clarendon Press, 1993); and Henry Tam, *Communitarianism: A New Agenda for Politics & Citizenship* (New York: NYU Press, 1998). Responsive (or new) communitarianism should not be confused with authoritarian communitarianism.

6. See, e.g., Richard Easterlin, "Income and Happiness: Towards a Unified Theory," *Economic Journal* 111 (2001): 465–484; Robert Frank, *Luxury Fever* (New York: Free Press, 1999); Jonathan L. Freedman, *Happy People: What Happiness Is, Who Has It, and Why* (New York: Harcourt Brace Jovanovich, 1978), 133–151; Ronald Inglehart, *Modernization and Postmodernization: Cultural, Economic, And Political Change in 43 Societies* (Princeton, NJ: Princeton University Press, 1997), 87; Robert E. Lane, *The Loss of Happiness in Market Democracies* (New Haven: Yale University Press, 2000); David G. Myers, *The Pursuit of Happiness: Who Is Happy – And Why* (New York: William Morrow and Company, 1992), 30–46; and Andrew J. Oswald, "Happiness and Economic Performance," *Economic Journal* 107 (1997): 1815–1831.

7. Pew Research Center for the People and the Press, *What the World Thinks in 2002: How Global Publics View Their Lives, Their Countries, The World, America* (Washington, D.C.: Pew Research Center for the People and the Press, 2002).

8. See Catherine E. Rudder, "Can Congress Govern?" in *Congress Reconsidered*, 5th ed., eds. Lawrence C. Dodd and Bruce I. Oppenheimer (Washington, D.C.: CQ Press, 1993), 365–374; and Elizabeth Drew, *Politics and Money: The New Road to Corruption* (New York: Collier, 1983).

Chapter 1

1. Legitimacy, as it is commonly treated in standard sources, is defined as the "foundation of such governmental power as is exercised both with a consciousness on the government's part that it has a right to govern and with some recognition by the governed of that right." *International Encyclopedia of the Social Sciences*, ed. David L. Sills (New York: Macmillan and Free Press, 1968), 244. Robert Jackson shows that there are recognized international norms that have implications for determining legitimate conduct by states. See Robert Jackson, *The Global Covenant: Human Conduct in a World of States* (Oxford: Oxford University Press, 2000).

2. See, for example, Francis Fukuyama, *The End of History and the Last Man* (New York: Free Press, 1992); Michael Mandelbaum, *The Ideas that Conquered the World: Peace, Democracy, and Free Markets in the Twenty-First Century* (New York: Public Affairs, 2002); and Fareed Zakaria, *The Future of Freedom: Illiberal Democracy at Home and Abroad* (New York: W. W. Norton, 2003).

3. George W. Bush, "Introduction," *The National Security Strategy of the United States of America*, September 2002, iv. Available at: http://www.whitehouse.gov/nsc/nss.pdf. Accessed 10/28/02.

4. Blair quoted in George F. Will " . . . Or maybe not at all," *Washington Post*, 17 August 2003, B7.

5. See Samuel P. Huntington, *The Clash of Civilizations and the Remaking of World Order* (New York: Simon & Schuster, 1996); and Bernard Lewis, "The Roots of Muslim Rage," *Atlantic Monthly*, September 1990, 47–60.

6. Samuel P. Huntington, "The Clash of Civilizations," *Foreign Affairs* 72, no. 3 (Summer 1993): 40.

7. For a good comparison of Huntington and Fukuyama, see Stanley Kurtz, "The Future of History, *Policy Review*, no. 113 (2002): 43–58.

8. Thomas L. Friedman, *The Lexus and the Olive Tree* (New York: Farrar, Straus & Giroux 1999).

9. There are some who argue that one can find within Asian cultural traditions values that are comparable to Western human rights. See, for example, *Human Rights in Asian Cultures: Continuity and Change*, ed. Jefferson R. Plantilla and Sebasti L. Raj, S. J. (Osaka: Hurights Osaka, 1997).

10. Bush quoted in William Kristol, "Morality in Foreign Policy," *Weekly Standard*, February 10, 2003, 7.

11. Fareed Zakaria, "Culture Is Destiny: A Conversation with Lee Kuan Yew," *Foreign Affairs* 73, no. 2 (1994): 111.

12. Hau Pei-tsun, *Straight Talk* (Taipai, Taiwan: Governmental Information Office, 1993), cited and quoted in Daniel A. Bell, *East Meets West: Human Rights and Democracy in East Asia* (Princeton, NJ: Princeton University Press, 2000), 149–150.

13. Suzanne Haneef, *What Everyone Should Know about Islam and Muslims* (Chicago: Kazi Publications/Library of Islam, 1996), 118.

14. Herbert Bronstein, "Mitzvah and Autonomy: The Oxymoron of Reform Judaism," *Tikkun* 14, no. 4 (1999): 41.

15. In addition to those listed, other sources depicting the main tenets of the Eastern belief system include Geir Helgesen, who found that nearly 90 percent of South Koreans agreed with the statement "a better future depends on the social morality in society" in the study *Democracy and Authority in Korea* (New York: St. Martin's Press, 1998), 94; and T. R. Reid, *Confucius Lives Next Door: What Living in the East Teaches Us about Living in the West* (New York: Vintage, 2000).

16. See the "Letter to the American People," reportedly written by Osama bin Laden in November 2002 and published in English on the website of the London *Observer*. Available at: http://www.observer.co.uk/Print/0,3858,4552895,00.html. Accessed 4/25/03.

17. Daniel A. Bell writes: "the view that a U.S.-style political system would lead to social breakdown is widely shared in Asia, and this undermines American moral authority in the region." See *East Meets West* (Princeton, NJ: Princeton University Press, 2000), 57.

18. Louis Hartz, *The Liberal Tradition in America: An Interpretation of American Political Thought since the Revolution* (New York: Harcourt Brace, 1995).

19. See, for instance, Bruce Ackerman, *We the People* (Cambridge, Mass.: Belknap, 1991); Bernard Bailyn, *The Ideological Origins of the American Revolution* (Cambridge, Mass.: Harvard University Press, 1967); J. G. A. Pocock, *The Machiavellian Moment : Florentine Political Thought and the Atlantic Republican Tradition* (Princeton, NJ: Princeton University Press, 1975); and Gordon Wood, *The Creation of the American Republic 1776–1787* (Chapel Hill: University of North Carolina Press, 1969).

20. See Amartya Sen, "Human Rights and Asian Values," *New Republic*, July 14 and 21, 1997, 38–39.

21. I write "extensive" because, as William A. Galston has shown, all states enforce some values, none is fully neutral. See William A. Galston, *Liberal Purposes: Goods, Virtues, and Diversity in the Liberal State* (Cambridge, Mass.: Cambridge University Press, 1991).

22. For further discussion, see Amitai Etzioni, *The New Golden Rule: Community and Morality in a Democratic Society* (New York: Basic Books, 1996), 85–159.

23. Jonathan Rauch, "Confessions of an Alleged Libertarian (and the Virtues of 'Soft' Communitarianism)," *The Responsive Community* 10, no. 3 (2000): 23.

24. On the differences between Chinese and American models of society, see Randall Peerenboom, *China's Long March toward Rule of Law* (New York: Cambridge University Press, 2002).

25. Liu Banyan and Perry Link, "A Great Leap Backward," *New York Review of Books*, October 8, 1998, 19.

26. Statistics compiled from the *World Factbook of Criminal Justice Systems* (1989–1993 numbers) and a report from the UNODC., Moscow Regional Office (1995–2001 numbers).

27. Paul Quinn-Judge, "Russian Roulette," *Time (International)*, September 7, 1998.

28. Patrick Richter, "US Expert Outlines Social and Environmental Disaster in Russia," *World Socialist Web Site*, October 29, 1999. Available at: http://www.wsws.org/articles/1999/oct1999/russ-a29.shtml. Accessed 7/15/03.

29. PBS Frontline, "Drug Abuse and Addiction," *Facts & Stats of the Yeltsin Era*. Available at: http://www.pbs.org/wgbh/pages/frontline/shows/yeltsin/etc/facts.html. Accessed 7/15/03.

30. Belinda Cooper, "The Fall of the Wall and the East German Police," in *Policing in Central and Eastern Europe: Comparing Firsthand Knowledge with Experience from the West*, ed. Milan Pagon (Ljubljana, Slovenia: College of Police and Security Studies, 1996). For a discussion of China's problems, see Banyan and Link, "Great Leap," 19; and Patrick E. Tyler, "China Battles a Spreading Scourge of Illicit Drugs," *New York Times*, November 15, 1995, A1. Regarding the increasing problems in the former Soviet Union, see John M. Kramer, "Drug Abuse in East-Central Europe," *Problems of Post-Communism* 44 (1997): 35–36; and Sharon L. Wolchik, "The Politics of Transition in Central Europe," *Problems of Post-Communism* 42 (1995): 38.

31. David Rohde, "Afghans Lead World again in Poppy Crop," *New York Times*, October 29, 2002, A8; Bureau for International Narcotics and Law Enforcement Affairs, *International Narcotics Control Strategy Report*, March 2003, VII-3.

32. April Witt, "Afghan Poppies Proliferate: As Drug Trade Widens, Labs and Corruption Flourish," *Washington Post*, July 10, 2003, A1.

33. "Dodge City on the Tigris," *Economist*, July 19, 2003, 19.

34. Thomas Carothers, *Aiding Democracy Abroad: The Learning Curve* (Washington, D.C.: Carnegie Endowment for International Peace, 1999); Robert Kaplan, "Was Democracy Just a Moment?," *The Atlantic Monthly*, December 1997, 55–71.

35. See Paul Berman, *Terror and Liberalism* (New York: W.W. Norton, 2003), and Amitai Etzioni, "Opening Islam," *Society* 39, no. 5 (Spring 2002): 29–35.

36. Jon Sawyer, "Iran Clerics' Rule Facing Opposition; Dissidents Openly Challenge the Revolution of 1979," *Saint Louis Post-Dispatch*, July 12, 2003, p. 4.

37. The U.S. Agency for International Development (USAID) is active in the promotion of Western democratic values abroad. Among its efforts to strengthen and "open" the civil societies of other nations are teacher training and exchange programs in Central Asia, education of girls in Jordan and India, and the airing of *Sesame Street* on Egyptian television stations.

38. Bill Bradley, "Civil Society and the Rebirth of Our National Community," *The Responsive Community* 5, no. 2 (1995): 4–10.

39. Jonathan Sacks argues that there is a religious global synthesis based on toler-
      ance and diversity. Jonathan Sacks, *Dignity of Difference: How to Avoid the Clash of
      Civilizations* (New York: Continuum, 2003).

40. The Carnegie Endowment for International Peace has an entire symposium
      dedicated to the issues surrounding reform in Islamic countries. See *Arab Reform
      Bulletin* 1, no. 4 (October 2003).

41. United States Department of State, *Background Notes: Bahrain* (Washington,
      D.C.: U.S. Department of State, February 2002). Available at: http://www.state.
      gov/r/pa/ei/bgn/5301.htm. Accessed 2/3/03.

42. Douglas Jehl, "Democracy's Uneasy Steps in Islamic World," *New York Times*,
      November 23, 2001, A1.

43. Barbara Slavin, "Arab Law Makers Get Close-Up View of Democracy," *USA
      Today*, December 12, 2002, 12A; Philip Dine, "Woman Breaks Ground in Run
      for Parliament Seat," *St. Louis Post-Dispatch*, November 8, 2002, A15.

44. Philip Dine, "U.S.-Iraqi Tension Takes Back Seat to Bahrain's Struggle to Im-
      prove Life," *St. Louis Post-Dispatch*, November 8, 2002, A1.

45. Somini Sengupta, "Bahrain Says 52% Vote Turnout Meets Democratic Goals,"
      New York Times, October 25, 2002, A6.

46. "Arabs Tiptoe to Democracy," *Economist*, August 7, 1999, 33.

47. Susan B. Glasser, "Qatar Reshapes Its Schools," *Washington Post*, February 2,
      2003, A20.

48. See "Saudi Arabia Announces First Local Council Elections, but No Date," *New
      York Times*, October 13, 2003, A3.

49. For a good discussion of the need to support the moderate Muslim majority, see
      Graham E. Fuller, *The Future of Political Islam* (New York: Palgrave Macmillan,
      2003).

50. Many scholars refer to these hardliners as "Islamists," which Noah Feldman has
      called "a comprehensive political, spiritual and personal world-view defined in
      opposition to all that is non-Islamic." Quoted in "A Survey of Islam and the
      West," *Economist*, September 13, 2003, 5.

51. See, for example, Charles Kurzman, who distinguishes liberal Islam from cus-
      tomary Islam and revivalist Islam, as well as defines three modes of liberal Islam
      (liberal, silent, and interpreted *sharia*) in "Introduction," *Liberal Islam: A Source-
      book*, ed. Kurzman (New York: Oxford University Press, 1998), 3–26; William E.
      Shepard discusses five forms of Islam (secular, modern, radical, traditional, and
      neotraditional) in "Islam and Ideology: Toward a Typology," *International Jour-
      nal of Middle East Studies* 19 (1987): 307–336; and Abdou Filali-Ansary notes that
      there are at least six names for "liberal" Islam, including reformed Islam, modern
      Islam, protestant Islam, positive Islam, the Islam of modernity, and enlightened
      Islam, in "The Sources of Enlightened Muslim Thought," *Journal of Democracy*
      14, no. 2 (2003): 19.

52. Muqtedar Khan, "Who Are Moderate Muslims," Available at: http://www.ijti-
      had.org/moderatemuslims.htm. Accessed 5/2/03.

53. Khaled M. Abou El Fadl, *Speaking in God's Name: Islamic Law, Authority, and
      Women* (Oxford: One World, 2001), 307.

54. Forough Jahanbakhsh, *Islam, Democracy, and Religious Modernism in Iran:
      1953–2000* (Leiden, Netherlands: Koninklijke Brill, 2001), 45–46.

55. Quoted in "Reformists Versus Conservatives in Iran," *Middle East Media Research
      Institute* (Inquiry and Analysis Series No. 55), May 9, 2001. President Karzai has

also presided over the creation of Afghanistan's new constitution, which balances Islamic law with democratic principles. For more, see Carlotta Gall, "New Afghan Constitution Juggles Koran and Democracy" *New York Times*, October 19, 2003, A3.

56. Khaled M. Abou El Fadl, *And God Knows the Soldiers: The Authoritative and Authoritarian in Islamic Discourse* (Lanham, Md.: University Press of America, 2001), 24.

57. Ayelet Savyon, "The Call for Islamic Protestantism: Dr. Hashem Aghajari's Speech and Subsequent Death Sentence," *Middle East Media Research Institute* (Special Dispatch Series No. 445), December 2, 2002.

58. Khan, "Moderate Muslims."

59. Abou El Fadl, *And God Knows the Soldiers*, 90, 134.

60. Geneive Abdo, "Some Moderate Islamic Clerics Take a New Hard Line Against US," *Boston Globe*, March 16, 2003, A20.

61. Hilary MacKenzie, "Clerics Vow to Wage a Holy War: Focus of Islamic Conference is to Appease Kurds and Form Front Against United States," *Gazette* (Montreal), December 24, 2002, A22.

62. An elaborate analysis of the implications of this term is provided by Shehzad Saleem, "Islam and Non-Muslims: A New Perspective," *Renaissance* 12, no. 3 (2003).

63. Khaled M. Abou El Fadl, "Peaceful Jihad," in *Taking Back Islam: American Muslims Reclaim Their Faith*, ed. Michael Wolfe (Emmaus, Pa.: Rodale, 2002), 37.

64. Seyyed Hossein Nasr, *The Heart of Islam* (New York: HarperSanFrancisco, 2002), 260.

65. The Pew Research Center for the People and the Press, *Global Attitudes: 44-Nation Major Survey (2002)*, June 3, 2003. Question 53b, T91.

66. Angel M. Rabasa, *Political Islam in Southeast Asia: Moderates, Radicals, and Terrorists* (New York: Oxford University Press/International Institute for Strategic Studies, 2003), 15–16.

67. Ibid., 16. Surveys and election results show that the number of Indonesians who want an Islamic state is no more than 15 percent of the total population of about 200 million; see R. William Liddle and Saiful Mujani, "The Real Face of Indonesian Islam," *New York Times*, November 10, 2003, A15.

68. Chandra Muzaffar, interview, October 10, 2001. *Muslims*, prod. by Graham Judd and Elena Mannes, 120 min., Independent Production Fund, 2002, videocassette. Available at: http://www.pbs.org/wgbh/pages/frontline/shows/muslims/interviews/muzaffar.html. Accessed 7/18/03.

69. Pew Research Center, *Global Attitudes*. Question 53a, T-91.

70. "It Could Be Worse," *Economist*, June 28, 2003, 15–16.

71. See, for instance, Thomas L. Friedman, "Drilling for Freedom," *New York Times*, October 20, 2002, sec. 4, p. 11.

72. I am indebted to Daniel A. Bell for this point. See Theodore De Bary, Irene Bloom, and Joseph Adler, eds., *Sources of Chinese Tradition* (New York: Columbia University Press, 2000). De Bary has written much about the "communitarian" aspects of Confucianism; see for instance William Theodore De Bary *Asian Values and Human Rights* (Cambridge, Mass. Harvard University Press, 1998). On Confucianism and Democracy, see Daniel A. Bell and Hahm Chaibong, eds., *Confucianism for the Modern World* (New York: Cambridge University Press, 2003). For the writings of Han Fei Tzu, see the short, excellent translation by Burton Watson, ed., *Basic Writings of Mo Tzu, Hsun Tzu, and Han Fei Tzu* (New York: Columbia University Press, 1967).

73. See for example Denny Roy, "Singapore, China, and the 'Soft Authoritarian Challenge'" *Asian Survey* 34, no. 3 (1994): 231–242; and Steven J. Hood, "The Myth of Asian-Style Democracy" *Asian Survey* 38, no. 9 (1998): 853–866.

74. Francis Fukuyama, *The Great Disruption: Human Nature and the Reconstitution of Social Order* (New York: Free Press, 1999).

75. The FBI's estimated number of Crime Index offenses decreased about 18 percent between 1992 and 2001. *Federal Bureau of Investigation, Crime in the United States 2001: Uniform Crime Reports* (Washington, D.C.: Government Printing Office, 2002), 10.

76. For teen birth rates, see Brady E. Hamilton, Joyce A. Martin, and Paul D. Sutton, "Births: Preliminary Data for 2002," *Centers for Disease Control and Prevention National Vital Statistics Reports* 51, no. 11 (2003). For data showing a decline in the use of marijuana over the last twenty years, see National Center for Health Statistics, *Health, United States, 1995* (Hyattsville, Md.: Public Health Service, 1996), 175–176 [Table 65]; National Center for Health Statistics, *Health, United States, 2002*, with Chartbook on Trends in the Health of Americans (Hyattsville, Md.: Public Health Service, 2003), 201–202 [Table 64].

77. Amitai Etzioni, *My Brother's Keeper: A Memoir and a Message* (Lanham, Md.: Rowman & Littlefield, 2003), 319–363.

78. Etzioni, *New Golden Rule*, 34–57.

79. "Human Rights at Fifty: Program 9849." Narr. Mary Gray Davidson. Prod. Stanley Foundation. Common Ground Radio. KWPC, Muscatine, Iowa, December 8, 1998. Transcript available at: http://www.commongroundradio.org/shows/98/9849.html. Accessed 1/27/03.

80. Bilahari Kausikan, "Asia's Different Standard," *Foreign Policy*, no. 92 (1993): 24.

81. For more on the Asian values debate, including criticism of the Universal Declaration of Human Rights, see Daniel A. Bell, *East Meets West* (Princeton: Princeton University Press, 2000), p. 67. See also Joanne R. Bauer and Daniel A. Bell, eds., *The East Asian Challenge for Human Rights* (Cambridge: Cambridge University Press, 1999).

82. Daniel A. Bell outlines the possibilities for nonlegal, communal enforcement of rights and responsibilities—for example, mediation—that is more common in Asian cultures. See Daniel A. Bell, *East Meets West* (Princeton: Princeton University Press, 2000), 76–78.

83. For my views on communitarian thinking, see *New Golden Rule*. For the text of the communitarian platform, those who endorse it, and information about the Communitarian Network, see http://www.communitariannetwork.org. Articles from a communitarian perspective can be found in *The Responsive Community*, the only journal of communitarian thought. For other major communitarian texts by sociologists, see especially Philip Selznick, *The Communitarian Persuasion* (Washington, D.C.: Woodrow Wilson Center Press, 2002) and *The Moral Commonwealth: Social Theory and the Promise of Community* (Berkeley: University of California Press, 1992); Robert N. Bellah, Richard Madsen, William M. Sullivan, Ann Swidler, and Steven M. Tipton, *Habits of the Heart: Individualism and Commitment in American Life* (Berkeley: University of California Press, 1985); as well as previous works by Martin Buber, Emile Durkheim, Robert Nisbet, and Ferdinand Tonnies. Political theorists writing about communitarianism include Michael Sandel, Charles Taylor, and Michael Walzer. A particularly well-written and well-documented book is Alan Ehrenhalt's *The Lost City: Discovering the Forgotten Virtues of Community in the Chicago of the 1950s* (New York: Basic Books, 1995). Other good books include Daniel A. Bell, *Communitarianism and Its Critics*

(Oxford: Clarendon Press, 1993); and Henry Tam, *Communitarianism: A New Agenda for Politics & Citizenship* (New York: New York University Press, 1998). Responsive (or new) communitarianism should not be confused with authoritarian communitarianism.

84. "A Universal Declaration of Human Responsibilities," *The Responsive Community* 8, no. 2 (1998): 71–77.

CHAPTER 2

1. Daniel Lerner, *The Passing of Traditional Society: Modernizing the Middle East* (New York: Free Press, 1958).

2. Amy Guttman, "Communitarian Critics of Liberalism," *Philosophy and Public Affairs* 14, no. 3 (Summer 1985): 319.

3. Ferdinand Tonnies, *Community and Society*, trans. Charles P. Loomis (New York: Harper & Row, 1963).

4. Joseph S. Nye, Jr. *The Paradox of American Power* (Oxford: Oxford University Press, 2002), 8–9; and Nye, *Soft Power: The Means to Success in World Politics* (New York: PublicAffairs, 2004).

5. See Amitai Etzioni, *A Comparative Analysis of Complex Organizations* (New York: The Free Press, 1961).

6. Ibid.

7. Joseph S. Nye, Jr., "U.S. Power and Strategy After Iraq," *Foreign Affairs* 82, no. 4 (2003): 66.

8. For the complexities involved in deciding what is liberal, see Hans Joas, *War and Modernity* (Cambridge: Polity Press, 2003); particularly pages 34–40.

9. For a comprehensive concept of the term, see *Routledge Encyclopedia of Philosophy*, Edward Craig, general ed. (London: Routledge, 1998), 584–586.

10. Simon, Herbert A., *Administrative Behavior* (New York: The Macmillan Company, 1957), 125.

11. Robert Kagan, "Looking for Legitimacy in All the Wrong Places," *Foreign Policy*, no. 137 (2003): 70.

12. George F. Will, "Shrinking the U.N.," *Washington Post*, February 20, 2003, A39.

13. Charles Krauthammer, "Victory Changes Everything . . . ," *Washington Post*, November 30, 2001, A41. See also Martin Kramer in *War on Terror: The Middle East Dimension*, ed. Robert B. Satloff (Washington, D.C.: Washington Institute for Near East Policy, 2002), 17–24.

14. For evidence of increased support for acting more legitimately, see Amitai Etzioni, *The Monochrome Society* (Princeton: Princeton University Press, 2001), 232–245.

15. There are many radical critiques of U.S. imperialism. Among the most recent are Tariq Ali, *Bush in Babylon: The Recolonisation of Iraq* (New York: Verso, 2003); Noam Chomsky, *Hegemony or Survival: America's Quest for Global Dominance* (New York: Metropolitan Books, 2003); Chalmers Johnson, *The Sorrows of Empire: Militarism, Secrecy, and the End of the Republic* (New York: Metropolitan Books, 2003); Robert Jay Lifton, *Superpower Syndrome: America's Apocalyptic Confrontation with the World* (New York: Thunder's Mouth Press, 2003); John Newhouse, *Imperial America: The Bush Assault on World Order* (New York: Knopf, 2003); and George Soros, *The Bubble of American Supremacy: Correcting the Misuse of American Power* (New York: Public Affairs, 2004).

CHAPTER 3

1. For a discussion, see Robert Gilpin, *The Challenge of Global Capitalism* (Princeton: Princeton University Press, 2000).

2. Jeffrey Sachs, *Poland's Jump to the Market Economy* (Cambridge, Mass.: Massachusetts Institute of Technology Press, 1993).

3. See, for instance, Robert Wuthnow's discussion of American attitudes toward money and materialism in Robert Wuthnow, *God and Mammon in America* (New York: Free Press, 1994), 117–189; and the compilation of Higher Education Research Institute survey data by the Center for Information & Research on Civic Learning and Engagement (CIRCLE), which demonstrates that college freshman are more concerned with being well-off financially than with developing a meaningful philosophy of life. See CIRCLE, "Changing Priorities: Money Counts." Available at: http://www.civicyouth.org/research/areas/youth_attit. htm. Accessed 7/17/03.

4. Although the GDP of former Communist countries is increasing, the percentage of those who felt that their nation was "going in the right direction in 2002" is relatively low: 18 percent in Bulgaria and Macedonia, 28 percent in Croatia, and 34 percent in Romania. Other figures along these lines indicate that, in this region, the "beneficiaries of reform consider themselves victims of change." See "Never Had It so Good: Trouble Is, It Doesn't Feel that Way," *Economist*, September 13, 2003, 69.

5. Frank M. Andrews and Stephen B. Withey, *Social Indicators of Well-Being: Americans' Perceptions of Life Quality* (New York: Plenum Press, 1976), 254–255.

6. Jonathan L. Freedman, *Happy People: What Happiness Is, Who Has It, and Why* (New York: Harcourt Brace Jovanovich, 1978).

7. David G. Myers and Ed Diener, "Who Is Happy?," *Psychological Science* 6 (1995): 12–14.

8. Richard A. Easterlin, "Income and Happiness: Towards a Unified Theory," *Economic Journal* 111 (2001): 469, 471.

9. Will Hutton, *A Declaration of Interdependence: Why America Should Rejoin the World* (New York: W. W. Norton & Company, 2003).

10. See, among many others, Daniel Doherty and Amitai Etzioni, eds., *Voluntary Simplicity* (Lanham, Md.: Rowman & Littlefield, 2003); and Amitai Etzioni, *The Monochrome Society* (Princeton: Princeton University Press, 2001), 48–78.

11. Abraham Maslow, *Toward a Psychology of Being*, 3d ed. (New York: John Wiley & Sons, 1998); and chapter 21 in Amitai Etzioni, *The Active Society* (New York: The Free Press, 1968), 617–654.

12. For a discussion of voluntary simplicity, see Etzioni, *Monochrome Society*, 48–78.

13. Robert Fogel, *The Fourth Great Awakening and the Future of Egalitarianism* (Chicago: University of Chicago Press, 1999).

14. For a discussion of the relevance of Confucianism to modern politics and society, see Daniel A. Bell and Hahm Chaibong, eds., *Confucianism for the Modern World* (Cambridge: Cambridge University Press, 2003.)

15. "Confucius and the Party Line," *Economist*, May 24, 2003, 38.

16. In addition to the books already mentioned, see Juliet Schor, *The Overworked American: Why We Want What We Don't Need* (New York: HarperPerennial, 1999), 111–142.

17. Paul Berman elaborates on the futility of confronting terrorists with secular arguments: "The followers of Qutb speak, in their wild fashion, of enormous

human problems, and they urge one another to death and murder. But the enemies of these people speak of what? The political leaders speak of UN resolutions, of unilateralism, of multilateralism, of weapons inspectors, of coercion and noncoercion. This is no answer to the terrorists. . . . Who will speak of the sacred and the secular, of the physical and the spiritual world?" Paul Berman, "The Philosopher of Islamic Terror," *New York Times*, March 23, 2003, sec. 6, p. 24.

18. Elizabeth Shakman Hurd, "The Hidden Life of Secularism: Implications for the U.S. in Iraq," 2003, unpublished manuscript.

19. Peter L. Berger, "The Desecularization of the World: A Global Overview," in *The Desecularization of the World: Resurgent Religion and World Politics*, ed. Berger (Washington, D.C.: Ethics and Public Policy Center, 1999), 2.

20. David B. Barrett, George T. Kunan, and Todd M. Johnson, *World Christian Encyclopedia*, vol. 1 (Oxford: Oxford University Press, 2001), 624.

21. Alan Aldridge, *Religion in the Contemporary World: A Sociological Introduction* (Cambridge, UK: Polity Press, 2000), 109–110.

22. Figures taken from Barrett, Kunan, and Johnson, *Christian Encyclopedia*, 793, 757, and 91, respectively.

23. See, for example, Rodney Stark and Roger Finke, *Acts of Faith Explaining the Human Side of Religion* (Berkeley: University of California Press, 2000), 74; David C. Lewis, *After Atheism: Religion and Ethnicity in Russia and Central Asia* (Surrey, U.K.: Curzon, 2000), 194; and Barrett, Kunan, and Johnson, *Christian Encyclopedia*, 603, 619.

24. Barrett, Kunan, and Johnson, *Christian Encyclopedia*, 191.

25. Philip Jenkins, *The Next Christendom: The Coming of Global Christianity* (Oxford: Oxford University Press, 2002), 71.

26. Figures taken from Barrett, Kunan, and Johnson, *Christian Encyclopedia*, 734 and 372, respectively.

27. Figures taken from ibid., 13, 13, 360, and 360, respectively.

28. Aldridge, *Religion in the Contemporary World*, 106–107.

29. Gabriel A. Almond, R. Scott Appleby, and Emmanuel Sivan, *Strong Religion: The Rise of Fundamentalisms Around the World* (Chicago: University of Chicago Press, 2003).

30. José Casanova, *Public Religions in the Modern World* (Chicago: University of Chicago Press, 1994), 5.

31. For additional discussion of the importance of Turkish politics and religion, see Noah Feldman, *After Jihad: America and the Struggle for Islamic Democracy* (New York: Farrar, Straus, and Giroux, 2003).

32. Asla Aydintasbas, "'Muslim Democrats,'" *Wall Street Journal*, October 30, 2002, A18.

33. Steven Lee Myers, "Russian Group Is Offering Values to Fill a Void," *New York Times*, February 16, 2003, sec. 1, p. 8.

34. For descriptions of American's experimentation with alternative forms of religion and spirituality, see Robert Wuthnow, *After Heaven: Spirituality in America Since the 1950s* (Berkeley: University of California Press, 1998).

35. For instance, in Scandinavia, fewer than 5 percent of people attend church regularly. "Happy Family," *Economist*, January 23, 1999, 3–7.

36. Christopher Lasch, *The Culture of Narcissism* (New York: W. W. Norton, 1978), xvi.

CHAPTER 4

1. Gareth Porter and Janet Welsh Brown, *Global Environmental Politics* (Boulder, CO: Westview Press, 1996), 69–105; Beth Simmons, "International Law and State Behavior: Commitment and Compliance in International Monetary Affairs," *American Political Science Review* 94, no. 4 (2000): 819–835.

2. Charles Taylor argues that there is a voluntary global consensus on human rights, though different cultures may disagree on the justifications for these universal norms. See Charles Taylor, "Conditions of an Unforced Consensus on Human Rights" in *The East Asian Challenge for Human Rights*, ed. Joanne R. Bauer and Daniel A. Bell (New York: Cambridge University Press, 1999).

3. Barbara Harff, "No Lessons Learned from the Holocaust? Assessing Risks of Genocide and Political Mass Murder Since 1955" *American Political Science Review* 97, no. 1 (2003): 57–73.

4. Several groups have begun to push for a "public diplomacy" solution to the perceived growth in anti-Americanism around the world. For instance, Christopher Ross writes, "I am delighted with the burgeoning recognition that how the U.S. government communicates abroad—and with whom—directly affects the nation's security and well-being." See Christopher Ross, "Public Diplomacy Comes of Age," *Washington Quarterly* 25, no. 2 (Spring 2002): 75; Antony J. Blinken, "Winning the War of Ideas," *Washington Quarterly* 25, no. 2 (Spring 2002): 101–114; and *Finding America's Voice: A Strategy for Reinvigorating U.S. Public Diplomacy*, The Council on Foreign Relations Independent Task Force Report (New York: The Council on Foreign Relations, 2003).

5. Robert Satloff, "How to Win Friends and Influence Arabs," *Weekly Standard*, August 18, 2003, 18.

6. Steven R. Weisman, "U.S. Must Counteract Image in Muslim World, Panel Says," *New York Times*, October 1, 2003, A1, A8.

7. Jane Perlez, "U.S. Asks Muslims Why It Is Unloved. Indonesians Reply," *New York Times*, September 27, 2003, A3. Italics added.

CHAPTER 5

1. For the most famous volume on neo-realist theory, see Kenneth Waltz *Theory of International Politics* (Reading, Mass.: Addison-Wesley, 1979). Stephen G. Brooks also outlines competing realist theories in "Dueling Realisms" *International Organization* 51, no. 3 (Summer 1997): 445–477.

2. Leslie H. Gelb and Justine A. Rosenthal, "The Rise of Ethics in Foreign Policy," *Foreign Affairs* 82, no. 3 (2003): 2–7. Audie Klotz argues that the international community's condemnation of apartheid indicates the existence of shared moral norms; see Audie Klotz, *Norms in International Relations: The Struggle Against Apartheid* (Ithaca, N.Y.: Cornell University Press, 1995).

3. See, for instance, George W. Bush, "Remarks: U.S. Humanitarian Aid to Afghanistan," Washington, D.C., October 11, 2002. Available at: http://www.whitehouse.gov/news/releases/2002/10/20021011-3.html. Accessed 2/11/03; and David E. Sanger and James Dao, "U.S. Is Completing Plan to Promote a Democratic Iraq," *New York Times*, January 6, 2003, A1.

4. For a discussion of U.S. efforts to democratize eighteen countries, see Minxin Pei and Sara Kasper, "The 'Morning After' Regime Change: Should US Force

Democracy Again?," *Christian Science Monitor,* January 15, 2003, 9. See also Amitai Etzioni, "A Self-Restrained Approach to Nation Building by Foreign Powers," 2003, unpublished manuscript.

5. On these elements see Graham Allison, "Deepening Russian Democracy: Progress and Pitfalls in Putin's Government," *Harvard International Review* 24, no. 2 (2002): 63–64; Archie Brown, "Russia and Democratization," *Problems of Post-Communism* 46, no. 5 (1999): 5–6; Robert A. Dahl, *Polyarchy: Participation and Opposition* (New Haven, CT: Yale University Press, 1971), 3; and Adeed Dawisha and Karen Dawisha, "How To Build a Democratic Iraq," *Foreign Affairs* 82, no. 3 (2003): 47.

6. Freedom House, which conducts an annual assessment of freedom and civil liberties in all nations, reported that there were 121 "electoral democracies" as of 2003. See Adrian Karatnycky, Aili Piano, and Arch Puddington, eds., *Freedom in the World: The Annual Survey of Political Rights and Civil Liberties 2003* (New York: Rowman & Littlefield, 2003), 707.

7. For an examination of the U.S. propensity to export democracy see Gideon Rose, "Democracy Promotion and American Foreign Policy," *International Security* 25, no. 3 (2000/2001): 186–203.

8. See, for instance, Robert D. Kaplan, *The Coming Anarchy* (New York: Random House, 2000).

9. Fareed Zakaria, *The Future of Freedom: Illiberal Democracy at Home and Abroad* (New York: W. W. Norton, 2003).

10. Fareed Zakaria argues that "the haste to press countries into elections over the last decade has been, in many cases, counterproductive." Zakaria, *Future of Freedom,* 155.

11. Mathews quoted in Lawrence F. Kaplan, "Democrats Against Democracy," *Wall Street Journal,* March 19, 2003, A14.

12. See Amy Chua, *World on Fire: How Exporting Free Market Democracy Breeds Ethnic Hatred and Global Instability* (New York: Doubleday, 2003).

13. See, for example, Larry Diamond, Juan J. Linz, and Seymour Martin Lipset, eds., *Politics in Developing Countries: Comparing Experiences with Democracy,* 2nd ed. (Boulder, Colo.: Lynne Rienner, 1995); Guillermo O'Donnell and Philippe C. Schmitter, *Transitions from Authoritarian Rule: Tentative Conclusions About Uncertain Democracies* (Baltimore: Johns Hopkins University Press, 1986); Dietrich Ryueschemeyer, Evelyne Huber Stephens, and John D. Stephens, *Capitalist Development and Democracy* (Chicago: University of Chicago Press, 1992); Samuel P. Huntington, *Political Order in Changing Societies* (New Haven, Conn.: Yale University Press, 1968); and Adam Przeworski et al., "What Makes Democracies Endure?," *Journal of Democracy* 7, no. 1 (1996): 37–55.

14. Ithiel de Sola Pool, *Technologies of Freedom* (Cambridge, Mass.: Belknap Press, 1983).

15. For a different viewpoint, see Mark Palmer, *Breaking the Real Axis of Evil* (Lanham, Md.: Rowman & Littlefield, 2003).

16. As a former French colony, the Ivory Coast allows French troops to be stationed within its borders. Until the 2002 coup, the Ivory Coast was a relatively stable former colony. However, after the coup, France increased its troop presence and, although it intended to remain neutral in the conflict, it did defend the government against an attempted overthrow.

17. For particularly solid reporting on the subject, see Glenn Kessler and Robin Wright, "Realities Overtake Arab Democracy Drive," *Washington Post,* December 3, 2003, A22–23.

18. *The Journal of Democracy,* published quarterly by the National Endowment for Democracy's International Forum for Democratic Studies and The Johns Hopkins University Press, is dedicated to these issues.

19. Pei and Kasper, "'Morning After' Regime Change," 9. Nancy Bermeo argues that the failure of democracies happens as a result of manipulation by political elites and not the stereotypical angry, polarized masses. See Nancy Bermeo, *Ordinary People in Extraordinary Times: The Citizenry and the Breakdown of Democracy* (Princeton: Princeton University Press, 2003).

20. For theorists who have identified many different prerequisites for democracy, see, among others, Allison, "Deepening Russian Democracy," 62–67; Brown, "Russia and Democratization," 3–13; Robert Dahl, *Democracy and Its Critics* (New Haven, Conn.: Yale University Press, 1989); Dahl, *Polyarchy*; Dawisha and Dawisha, "Build a Democratic Iraq," 36–50; Larry Diamond, Juan J. Linz, and Seymour Martin Lipset, eds., *Politics in Developing Countries: Comparing Experiences with Democracy*, 2nd ed. (Boulder, Colo.: Lynne Rienner, 1995); Juan J. Linz and Alfred Stepan, *Problems of Democratic Transition and Consolidation: Southern Europe, South America, and Post-Communist Europe* (Baltimore: Johns Hopkins University Press, 1996); Guillermo O'Donnell and Philippe C. Schmitter, *Transitions from Authoritarian Rule: Tentative Conclusions about Uncertain Democracies* (Baltimore: Johns Hopkins University Press, 1986); and Adam Przeworski et al., "What Makes Democracies Endure?," *Journal of Democracy* 7, no. 1 (1996): 37–55.

21. Max Boot, "What Next? The Bush Foreign Policy Agenda Beyond Iraq," *Weekly Standard*, May 5, 2003, 29.

22. See, for instance, Stephen E. Ambrose, "The Master (Nation) Builder," *National Review*, March 11, 2002, 30–32; Bob Geldof, "A Continent in Crisis: We Must Act Now to Prevent Apocalypse," *Observer* (London), June 15, 2003, 20; and Gordon Brown, "Marshall Plan for the Next 50 Years," *Washington Post*, December 17, 2001, A23.

23. See Niall Ferguson, "Empire on a Shoestring," *Washington Post*, July 20, 2003, B1, and Ferguson, "The Empire Slinks Back," *New York Times Magazine*, April 27, 2003, 52–57.

24. Paul M. Kennedy, *The Rise and Fall of Great Powers* (New York: Random House, 1987). Others argue that Kennedy's predictions of fiscal overstretch may come true today not because of an over-commitment of military troops overseas but rather because of changing domestic demographics, for example an aging population and chronic budget deficits. See Niall Ferguson and Laurence J. Kotlikoff, "Going Critical: American Power and the Consequences of Fiscal Overstretch," *National Interest* no. 73 (Fall 2003): 22–32.

25. Chalmers A. Johnson, *Blowback: The Costs and Consequences of American Empire* (New York: Metropolitan Books, 2000).

26. Charles Krauthammer points out that "economically the U.S. is not overstretched. But psychologically, we are coming up against our limits," in Charles Krauthammer, "Help Wanted: Why America Needs To Lean Hard on its Allies to Lend a Hand in Iraq," *Time*, September 1, 2003, 72.

27. Jane Perlez, "Saudis Quietly Promote Strict Islam in Indonesia," *New York Times*, July 5, 2003, A3.

28. Richard N. Haass, "Sanctioning Madness," *Foreign Affairs* 76 (1997): 75–79. See also Puneet Talwar, "Iran in the Balance," *Foreign Affairs* 80 (2001): 58–71; Richard N. Haass and Meghan L. O'Sullivan, eds., *Honey and Vinegar: Incentives, Sanctions, and Foreign Policy* (Washington, D.C.: Brookings, 2000); and Suzanne Maloney, "America and Iran: From Containment to Coexistence," *Policy Brief No. 87* (Washington, D.C.: Brookings, August 2001).

29. For case studies supporting the effectiveness of engagement in countries as diverse as China, Iraq, North Korea, South Africa, the Soviet Union, and Vietnam, see the articles in Haass and O'Sullivan, *Honey and Vinegar*. Other pro-engagement pieces include Talwar, "Iran in the Balance," 58–71; Haass, "Sanctioning Madness," 74–85; and Joseph S. Nye Jr., "The Case for Deep Engagement," *Foreign Affairs* 74, no. 4 (1995): 90–102. The classic case for isolation is made by former Senator Jesse Helms in "What Sanctions Epidemic?," *Foreign Affairs* 78, no. 1 (1999): 1–7.

30. The Chinese government has continued to open in response to economic pressures. For instance, though in the past China has kept most government information secret, in order to join the WTO it was forced to make public all of its rules relating to internal trade and investment. Since then, China has started to create a freedom of information act that will enable citizens to obtain a whole host of previously secret information. See "The Right To Know," *Economist* October 25, 2003, 40.

31. "U.S. Gains Libyan Nuclear Gear And Flies It to Knoxville, Tenn.," *New York Times*, January 28, 2004, A4.

32. Helms, "What Sanctions Epidemic?," 5.

33. Katherine Marshall, "Development and Religion: A Different Lens on Development Debates," *Peabody Journal of Education* 76 (2001): 339.

34. Anshuman A. Mondal, "Liberal Islam?," *Prospect*, January 2003, 31.

35. For an argument about the importance of religion in public life, see Ashis Nandy, "An Anti-Secularist Manifesto," in *The Romance of the State: And the Fate of Dissent in the Tropics* (New York: Oxford University Press, 2002), 34–60.

36. Mary Ann Glendon, *Rights Talk: The Impoverishment of Political Discourse* (New York: Free Press, 1991).

37. Joseph R. Biden Jr., "Statement on Afghan Relief and Reconstruction," October 3, 2001. Available at: http://foreign.senate.gov/Democratic/press/statements/statements_011003.html. Accessed 5/5/03.

38. Deborah Loh, "Malaysian Education System Can Be Good Model for Afghanistan," *New Straits Times* (Malaysia), January 9, 2002, 7.

39. In September 2003, President Bush drafted regulations to expand his faith-based initiative effort by allowing more charitable, religious groups to compete for federal grants. Already during Bush's administration the Department of Health and Human Services has granted $30.5 million to over eighty faith-based organizations in forty-five states. For more, see Deb Riechmann, "U.S. Allowing Funds to Religious Groups" *Associated Press*, September 22, 2003.

40. Michael Tanner, "Corrupting Charity," *USA Today Magazine*, September 2001, 16.

41. Catholic Charities, "Frequently Asked Questions: General." Available at: http://www.catholiccharitiesinfo.org/faqs/general.htm. Accessed 5/6/03.

42. Joseph R. Hagal, "Faith-Based Community Development: Past, Present, Future," *America*, April 23, 2001, 15.

43. See Sophie van Bijsterveld, *The Empty Throne: Democracy and the Rule of Law in Transition* (Utrecht, Netherlands: Lemma, 2002).

44. The two best-known definitions of multilateralism come from Robert O. Keohane and John G. Ruggie. Keohane defines multilateralism as "the practice of coordinating national policies in groups of three or more states," in Robert O. Keohane, "Multilateralism: An Agenda for Research," *International Journal* 45 (1990): 731. Ruggie distinguishes between this nominal definition and his own qualitative definition of multilateralism: "an institutional form that coordinates

relations among three or more states on the basis of generalized principles of conduct: that is, principles which specify appropriate conduct for a class of actions, without regard to the particularistic interests of the parties or the strategic exigencies that may exist in any specific occurrence." John Gerard Ruggie, "Multilateralism: The Anatomy of an Institution," in *Multilateralism Matters: The Theory and Praxis of an Institutional Form*, ed. John Gerard Ruggie (New York: Cambridge University Press, 1993), 11. In a later work, Ruggie identifies multilateralism as an "international order in which the United States seeks to institute and live by certain mildly communitarian organizing principles." John Gerard Ruggie, *Winning the Peace: America and World Order in the New Era* (New York: Columbia University Press, 1996), 4.

45. Joseph S. Nye Jr., *The Paradox of American Power: Why the World's Only Superpower Can't Go It Alone* (New York: Oxford University Press, 2002), 158.

46. The classic work on this subject is E. Allen Lind and Tom R. Tyler, *The Social Psychology of Procedural Justice* (New York: Plenum Press, 1988).

47. Stephen Zunes, "United Nations Security Council Resolutions Currently Being Violated by Countries Other than Iraq," *Foreign Policy in Focus*, February 28, 2003. Available at http://www.globalpolicy.org/security/issues/israel-palestine/2003/0228vio.htm. Accessed 11/21/03.

48. Ibid.

49. For instance, the Hutus broadcast their intentions on the radio long before the genocide began. See Philip Gourevitch, *We Wish To Inform You that Tomorrow We Will Be Killed with our Families: Stories from Rwanda* (New York: St. Martin's Press, 1999) and Fergal Keane, *Season of Blood: A Rwandan Journey* (New York: Viking, 1995).

50. See, among others, William Alonso, "Citizenship, Nationality, and Other Identities," *Journal of International Affairs* 48 (1995): 585–599; Rainer Baubock, *Transnational Citizenship: Membership and Rights in International Migration* (Brookfield, Vt.: Edward Elgar, 1995); Richard Munch, *Nation and Citizenship in the Global Age: From National to Transnational Ties and Identities* (New York: Palgrave, 2001); Daniel M. Weinstock, "Prospects for Transnational Citizenship and Democracy," *Ethics & International Affairs* 15, no. 2 (2001): 53–66. See also the website of the World Service Authority, which issues passports and other documents for "world citizens": http://www.worldgovernment.org.

51. Max Boot, "America's Destiny Is to Police the World," *Financial Times* (London), February 17, 2003, 21; Boot, "American Imperialism? No Need to Run Away from Label," *USA Today*, May 5, 2003, 15A; and Boot, *The Savage Wars of Peace: Small Wars and the Rise of American Power* (New York: Basic Books, 2002). See also Niall Ferguson, *Empire: The Rise and Demise of the British World Order and the Lessons for Global Power* (New York: Basic Books, 2003).

52. Joshua Muravchik, *The Imperative of American Leadership: A Challenge to Neo-Isolationism* (Washington, D.C.: American Enterprise Institute Press, 1996.)

53. Wright argues that although history seems to predict that America will follow this course, inherent in its evolving global mission will be the moral challenge to accept humanity's interdependence, where "our welfare is crucially correlated with the welfare of the other, and our freedom depends on the sympathetic comprehension of the other." Robert Wright, "Two Years Later, a Thousand Years Ago," *New York Times*, September 11, 2003. On the idea of America's accidental empire, see, for instance, "Show Me the Way to Go Home," *Economist*, August

15, 2003, 10; and Sebastian Mallaby, "The Reluctant Imperialist: Terrorism, Failed States, and the case for American Empire," *Foreign Affairs* 81, no. 2 (2002): 2–7.

54. For coverage of Bush's remarks, see Peter Ford, "Europe cringes at Bush 'crusade' against terrorists" *Christian Science Monitor* September 19, 2001, 12. For coverage on Lieutenant General William G. Boykin's remarks, see Douglas Jehl, "The Struggle for Iraq: Pentagon; U.S. General Apologizes for Remarks About Islam" *New York Times* October 18, 2003, A6.

CHAPTER 6

1. G. John Ikenberry, "America's Imperial Ambition," *Foreign Affairs* 81, no. 5 (2002): 44–60.

 2. Michele Kelemen, summarizing Robert Kagan, *All Things Considered,* National Public Radio, June 5, 2003, Lexis/Nexis.

 3. Martin Walker, "America's Virtual Empire," *World Policy Journal* 19, no. 2 (2002): 13–20.

 4. Michael Ignatieff, "The Burden," *New York Times Magazine,* January 5, 2003, 24.

 5. For an earlier discussion of this matter see Amitai Etzioni, *The Active Society: A Theory of Societal and Political Processes* (New York: Free Press, 1968).

 6. For a discussion of the implications, see Steven E. Miller, "The End of Unilateralism or Unilateralism Redux?," *Washington Quarterly* 25, no. 1 (2002): 15–29.

 7. Quoted in Michael Hirsh, "Bush and the World," *Foreign Affairs,* September/October 2002, 26.

 8. See, for instance, Michael Hardt and Antonio Negri, *Empire* (Cambridge, Mass.: Harvard University Press, 2000); Andrew J. Bacevich, *American Empire: The Realities and Consequences of U.S. Diplomacy* (Cambridge, Mass.: Harvard University Press, 2002); and Robert N. Bellah, "The New American Empire," *Commonweal,* October 25, 2002, 12–14.

 9. For further discussion on the emergence of the Bush doctrine, see Hirsh, "Bush and the World," 18–43.

10. For more on the evolution of Bush's foreign policy, see James M. Lindsay and Ivo H. Daalder, *America Unbound: The Bush Revolution in Foreign Policy* (Washington, D.C.: Brookings, 2003).

11. Oran R. Young, *Governance in World Affairs* (Ithaca, N.Y.: Cornell University Press, 1999).

12. Although there was a great deal of American public discourse on the war, Leon Gordenker argues that the quality of the debate was remarkably thin and that both supporters of and opponents to the war relied more on "ideological assertions about strategic goals and national interest, tactical preoccupations, military images, and rumors from diplomatic corridors." Leon Gordenker, "What UN Principles? U.S. Debate on Iraq," *Global Governance* 9 (2003): 283–289.

13. Judy Dempsey, Krishna Guha, and George Parker, "Chirac Plans to Resist the Control of Postwar Iraq by US Allies," *Financial Times* (London), March 22, 2003, 6.

14. Schroeder is quoted in James Rubin, "Stumbling into War," *Foreign Affairs* 82, no. 5 (2003): 49.

15. "Pan-European Body Condemns War in Iraq," *Agence France Presse,* April 3, 2003, Lexis/Nexis.

16. *Suddeutsche Zeitung* cited in "European Press Slams Bush's 'Heathen' New World Order," *Agence France Presse*, March 21, 2003, Lexis/Nexis.

17. The article accusing Bush echoed a prediction that other nations would come to view nuclear weapons as the only means of defense against a similar U.S.-led attack against their own regimes. *Der Spiegel*, cited in "US Has Sparked Arms Race by Launching Iraq War," *Agence France Presse*, March 20, 2003, Lexis/Nexis.

18. The Pew Research Center for the People & the Press, *America's Image Further Erodes, Europeans Want Weaker Ties*, March 18, 2003. Available at: http://people-press.org/reports/pdf/175.pdf. Page 1. Accessed 7/16/03.

19. "Media Watch: EU Opinion Polls," *Irish Times*, April 5, 2003, 12.

20. Ibid.

21. Quoted in Christopher Marquis, "After the War: Opinion; World's View of U.S. Sours After Iraq War, Poll Finds," *New York Times*, June 4, 2003, A19.

22. Emmanuel Todd argues that the global distaste for American unilateralism will ultimately lead to the downfall of its international hegemony. See Emmanuel Todd, *After the Empire: The Breakdown of the American Order*, trans. C. Jon Delogu (New York: Columbia University Press, 2004).

23. "The World Out There," *Economist*, June 7, 2003, 26–27.

24. Ibid.

25. Angelique Chrisafis et al, "Millions Worldwide Rally for Peace," *Guardian* (London), February 17, 2003, 6.

26. Karl Ritter, "In the Nordics, Thousands Protest U.S. Attacks on Iraq," Associated Press Worldstream, March 20, 2003, Lexis/Nexis.

27. Quoted in Thomas L. Friedman, "Have I Got Mail," *New York Times*, June 8, 2003, sec. 4, p. 13.

28. For a discussion of the American public's views on empire, see Carl F. Bowman, "Survey Report: The Evidence for Empire," *The Hedgehog Review* 5, no. 1 (2003): 69–81.

29. Gary Younge, "Threat of War: Americans Want UN Backing before War," *Guardian* (London), February 26, 2003, 5.

30. Richard Morin, "Public Backs U.N. Assent on Iraq; Poll Finds Americans Willing to Delay War to Gain Support," *Washington Post*, February 25, 2003, A17.

31. Amy Kaslow and George D. Moffett III, "Most Donors Honoring Pledges," *Christian Science Monitor*, June 11, 1991, 6.

32. The cost of keeping troops in Iraq was estimated by the Pentagon to be $3.9 billion a month. Eric Schmitt, "Senators Assail 2 Officials For Lack of Postwar Details," *New York Times*, July 30, 2003, A9.

33. Marianne Brun-Rovet and Peter Spiegel, "Pentagon Goes Cap-in-Hand to Congress as War Costs Mount," *Financial Times* (London), August 1, 2003, 9.

34. Cited in Niall Ferguson, "Empire on a Shoestring," *Washington Post*, July 20, 2003, B1.

35. Elisabeth Bumiller, "The Struggle for Iraq: The President; Bush Seeks $87 Billion and U.N. Aid for War Effort," *New York Times*, September 7, 2003, A1.

36. Douglas Jehl, "High Cost of Occupation: U.S. Weighs a U.N. Role," *New York Times*, August 29, 2003, A10.

37. President George W. Bush, quoted in "A Kindler, Gentler Bush Appeals to UN for Iraq Aid," *USA Today*, September 24, 2003, A20; and George Bush, *Address to the United Nations General Assembly*, New York, September 23, 2003.

38. For more on the state of American credibility abroad, see Zbigniew Brzezinski, "Another American Casualty: Credibility," *Washington Post*, November 9, 2003, B1.
39. *Charter of the United Nations*, Article 2, Section 4.
40. Simon Schama, "The Unloved American," *New Yorker*, March 10, 2003, Lexis/Nexis.
41. "Pre-emption, Iraq, and Just War: A Statement of Principles." Available at: http://www.americanvalues.org/html/1b___pre-emption.html. Accessed 7/24/03.
42. "What We're Fighting For: A Letter from America," *The Responsive Community* 12, no. 4 (2002): 30–42.
43. For insight into just war theory and its application, see, among others, Jean Bethke Elshtain, *Just War Against Terror* (New York: Basic Books, 2003); J. Bryan Hehir, "The Just War Ethic Revisited," in *Ideas & Ideals: Essays on Politics in Honor of Stanley Hoffman*, ed. Linda B. Miller and Michael Joseph Smith (Boulder, CO: Westview Press, 1993), 144–161; and J. Bryan Hehir, "Just War Theory in a Post–Cold War World," *Journal of Religious Ethics* 20 (1992): 237–257.
44. "President Bush's Address to the Nation," *New York Times*, September 8, 2003, A22.
45. Warren Vieth, "U.S., Key Allies Discuss Debt Relief," *Los Angeles Times*, April 13, 2003, sec. 1, p. 10.
46. CIA World Factbook, cited in Helle Dale, "No Blood for French Oil," *Washington Times*, March 5, 2003, A19.
47. As defined by Gabriel Almond, the attentive public is comprised of people who are "informed and interesting in foreign policy problems, and [who constitute] the audience for foreign policy discussions among the elites." Gabriel A. Almond, *The American People and Foreign Policy* (New York: Frederick A. Praeger, 1960 [1950]), 138.
48. Ivo H. Daalder calls this "democratic imperialism." Quoted in Dan Morgan, "A Debate Over U.S. 'Empire' Builds in Unexpected Circles," *Washington Post*, August 10, 2003, A3. For more analysis of American "democratic imperialism," including its British historical counterpart, see Stanley Kurtz, "Democratic Imperialism: A Blueprint," *Policy Review*, no. 118 (2003): 3–20; and Simon Schama, *A History of Britain 1776–2000* (New York: Miramax Books/Hyperion, 2003).
49. Brooks and Wohlforth argue that though the United States is far and away the most powerful nation in the world, it can still "afford to reap the greater gains that will eventually come from magnanimity. . . . Unilateralism may produce results in the short term, but it is apt to reduce the pool of voluntary help from other countries that the United States can draw on down the road, and thus in the end to make life more difficult rather than less." Stephen G. Brooks and William C. Wohlforth, "American Primacy in Perspective," *Foreign Affairs* 81, no. 4 (2002): 31.
50. James Risen and Tim Weiner, "CIA Is Said to Have Sought Help from Syria," *New York Times*, October 30, 2001, B3.
51. Bryan Bender, "U.S. Welcomes Support from Its Former Foes," *Boston Globe*, November 11, 2001, A32.
52. Bob Drogin and Josh Meyer, "Yemen Aiding Terror Inquiry," *Los Angeles Times*, October 17, 2001, A1.
53. Caroline Lambert, "A Survey of Central Asia: At the Crossroads," *Economist*, July 26, 2003, 3.
54. Bob Woodward "50 Countries Detain 360 Suspects at CIA's Behest," *Washington Post*, November 22, 2001, A1; Alan Sipress, "55 Nations Endorse Measures to Fight Terrorism," *Washington Post*, December 5, 2001, A14.

55. Patrick E. Tyler "Rebels in Control in Kabul as Taliban Troops Retreat," *New York Times*, November 14, 2001, A1; Harry Sterling, "Turkey Takes Risk in Joining Allies," *Gazette* (Montreal), November 17, 2001, B7.

56. Alison O'Connor, "Leaders Expected to Agree on European Arrest Warrant," *Irish Times*, December 14, 2001, 8; "Member States Agree Thirty Crimes for EU Arrest Warrant," *European Report*, November 17, 2001, Lexis/Nexis.

57. Bertrand Benoit and Margaret Heckel, "Berlin Deal on Security Measures," *Financial Times* (London), October 29, 2001, 7; Steven Erlanger, "German Cabinet Supports New Immigration Laws," *New York Times*, November 8, 2001, A12.

58. Paul Waugh, "Terror Suspects to Be Rounded Up under New Law," *Independent* (London), December 15, 2001, 14.

59. "Japan Need Not Be in a Hurry to Show Its Will to Send SDF," *Asahi News Service*, October 31, 2001, Lexis/Nexis.

60. Peter Ford "European Nations Broaden Police Powers," *Christian Science Monitor*, November 15, 2001, 8.

61. Somini Sengupta, "Indian Leader Feels Pressure from All Sides over Violence," *New York Times*, March 19, 2002, A5.

62. Although no comprehensive list of deployments is maintained, 170 countries is the generally accepted number. For a partial list, see Robert D. Kaplan, "Supremacy by Stealth: Ten Rules for Managing the World," *The Atlantic Monthly* 292, no. 1 (2003): 66–83; and "U.S. Military Bases and Empire," *Monthly Review* 35, no. 10 (2002): 1–14.

63. Max Boot, "America's Destiny is to Police the World," *Financial Times* (London), February 17, 2003, 21.

64. "U.S. Military Bases," 6.

65. Eric Schmitt, "Pentagon Seeking New Access Pacts for Africa Bases," *New York Times*, July 5, 2003, A6.

66. "U.S. Military Bases," 6.

67. See the report on the Echelon system by the European Parliament that states: "That a global system for intercepting communications exists, operating by means of cooperation proportionate to their capabilities among the USA, the UK, Canada, Australia and New Zealand under the UKUSA Agreement, is no longer in doubt. It may be assumed, in view of the evidence and the consistent pattern of statements from a very wide range of individuals and organizations, including American sources, that the system or parts of it were, at least for some time, code-named ECHELON. What is important is that its purpose is to intercept private and commercial communications, and not military communications." Temporary Committee on the ECHELON Interception System, *Report on the Existence of a Global System for the Interception of Private and Commercial Communications*, A5–0264/2001 PAR1, July 11, 2001, 133. Available at: http:// www.europarl.eu.int/tempcom/echelon/pdf/rapport_echelon_en.pdf. Accessed 8/6/03. See also the news report on the article, Kim Sengupta and Stephen Castle, "Secrecy, Spy Satellites and a Conspiracy of Silence: The Disturbing Truth about ECHELON," *Independent* (London), May 30, 2001, 3.

68. Even before the advent of the antiterrorism coalition, governments collaborated on these matters. Ken Guggenheim, "Mexican Appointee Raises Concerns Among U.S. Conservatives," Associated Press, November 23, 2000, Lexis/Nexis.

69. "What's News: World-wide," *Wall Street Journal*, June 25, 2003, A1.

70. Peter Calamai, "Detained Canadian Released from Jail in Syria," *Toronto Star*, October 6, 2003, A10.

71. "Australian Spies Key to Capture," *Sunday Mail* (Queensland), August 17, 2003, 4.

72. Ellen Nakashima and Alan Sipress, "Tips, Traced Call Led to Fugitive; Al Qaeda Suspect Was Tracked Through Four Countries," *Washington Post*, August 17, 2003, A16.

73. David Filipov, "Arms Sting Ameliorates US-Russia Relations," *Boston Globe*, August 14, 2003, A1.

74. Rana Jawad, "Top al-Qaeda operative Khalid Shaikh Mohammed arrested in Pakistan," *Agence France Presse*, March 2, 2003.

75. David Johnston, "Citing Low Threat Level, Officials Plan No Special Terror Alert for Holiday Weekend," *New York Times*, July 3, 2003, A11.

76. The term "authority" is used in this way by many social scientists; see, for example, Leslie Green, *Routledge Encyclopedia of Philosophy*, vol. 1, s.v. "authority."

77. For instance, the UN Security Council passed a resolution the day after the September 11 terrorist attack strongly condemning terrorism and it later established the UN Counter-Terrorism sub-committee to address the issue. Kofi Annan wrote that no one should "question the worldwide resolve to fight terrorism as long as is needed." Kofi Annan, "Fighting Terrorism on a Global Front," *New York Times*, September 21, 2001, A35.

78. Paul Blustein, "Aid to Turkey Raising Issue of Motive," *Washington Post*, November 23, 2001, E1; Christopher Cooper, "Allies in War on Terror Get a Helping of U.S. Largess," *Wall Street Journal*, December 12, 2001, A8.

79. Shefali Rekhi, "Web of Terror," *Straits Times* (Singapore), November 11, 2001, 40; Brendan Pereira, "KL Signals It's No More a Safe Haven," *Straits Times* (Singapore), November 27, 2001, A2.

80. "Outpouring of Grief and Sympathy Sweeps across Globe," *St. Petersburg Times*, September 14, 2001, 21A.

81. "A World in Mourning," *Ottawa Citizen*, September 14, 2001, C6.

82. Audrey Woods, "The World Also Takes Time Out to Remember," *Seattle Times*, September 15, 2001, A6.

83. Alastair MacDonald, "Europe Joins Americans in Grief, Anger," *Reuters*, September 14, 2001, Factiva.

84. Colin Nickerson, "Nations Join Us in Prayer," *Boston Globe*, September 15, 2001, A10.

85. Charles M. Sennott, "Nations Mark Sept. 11 with Mixed Feelings," *Boston Globe*, September 12, 2002, A24.

86. Michael R. Gordon, "A Month in a Difficult Battlefield: Assessing U.S. War Strategy," *New York Times*, November 8, 2001, A1.

87. Deborah Cole, "Greens Back Deployment in War on Terror, Save German Government," *Agence France Presse*, November 25, 2001, Lexis/Nexis.

88. Audrey Gillan, Jon Henley, Suzanne Goldberg, and Rebecca Allison, "World Leaders Rally Around Allies: West Gives Full Support for Strikes," *Guardian* (London), October 8, 2001, 6.

89. Sennott, "Nations Mark," A24.

90. Selcan Hacaoglu, "Turkey—NATO's Only Muslim Member—to Send 90-Member Special Force to Afghanistan," *Associated Press*, November 1, 2001, Lexis/Nexis.

91. Pew Research Center, *Global Attitudes (2003)*, Question 16, page T-141.

92. Stephen Castle and Andrew Grice, "EU Leaders Give Their Backing to Strikes," *Independent* (London), September 22, 2001, 2.

93. Ron Hutcheson and Michael Dorgan, "Bush Gets Pacific Rim Nations to Back War Against Terrorism," *Milwaukee Journal-Sentinel*, October 21, 2001, 4A; Indira A.R. Lakshmanan, "Pakistan Back US, Despite Warning by Afghanistan," *Boston Globe*, September 16, 2001, A5; and "Hong Kong Expresses Support for Strikes Against Terror," *Deutsche Presse-Agentur*, October 8, 2001, Lexis/Nexis.

94. Jonathan Steele, "Right to Self-Defence Basis of Attacks: Raids Justified by UN Resolutions, US Says," *Guardian* (London), October 9, 2001, 12.

95. Our letter, which drew directly on St. Augustine and other just war doctrines, was fairly well received. See "What We're Fighting For," 30–42. Although it drew an angry response from a few on the American left ("A Critical Response: 'A Letter from United States Citizens to Friends in Europe,'" *The Responsive Community* 12, no. 4 (2002): 43–48) and some on the German left ("A World of Peace and Justice Would Be Different." Available at: http://www.americanvalues.org/html/german_statement.html. Accessed 7/16/03. Originally published in *Frankfurter Allgemeine Zeitung* as "Eine Welt der Gerechtigkeit und des Friedens sieht anders aus," May 2, 2002), the response of more than 100 Saudi Arabian intellectuals was much more moderate ("How We Can Coexist," *The Responsive Community* 13, no. 1 (2002/2003): 66–81).

96. See Elshtain, *Just War Against Terror*, and Hehir, "Just War Ethic Revisited," 144–161.

97. For a comprehensive account of the changing dynamics of modern warfare, see Bruce Berkowitz, *The New Face of War: How War Will Be Fought in the 21st Century* (New York: The Free Press, 2003.)

98. On international norms, see Hedley Bull, *Anarchical Society: A Study of Order in World Politics* (New York: Columbia University Press, 1977); and Robert Jackson, "International Community Beyond the Cold War," in Gene M. Lyons and Michael Mastanduno, *Beyond Westphalia: State Sovereignty and International Intervention* (Baltimore, Md.: Johns Hopkins University Press, 1995). For a sociological perspective, see John W. Meyer, "The World Polity and the Authority of the Nation-State," in George M. Thomas, John W. Meyer, Francisco O. Ramirez, and John Boli, *Institutional Structure: Constituting the State, Society and the Individual* (Newbury Park, Calif.: Sage, 1987), 41. See also Bruce Cronin, "The Two Faces of the United Nations: The Tension Between Intergovernmentalism and Transnationalism," *Global Governance* 8 (2002): 52–71.

99. Amitai Etzioni, *My Brother's Keeper: A Memoir and a Message* (Lanham, Md.: Rowman & Littlefield, 2003).

100. The term "attentive public" was first used by Almond, *The American People and Foreign Policy*, 138. For other texts on the attentive public, see Jon D. Miller, "Reaching the Attentive and Interested Publics for Science," in *Scientists and Journalists: Reporting Science as News*, ed. Sharon M. Friedman, Sharon Dunwoody, and Carol L. Rogers (New York: Free Press, 1986), 55–69; and Donald J. Devine, *The Attentive Public: Polyarchical Democracy* (Chicago: Rand McNally, 1970).

101. Shalom H. Schwarz and Anat Bardi, "Moral Dialogues across Cultures: An Empirical Perspective," in *Autonomy and Order: A Communitarian Anthology*, ed. Edward W. Lehmann (Lanham, Md.: Rowman & Littlefield, 2000), 155–179.

102. The Pew Research Center for the People and the Press, *2002 Global Attitudes Survey*, December 4, 2002. Available at: http://people-press.org/reports/pdf/165topline.pdf. Question 15d, T-21. Accessed 7/16/03.

103. Ibid., Question 64, T-51.

104. Michael Walzer, *Thick and Thin: Moral Argument at Home and Abroad* (Notre Dame, Ind.: University of Notre Dame Press, 1994); and Frances V. Harbour, "Basic Moral Values: A Shared Core," *Ethics and International Affairs* 9 (1995): 155–170.

105. John Tagliabue, "Group of 8 Finds Unity on the Threat of Terrorism," *New York Times*, May 6, 2003, A20.

106. Nicolas Sarkozy, quoted in ibid.

107. "8 Killed in Saudi Sweep Against Militants," *New York Times*, July 29, 2003, A14.

108. "U.S. and Saudis Join in Anti-war Efforts," *New York Times*, August 26, 2003, A10.

109. Josh Meyer, "Saudi Police Kill 2 Al Qaeda Leaders, 2 Others in Clash," *Los Angeles Times*, July 4, 2003, sec. 1, p. 6.

110. "Iranians Confirm Al Qaeda Arrests," *Washington Post*, July 24, 2003, A16.

111. "Iran Sends Al Qaeda Members to Saudi Arabia; Few Details on those Extradited," *San Diego Union-Tribune*, August 24, 2003, A20.

112. "What's News—World-wide," *Wall Street Journal*, September 12, 2003, A1.

113. Michael Brzezinski, "Who's Afraid of Norway?," *New York Times Magazine*, August 24, 2003, 26.

CHAPTER 7

1. After Vietnam the United States became increasingly afraid of involving its military in the internal conflicts of other countries, or of "mission creep." This phrase gained particular currency after the debacle in Somalia; see, for example, John R. Bolton, "Wrong Turn in Somalia," *Foreign Affairs* 73, no. 1 (1994): 56–66 and Susan D. Miller, "Locating Accountability: The Media and Peacekeeping," *Journal of International Affairs* 55 (2002): 369–390.

2. Marrack Goulding evaluates the various instruments that can be used to cope with tyrannical governments, including diplomacy, economic sanctions, international courts, and military interventions. See Marrack Goulding, "Deliverance from Evil," *Global Governance* 9, no. 2 (April/June 2003): 147–152.

3. Application of encompassing sanctions of the kind employed to cow Saddam's Iraq and Castro's Cuba are also coercive. Hence, they should be treated similarly. I use the term "encompassing" because limited sanctions, say banning the importation of genetically modified foods, are used very wisely as part of trade negotiations among free countries and do not raise the same issues that encompassing ones do.

4. I use the term as it is very widely used both in political science literature and in common parlance. See, for instance, Dolf Sternberger, *International Encyclopedia of the Social Sciences*, vol. 9, s.v. "legitimacy." I am aware of the issues it raises, especially concerning whose values are involved and issues raised by relativism. I have dealt with those elsewhere; see chapter 8 of *The New Golden Rule: Community and Morality in a Democratic Society* (New York: Basic Books, 1996), and hope to return to them in the future.

5. Etzioni, *New Golden Rule*, 217–257.

6. See, for instance, G. John Ikenberry, *After Victory: Institutions, Strategic Restraint, and the Rebuilding of Order after Major Wars* (Princeton: Princeton University Press, 2001); and Joseph S. Nye, Jr., *The Paradox of American Power: Why the World's Only Superpower Can't Go It Alone* (New York: Oxford University Press, 2002).

7. Lawrence J. Korb points out that America's right to defend itself against "the recent intersection of radicalism with destructive technologies" should need not prevent it from cooperating with other nations to reduce global security threats. Lawrence J. Korb, *A New National Security Strategy in an Age of Terrorists, Tyrants, and Weapons of Mass Destruction*, A Council on Foreign Relations Policy Initiative (New York: Council on Foreign Relations, 2003), 35.

8. For analysis on the need for safety and order in addition to a moral foreign policy, see Stanley Hoffmann, "In Defense of Mother Teresa: Morality in Foreign Policy," *Foreign Affairs* 75, no. 2 (1996): 172–175.

9. Cf. Hedley Bull, *The Anarchical Society: A Study of Order in World Politics* (New York: Columbia University Press, 1977), 46.

10. See, for example, Daniel Kahneman and Amos Tversky, "Prospect Theory: An Analysis of Decision Under Risk," *Econmetrica* 47 (1979): 263–291.

11. For an excellent discussion of these points, see Ashton B. Carter, "Overhauling Counterproliferation," forthcoming in *Technology in Society*, 26, no. 2 and 3 (April/July 2004); Scott D. Sagan, "The Perils of Proliferation in South Asia," *Asian Survey*, November/December 2001, 1064–1086; and Tod Lindberg, "Deterrence and Prevention: Why a War against Saddam Is Crucial to the Future of Deterrence," *Weekly Standard*, February 2, 2003, Lexis-Nexis.

12. Henry Sokolski argues that Algeria's nuclear weapons program should be addressed by the U.S. government before those of North Korea and Iran. See Henry Sokolski, "The Qaddafi Precedent," *Weekly Standard*, January 26, 2004, 12–13.

13. On the other hand, Matake Kamiya argues that Japan is both unwilling and unable to ever become a nuclear power. See Matake Kamiya, "Nuclear Japan: Oxymoron or Coming Soon?" *Washington Quarterly* 26, no. 1 (2003): 63–75.

14. Praful Bidwai and Achin Vanaik argue that India's nuclear program was originally viewed as a trophy by the Bharatiya Janata Party (BJP) and was pursued without much consideration for its strategic implications. See Praful Bidwai and Achin Vanaik, *New Nukes: India, Pakistan, and Global Nuclear Disarmament* (New York: Olive Branch Press, 2000).

15. K. Shankar Bajpai outlines the case for American involvement in "Untangling India and Pakistan," *Foreign Affairs* 82, no. 3 (2003): 112–126.

16. Especially problems surrounding domestic inter-religious violence. Recent elections in the Indian state of Gujarat brought in a wave of Hindu nationalists who may exacerbate existing tensions in the wake of Muslim riots that caused the deaths of 59 Hindus. For more, see Amy Waldman, "A Secular India, or Not? At Strife Scene, Vote Is Test," *New York Times*, December 12, 2002, A16. See also John Lancaster, "Hindu Nationalists Win Indian State Election; Riot-Torn Gujarat Picks Hard-Liners," *Washington Post*, December 16, 2002, A16.

17. Carla Anne Robbins, "The U.N.: Searching for Relevance—Operation Bypass: Why U.S. Gave U.N. No Role in Plan To Halt Arms Ships—Sole Superpower's Approach To Fighting Proliferation Challenges the World Body—A Boarding on the High Seas," *Wall Street Journal*, October 21, 2003, A1.

18. Mark Valencia, "Pressing for Sea Change," *Washington Times*, August 25, 2003, A15.

19. Philip Shenon, "U.S. Reaches Deal to Limit Transfers of Portable Missiles," *New York Times*, October 21, 2003, A1.

20. Judy Dempsey, "EU Foreign Ministers Agree Policy on WMD Strategy Document," *Financial Times* (London), June 17, 2003, 9.

21. These activities are part of the Nunn-Lugar Cooperative Threat Reduction Program. For more information on this program, see, among others, Gilles Andréani, "The Disarray of US Non-Proliferation Policy," *Survival* 41, no. 4 (1999–2000): 42–61

22. For information on the catch-all control program in the United States and the European Union and on the U.S. Enhanced Proliferation Control Initiative, see Henry D. Sokolski, *Best of Intentions: America's Campaign Against Strategic Weapons Proliferation* (Westport, Conn.: Praeger, 2001), 108; and David A. Cooper, *Competing Western Strategies against the Proliferation of Weapons of Mass Destruction* (Westport, Conn.: Praeger, 2002), 64.

23. For more discussion, see Graham Allison, "How to Stop Nuclear Terror," *Foreign Affairs* 83, no. 1 (2004): 64–74; and Lee Feinstein and Anne-Marie Slaughter, "A Duty to Prevent," *Foreign Affairs* 83, no. 1 (2004): 136–150.

24. Henry Sokolski, "Nukes on the Loose," *Weekly Standard*, June 23, 2003, 21.

25. Robert Wright, "A Real War on Terrorism: The Threat of Terrorism Naturally Grows," *Slate*, September 4, 2002. Available at: http://slate.msn.com/id/2070210/entry/2070799. Accessed 7/24/03.

26. For more on the START treaties, see Amy F. Woolfe, "91139: Strategic Arms Reduction Treaties (START I & II): Verification and Compliance Issues," *Congressional Research Service Reports*, November 22, 1996. Available at: Accessed 8/26/03. For information on the Moscow Treaty, see Drake Bennett, "Critical Mess: How the Neocons are Promoting Nuclear Proliferation," *American Prospect*, July 1, 2003, 49. For more information on efforts to discourage the use and proliferation of WMD, the Nuclear Threat Initiative (NTI) is a valuable resource. Their website, which offers daily news as well as more in-depth reports, can be found at http://www.nti.org.

27. Victor Zaborsky, "What to Control and How to Control: Nonproliferation Dilemmas," *World Affairs* 161, no. 2 (1998): 96. For a complete list of nations that have either given up on their nuclear programs or chosen to abandon it, see Ariel E. Levite, "Never Say Never Again," *International Security* 27, no. 3 (2002/2003): 62.

28. Bennett, "Critical Mess," 50.

29. Zaborsky, "What to Control," 97.

30. Carlos Feu Alvim, "2000 NPT Review Conference: Statements," April 27, 2000. Available at: Accessed 8/26/03.

31. *The Nunn-Lugar Vision 1992–2002* (Washington, D.C.: Nuclear Threat Initiatives, n.d.), various pages.

32. Ibid.

33. Ibid., 2.

34. Ibid., 3.

35. Ibid.

36. In August 2002 the "Project Vinca" operation removed 48 kilograms of highly enriched uranium (HEU) from a plant in Yugoslavia and moved it to safer stor-

age in Russia. For an examination of the benefits of purchasing highly enriched uranium (HEU) from vulnerable nations, as well as other valuable procedures, see Matthew Bunn, Anthony Wier, and John Holdren, *Controlling Nuclear Warheads and Materials: A Report Card and Action Plan* (Washington, D.C.: Nuclear Threat Initiative and the Project on Managing the Atom, Harvard University, March 2003), 115–118.

37. Susan B. Glasser, "Russia Takes Back Uranium from Romania; U.S. Paid for Move to Avert Threat," *Washington Post*, September 22, 2003, A16.

38. The IAEA needs hard power not only to ensure proper inspections but also to uphold the provisions of the Nuclear Non-Proliferation Treaty (NPT); for example, to keep nations like Iran from obtaining the materials used to make nuclear weapons. See "Iran's Nuclear Ambitions: Tightening the Rein," *Economist*, September 13, 2003, 12.

39. "United Nations Peacekeeping Operations: Background Note," June 18, 2003. Available at: http://www.un.org/peace/bnote010101.pdf. Accessed 8/27/03.

40. David Rohde, "Dutch UN Peacekeepers Questioned as US, NATO Prep for Bosnia Mission," *Christian Science Monitor*, October 25, 1995, 7.

41. For a discussion of what I mean by these deontological terms, see Etzioni, *New Golden Rule*, 217–257.

42. See, for instance, Samantha Power, *A Problem from Hell: America and the Age of Genocide* (New York: Basic Books, 2002). See also Nicholas J. Wheeler, *Saving Strangers: Humanitarian Intervention in International Society* (Oxford: Oxford University Press, 2003); and Gareth Evans and Mohamed Sahnoun, "The Responsibility to Protect" *Foreign Affairs* 81, no. 6 (November/December 2002): 99–110.

43. For further discussion of these issues, see Mohammed Ayoob, "Humanitarian Intervention and International Society," *Global Governance* 7, no. 3 (July-September 2001): 225–230; Fiona Terry, *Condemned to Repeat? The Paradox of Humanitarian Intervention* (Ithaca: Cornell University Press, 2002); Larry Minear, *The Humanitarian Enterprise: Dilemmas and Discoveries* (Bloomfield: Kumarian Press, 2002); and David Rieff, *A Bed for the Night: Humanitarianism in Crisis* (New York: Simon & Schuster, 2002).

44. Although David Frumkin argues that humanitarian interventions in Kosovo and elsewhere were relatively easy compared to the enormous difficulties involved in maintaining peace in areas plagued by conflict. See David Frumkin, *Kosovo Crossing: American Ideals Meet Reality on the Balkan Battlefields* (New York: The Free Press, 1999.)

45. See the essays in "A Decade of Humanitarian Intervention," *Orbis* 45 (2001): 495–578; Rieff, *A Bed for the Night*; and Nicholas J. Wheeler, *Saving Strangers: Humanitarian Intervention in International Society* (New York: Oxford University Press, 2000).

46. Kenneth L. Cain, "Send in the Marines," *New York Times*, August 8, 2003, A21; and Colum Lynchm, "Rights Activists Worried By African Peacekeepers," *Washington Post*, August 5, 2003, A10; Rachel Bronson advocates this standby solution in "When Soldiers Become Cops," *Foreign Affairs* 81, no. 6 (November/December 2002): 122–132.

47. Nicholas J. Wheeler and Tim Dunne, "East Timor and the New Humanitarian Interventionism," *International Affairs* 77 (2001): 805–827.

48. Douglas Farah, "Sierra Leone Gets Pledge of British Aid; Official Says Ships Will Stay after Most Troops Leave," *Washington Post*, June 9, 2000, A28.

49. Lawrence Freedman and Efraim Karsh, *The Gulf Conflict: 1990–1991* (Princeton, NJ: Princeton University Press, 1993), xxix.

50. Michael Ignatieff, "The Burden," *New York Times Magazine*, January 5, 2003, 22–27+.

51. Stockholm International Peace Research Institute, "Recent Trends in Military Expenditure." Available at: http://projects.sipri.org/milex/mex_trends.html. Accessed 9/8/03.

52. Immanuel Kant was perhaps the first to write of the possibilities for peace among like-minded states in *Perpetual Peace* (New York: Columbia University Press, 1939 [1796]); see also Bruce Russett and John Oneal, *Triangulating Peace: Democracy, Interdependence, and International Organizations* (New York: Norton, 2001). On the democratic peace theory, see, among others, Michael J. Doyle, "Liberalism and World Politics," *American Political Science Review* 80 (1986): 1151–1169; David Lake, "Powerful Pacifists: Democratic States and War," *American Political Science Review* 86 (1992): 24–38; and John Owen, "How Liberalism Produces Democratic Peace," *International Security* 19, no. 2 (1992):87–125. For criticisms of the democratic peace theory, see, among others, Henry Farber and Joanne Gowa, "Polities and Peace," *International Security* 20, no. 2 (1995):123–147; Errol A. Henderson, *Democracy and War: The End of an Illusion?* (Boulder, Colo.: Lynne Rienner Publishers, 2002); Christopher Layne, "Kant or Cant: The Myth of the Democratic Peace," *International Security* 19, no. 2 (1994): 5–94; and David Spiro, "The Insignificance of the Democratic Peace," *International Security* 19, no. 2 (1994): 50–86.

53. Kenneth A. Schultz adds nuance to the world peace argument by using game theory to prove that the existence of democratic institutions makes it less probable that a state will initiate conflict. Kenneth A. Schultz, *Democracy and Coercive Diplomacy* (Cambridge: Cambridge University Press, 2001).

54. Tony Smith, quoted in Gary T. Dempsey, "Fool's Errands: America's Recent Encounters with Nation Building," *Mediterranean Quarterly* 12, no. 1 (2001): 61.

CHAPTER 8

1. For an overview of contemporary challenges to the Westphalia system, see Chris Brown, *Sovereignty, Rights and Justice* (Cambridge: Polity Press, 2002.) For a realist perspective, see Stephen D. Krasner, *Sovereignty: Organized Hypocrisy* (Princeton: Princeton University Press, 1999); and his critics, Christian Reus-Smit, *The Moral Purpose of the State: Culture, Social Identity, and Institutional Rationality in International Relations* (Princeton: Princeton University Press, 1999), and finally, Daniel Philpott, *Revolutions in Sovereignty: How Ideas Shaped Modern International Relations* (Princeton: Princeton University Press, 2001).

2. Lee Feinstein and Anne-Marie Slaughter, "A Duty to Prevent," *Foreign Affairs* 83, no. 1 (2004): 136–150.

CHAPTER 9

1. Alexander Wendt presents a teleological argument for the inevitability of world government, wherein anarchy and international instability will cause states to move towards increasingly universal political and military organization. See Alexander Wendt, "Why a World State is Inevitable: Teleology and the Logic of Anarchy," *European Journal of International Relations* 9, no. 4 (2003): 491–542.

2. See David R. Johnson and David Post, "Law and Borders—The Rise of Law in Cyberspace," *Stanford Law Review* 48 (1996): 1367–1402; Lawrence Lessig, *Code, and Other Laws of Cyberspace* (New York: Basic Books, 1999); on the limits of recent cooperative efforts to control Internet pornography, see Warren Hoge, "19 Countries Join in Raids on Internet Pornography," *New York Times*, November 29, 2001, A11.

3. Robert E. Hudec, *Enforcing International Trade Law: The Evolution of the Modern GATT Legal System* (Austin, Tex.: Butterworth Legal Publishers, 1991); Alec Stone Sweet, "The New GATT: Dispute Resolution and Judicialization of the Trade Regime," in *Law above Nations: Supranational Courts and the Legalization of Politics*, ed. Mary L. Volcansek (Gainesville: University of Florida Press, 1997), 118–141; Robert E. Hudec, "The New WTO Dispute Settlement Procedure: An Overview of the First Three Years," *Minnesota Journal of Global Trade* 8 (1999): 1–53.

4. A study of the special factors involved in trade would take us far afield. Briefly, trade seems to be supported by supranational corporations that have no investment in the treatment of many other problems, and it promises to pay off for all parties in relatively short order.

5. James H. Mittelman and Robert Johnston, "The Globalization of Organized Crime, the Courtesan State, and the Corruption of Civil Society," *Global Governance* 5 (1999): 113.

6. United States National Security Council, *International Crime Threat Assessment* (Washington, D.C.: National Security Council, 2000). Available at: http://clinton4.nara.gov/WH/EOP/NSC/html/NSC_Documents.html. Accessed 8/15/03.

7. "BCCI Committed Fraud Worldwide, Panel Finds," *St. Louis Post-Dispatch*, October 2, 1992, 13A; and Mark Galeotti, "Underworld and Upperworld: Transnational Organized Crime," in *Non-State Actors in World Politics*, ed. Daphné Josselin and William Wallace (Hampshire, U.K.: Palgrave, 2001), 204.

8. Mittelman and Johnston, "Globalization of Organized Crime," 113.

9. David Bickford, of Inter Access Risk Management, quoted in Vincent Boland, "Earnings from Organized Crime Reach $1,000bn," *Financial Times* (London), February 14, 1997, 16.

10. Louise I. Shelley, "Transnational Organized Crime: An Imminent Threat to the Nation-State?" *Journal of International Affairs* 48 (1995): 488–489, emphasis added.

11. National Intelligence Council, "Global Trends 2015: A Dialogue about the Future with Nongovernment Experts," December 2000, 41. Available at: http://www.cia.gov/cia/reports/globaltrends2015/index.html. Accessed 3/21/03.

12. Christopher Sulavik, "Facing Down Traffickers," *Time*, August 25, 2003, 31.

13. Quoted in Christopher Marquis, "A Crackdown on the Traffic in Humans," *New York Times*, February 26, 2003, A3; and quoted in Carolyn Lochhead, "Sex Trade Uses Bay Area to Bring in Women, Kids," *San Francisco Chronicle*, February 26, 2003, A3.

14. Elizabeth Fernandez and Stephanie Salter, "Ugly Americans: Sex Tourists," *San Francisco Chronicle*, February 17, 2003, A1.

15. Attorney General John Ashcroft, quoted in Lochhead, "Sex Trade," A3.

16. Vanda Carson, "Sex Tour Laws Failing to Stop Trade," *The Weekend Australian*, March 1, 2003, 8.

17. Audrey Gillan, "Special Investigation: The Teenagers Traded for Slave Labor and Sex," *Guardian* (London), July 30, 2003, 1.

18. Gary Gardner, "Accelerating the Shift to Sustainability," in *State of the World 2001*, ed. Linda Starke (New York: W. W. Norton, 2001), 190.

19. Maude Barlow and Tony Clarke, "Who Owns Water?," *Nation*, September 2–9, 2002, 12.

20. Food and Agriculture Organization, *State of the World's Forests 2001* (Rome: FAO, 2001), 46.

21. "Fisheries Depletion," *The Ecologist* 32 (2002): 8.

22. World Health Organization, "HIV/AIDS in Sub-Saharan Africa," PowerPoint Presentation, July 2002. Available at: http://www.who.int/hiv/facts/ppt1/en. Accessed 3/20/03.

23. UNAIDS and World Health Organization, *AIDS Epidemic Update*, December 2002. Statistics Worldwide: 4. Statistics Russia: 12. Statistics elsewhere: 7. Available at: http://www.who.int/hiv/facts/en/epiupdate_en.pdf. Accessed 6/20/03.

24. Andy Ho, "Why Epidemics Still Surprise Us," *New York Times*, April 1, 2003, A23.

25. Jack Woodall quoted in "World Health Organization's Efforts to Develop a Worldwide Alert System to Catch Diseases Earlier," interview by Brenda Wilson, *Morning Edition*, National Public Radio, May 13, 2003, Lexis/Nexis.

26. Cited in "Imitating Property Is Theft," *Economist*, May 17, 2003, 53.

27. Ellen McCarthy, "A New Focus on Movie Piracy," *Washington Post*, October 14, 2002, E5; Josh Fineman, "Fast Action Could Benefit Record Labels," *Gazette* (Montreal), February 13, 2001, C2; "Pirates of the Information Age," *Weekly Standard*, March 18, 2003, 1.

28. Jamie Smyth, "40% of Business Software Programs Illegal Copies, Survey Shows," *Irish Times*, June 4, 2003, 16.

29. "Pirate King Khan Gets Jail Sentence," *Computer Reseller News*, July 14, 2003, 4.

30. "Imitating Property," 54.

31. Data extrapolated from CERT Coordination Center and mi2g graphs and tables in Bob Tedeschi, "E-Commerce Report: Crime Is Soaring in Cyberspace, but Many Companies Keep It Quiet," *New York Times*, January 27, 2003, C4.

32. Cited in John Schwartz, "Securing the Lines of a Wired Nation," *New York Times*, October 4, 2001, G1.

33. Symantec Internet Security Threat Report, cited in Ariana Eunjung Cha, "Despite U.S. Efforts, Web Crimes Thrive," *Washington Post*, May 20, 2003, A14 (table).

34. Computer crimes encompass more than just hacking. For example, officials in Germany uncovered an international child pornography ring that involved over 26,000 suspects who are accused of posting illegal images on the Internet in 166 countries. See Richard Bernstein, "Germany Says it Uncovered Huge Child Pornography Ring," *New York Times*, September 22, 2003, A3.

35. James Adams argues that as governments and militaries rely more on computers, they become more vulnerable than ever to virtual attack. In the future, cyberspace may become the "new front line of warfare." See James Adams, "Virtual Defense," *Foreign Affairs* 80, no. 3 (2001): 98–112.

36. Vincent Kong, "'GateSecure' Against Viruses," *New Straits Times* (Malaysia), June 20, 2002, 45.

37. Ariana Eunjung Cha, "Internet Dream Turn to Crime: Russian Start-Up Firm Targeted U.S. Companies," *Washington Post*, May 18, 2003, A18.

38. "Why The Internet May Make Outlaws Of Us All," *The Age* (Melbourne), July 29, 2000, 11.

39. Quoted in Jennifer S. Lee, "130 Arrested Since Jan. 1 in Internet Frauds That Snared 89,000 Victims, Ashcroft Says," *Washington Post*, May 17, 2003, A11.

40. For a collection of international treaties, see *Focus 2003: Treaties Against Transnational Organized Crime and Terrorism*. Available at: http://untreaty.un.org/English/TreatyEvent2003/index.htm. Accessed 8/29/03.

CHAPTER 10

1. For a general discussion of INGOs, see Daphné Josselin and William Wallace, "Non-state Actors in World Politics: A Framework" and "Non-state Actors in World Politics: The Lessons," in *Non-State Actors in World Politics*, ed. Josselin and Wallace (New York: Palgrave, 2001), 1–20 and 251–260.

2. See, for instance, James N. Rosenau and Ernst-Otto Czempiel, eds., *Governance without Government: Order and Change in World Politics* (Cambridge: Cambridge University Press, 1992); Oran R. Young, *Governance in World Affairs* (Ithaca, N.Y.: Cornell University Press, 1999); Thomas G. Weiss and Leon Gordenker, eds., *NGOs, the UN, and Global Governance* (Boulder, Colo.: Lynne Rienner Publishers, 1996).

3. John Keane, *Global Civil Society?* (Cambridge: Cambridge University Press, 2003). See also Helmut Anheier, Marlies Glasius, and Mary Kaldor, eds., *Global Civil Society 2001* (Oxford: Oxford University Press, 2001).

4. Sometimes governance is defined as defined as including only government, see, for instance, Wolfgang H. Reinicke, *Global Public Policy: Governing without Government?* (Washington, D.C.: Brookings, 1998), 4.

5. See Fred Halliday, "The Romance of Non-State Actors," in *Non-State Actors*, 21–37; see also Jessica Mathews, "Power Shift," *Foreign Affairs* 76, no. 1 (1997): 50–66; Peter Spiro, "New Global Communities: Nongovernmental Organizations in International Decision-Making Institutions," *Washington Quarterly* 18, no. 1 (1995): 45–56; and James N. Rosenau, "Governance in the Twenty-first Century," *Global Governance* 1 (1995): 13–43.

6. Lester M. Salamon, "Rise of the Nonprofit Sector," *Foreign Affairs* 73, no. 4 (1994): 109–110.

7. Cf. David Held, *Democracy and the Global Order* (Stanford, Calif.: Stanford University Press, 1995).

8. Wolfgang Reinicke and Francis Deng, *Critical Choices: The United Nations, Networks, and the Future of Global Governance* (Ottawa: International Development Research Centre, 2000), 27.

9. For a definition of soft laws, see Michael L. McKinney and Robert M. Schoch, *Environmental Science Systems and Solutions*, 3rd ed. (Boston: Jones & Bartlett, 2003).

10. Ethan A. Nadelmann, "Global Prohibition Regimes: The Evolution of Norms in International Society," *International Organization* 44, no. 4 (1990): 515–517.

11. For more on the international application of norms and laws, see the body of work by Harold Hongju Koh, in particular, "How is International Human Rights Law Enforced?," *Indiana Law Journal* 74 (1999): 1397–1417; and "Why Do Nations Obey International Law?" *Yale Law Journal* 106 (1997): 2598–2659.

12. For an examination of the emerging role of INGOs in the formulation of UN treaties, as well as their limitations, see Anne Marie Clark, Elisabeth J. Friedman, and Kathryn Hochstetler, "The Sovereign Limits of Global Civil Society: A Comparison of NGO Participation in UN World Conferences on the Environment, Human Rights, and Women," *World Politics* 51, no. 1 (1998): 1–35. For

more on the successes of transnational social movements regarding human rights, see Susan Burgerman, *Moral Victories: How Activists Provoke Multilateral Action* (Ithaca, N.Y.: Cornell University Press, 2001). The classic text on transnational social movements in general is Margaret Keck and Kathryn Sikkink, *Activists Beyond Borders: Advocacy Networks in International Relations* (Ithaca, N.Y.: Cornell University Press, 1998). For examples of successful INGO protests and boycotts, see "Non-Governmental Organisations and Business: Living with the Enemy," *Economist*, August 9, 2003, 49.

13. Thomas Risse, Stephen C. Ropp, and Kathryn Sikkink, eds., *The Power of Human Rights: International Norms and Domestic Change* (Cambridge: Cambridge University Press, 1999).

14. Sanjeev Khagram, James V. Rikker, and Kathryn Sikkink, eds. *Restructuring World Politics: Transnational Social Movements, Network, and Norms* (Minneapolis: University of Minnesota Press, 2002).

15. Elizabeth A. Donnelly, "Proclaiming Jubilee: The Debt and Structural Adjustment Network," in *Restructuring World Politics*, 164; and "Debt Relief Coalition Says Work Still Ahead," *Christian Century*, February 18, 2001, 11.

16. Sanjeev Khagram, "Restructuring the Global Politics of Development: The Case of India's Narmada Valley Dams," in *Restructuring World Politics*, 206–230.

17. Maggie Black, "Narmada River Rising," *New Internationalist* 350 (2002): 8. In response to the massive demonstrations against large dam projects in the Narmada Valley, the World Commission on Dams was created. For a discussion of this commission, see Jennifer M. Brinkerhoff, "Global Public Policy, Partnership, and the Case of the World Commission on Dams," *Public Administration Review* 62 (2002): 324–336.

18. Benjamin R. Barber, "Globalizing Democracy," *American Prospect*, September 11, 2000, 16.

19. On the growth and power of these bodies see David Bollier, *The Rise of Netpolitik: How the Internet Is Changing International Politics and Diplomacy* (Washington, D.C.: Aspen Institute, 2002).

20. For a look at the issues affecting NGOs in former communist coutries, see Sarah E. Mendelson and John K. Glenn, *The Power and Limits of NGOs: A Critical Look at Building Democracy in Eastern Europe and Eurasia* (New York: Columbia University Press, 2002).

21. On the role and growth of environmental NGOs, see especially Thomas Princen and Matthias Finger, *Environmental NGOs in World Politics: Linking the Local and the Global* (London: Routledge, 1994).

22. Nadelmann, "Global Prohibition Regimes," 525.

CHAPTER 11

1. For a highly relevant examination of the functions and procedures needed in international institutions, see Robert O. Keohane, "Governance in a Partially Globalized World," *American Political Science Review* 95, no. 1 (2001): 1–13.

2. In the United States the group is the World Federalist Association (formerly the United World Federalists), http://www.wfa.org. Worldwide, see the website of the World Federalist Movement, http://www.worldfederalist.org. For other writings on world government, see, among numerous others, Richard Falk, *Positive Prescription for the Near Future: A World Order Perspective, World Order Series*

Program Occasional Paper No. 20 (Princeton: Princeton University Center for International Studies, 1991); and James A. Yunker, *World Union on the Horizon: The Case for Supernational Federation* (Lanham, Md.: University Press of America, 1993).

3. One of the most comprehensive undertakings in ideas to reform the United Nations can be found in Commission on Global Governance, *Our Global Neighborhood* (New York: Oxford University Press, 1995).

4. See David Mitrany, *A Working Peace System* (London: Royal Institute of International Affairs, 1943).

5. Anne-Marie Slaughter, "The Real New World Order," *Foreign Affairs* 76, no. 5 (1997): 183–197; Robert O. Keohane and Joseph S. Nye, "Transgovernmental Relations and International Organizations," *World Politics* 27, no. 1 (1974): 39–62; Samuel P. Huntington, "Transnational Organizations in World Politics," *World Politics* 25 (1973): 333–368. See also Ariel Colonomos, "Non-State Actors as Moral Entrepreneurs: A Transnational Perspective on Ethics Networks," in *Non-State Actors in World Politics*, ed. Daphné Josselin and William Wallace (New York: Palgrave, 2001), 76–89.

6. Keohane and Nye, "Transgovernmental Relations," 39–62. See also Diane Stone "The 'Policy Research' Knowledge Elite and Global Policy Processes," in *Non-State Actors*, 113–132.

7. Anne-Marie Slaughter, "The Accountability of Government Networks," *Indiana Journal of Global Legal Studies* 8 (2001): 347 and "Governing the Global Economy through Government Networks," *The Role of Law in International Politics*, ed. Michael Byers (New York: Oxford University Press, 2000), 179–180.

8. See Slaughter, "The Real New World Order," 186–189; idem, "Governing the Global Economy," 181–191; and Sol Picciotto, "Networks in International Economic Integration: Fragmented States and the Dilemmas of Neo-Liberalism," *Northwestern Journal of International Law & Business* 17 (1996/1997): 1043.

9. Ann Florini, *The Coming Democracy: New Rules for Running a New World* (Washington, D.C.: Island Press, 2003).

10. For an especially fine discussion of the issues involved, see John Keane, *Global Civil Society?* (Cambridge: Cambridge University Press, 2003), 175–209.

11. See, for example, Wole Akande, "Agricultural Subsidies in Rich Countries: Barriers to Fair Trade for Africa," *Yellow Times*, April 6, 2002. Available at: http://www.yellowtimes.org/article.php?sid=197. Accessed 7/18/03; Edmund L. Andrews, "Rich Nations Are Criticized for Enforcing Trade Barriers," *New York Times*, September 30, 2002, A8; Harry Dunphy, "Cut Trade Barriers, World Bank Urges," *Deseret News* (Salt Lake City), April 14, 2003, A9; and Conn Hallinan, "The 'Buy American' Package," *Global Affairs Commentary*, November 27, 2002. Available at: http://fpif.org/pdf/gac/0211aid.pdf. Accessed 7/17/03.

12. For a comprehensive critique of the idea that poverty is the cause of terrorism, see Walter Laqueur, *No End to War: Terrorism in the Twenty-First Century* (New York: Continuum, 2003).

13. Global AIDS Alliance, "US Senators Durbin and Specter Spearhead Letter from More Than 13 US Senators Urging Emergency Spending to Stop Global AIDS," *Press Release*, March 5, 2002. Available at: http://www.globalaidsalliance.org/durbin_specter.html. Accessed 7/17/03. See further Paula J. Dobriansky, Remarks to an INR Conference on War Instability and Public Health in Sub-Saharan Africa, Washington, D.C., June 7, 2001. For a good overview

of HIV, see Stefan Elbe, *Strategic Implications of HIV/AIDS*, *Adelphi Paper 357* (New York: Oxford University Press/International Institute for Strategic Studies, 2003).

14. For an additional discussion, see Solomon R. Benatar, Abdallah S. Daar, and Peter A. Singer, "Global Health Ethics: The Rationale for Mutual Caring," *International Affairs* 79, no. 1 (2003): 107–138.

15. Alan Krueger and Jitka Maleckova, *Education, Poverty, Political Violence and Terrorism: Is There a Causal Connection? NBER Working Paper 9074*, July 2002. Available at: http://www.nber.org/papers/w9074. Accessed 8/13/03.

16. George Soros, "The Bubble of American Supremacy," *Atlantic Monthly*, December 2003, 63–66. Joseph E. Stiglitz, *Globalization and its Discontents* (New York: W. W. Norton, 2003).

17. T. H. Marshall, *Citizenship and Social Class* (Cambridge: Cambridge University Press, 1950).

18. See, for instance, *National Statistics*, "Income Inequality Gap Widens Slightly from Mid-1990s," April 11, 2003. Available at: http://www.statistics.gov.uk/CCI/nugget.asp?ID=332&Pos=&ColRank=1&Rank=374. Accessed 9/11/03.

19. Philip Selznick, "Social Justice: A Communitarian Perspective," *The Responsive Community* 6, no. 4 (1996): 13–25.

20. Rob Stein, "WHO Gets Wider Power to Fight Global Health Threats," *Washington Post*, May 28, 2003, A15.

21. See Richard Benedick, *Ozone Diplomacy: New Directions in Safeguarding the Planet*, enlarged ed. (Cambridge, Mass.: Harvard University Press, 1998).

22. Nicole Itano, "Bush Touts African AIDS Triumphs," *Christian Science Monitor*, July 8, 2003, 6. On Uganda, see specifically Janice A. Hogel, ed., *What Happened in Uganda?: Declining HIV Prevalence, Behavior Change, and the National Response* (Washington, D.C.: United States Agency for International Development/The Synergy Project, 2002).

23. Angus Maddison, *The World Economy: A Millennial Perspective* (Paris: Organization for Economic Cooperation and Development, 2001), Table C3-C.

24. For various criticisms of transnational government networks, see Philip Alston, "The Myopia of the Handmaidens: International Lawyers and Globalization," *European Journal of International Law* 8 (1997): 435–448; Picciotto, "Networks in International Economic Integration," 1014–1056; Stephen J. Toope, "Emerging Patterns of Governance and International Law," in *The Role of Law in International Politics*, ed. Michael Byers (New York: Oxford University Press, 2000), 91–108; and John Peterson, "Get Away from Me Closer, You're Near Me Too Far: Europe and America after the Uruguay Round," in *Transatlantic Governance in the Global Economy*, ed. Mark A. Pollack and Gregory C. Shaffer (Lanham, Md.: Rowman & Littlefield, 2001): 45–72.

25. Information on the importance of wars has been drawn from Paul Kennedy, *The Rise and Fall of Great Powers: Economic Change and Military Conflict from 1500 to 2000* (New York: Random House, 1987), and Michael Geyer and Charles Bright, "Global Violence and Nationalizing Wars in Eurasia and America: The Geopolitics of War in the Mid-Nineteenth Century," *Comparative Studies in Society & History* 38 (1996): 619–657.

26. *World Encyclopedia of Peace*, 2d ed., s.v. "world government."

27. See, for example, James N. Rosenau and Ernst-Otto Czempiel, eds., *Governance without Government: Order and Change in World Politics* (Cambridge: Cambridge

University Press, 1992); Keohane and Nye, "Transgovernmental Relations," 39–62; Jessica Mathews, "Power Shift," *Foreign Affairs* 76, no. 1 (1997): 50–66.

28. Kofi Annan, "Problems without Passports," *Foreign Policy*, no. 132 (2002): 30.

CHAPTER 12

1. For other developments in international laws and courts and in their relationships with national laws and courts, see Joseph H. H. Weiler, "The Democracy Deficit of Transnational Governance: What Role for Technology?" presented at the International Political Science Association congress in Quebec City, August 1–5, 2000. For a detailed discussion of the importance of enforcement capabilities of supranational bodies, their development in the European Union, and the implications for world courts, see Anne-Marie Slaughter and Laurence R. Helfer, "Toward a Theory of Effective Supranational Adjudication," *Yale Law Journal* 107 (1997): 273–328; and also Anne-Marie Slaughter, "Fortieth Anniversary Perspective: Judicial Globalization," *Virginia Journal of International Law* 40 (2000): 1103–1123; Slaughter, "The Real New World Order," *Foreign Affairs* 76, no. 5 (1997): 183–197; William J. Aceves, "Liberalism and International Legal Scholarship: The Pinochet Case and the Move Toward a Universal System of Transnational Law Litigation," *Harvard International Law Journal* 41, no. 1 (2000): 129–184; and Mary L. Volcansek, ed., *Law above Nations: Supranational Courts and the Legalization of Politics* (Gainesville: University of Florida Press, 1997).

2. Radmila May, "The Yugoslav War Crimes Tribunal: Part Two," *Contemporary Review*, October 1999, 174–179.

3. Sean D. Murphy, "Progress and Jurisprudence of the International Criminal Tribunal for the Former Yugoslavia," *American Journal of International Law* 93 (1999): 57–97.

4. Alec Stone Sweet, "The New GATT: Dispute Resolution and Judicialization of the Trade Regime," in *Law above Nations*, 118–141.

5. Mary L. Volcansek, "Supranational Courts in a Political Context," in *Law Above Nations*, 1–19.

6. Ibid., 3.

7. It is not clear to what extent ICANN is truly supranational. According to the former chairman of ICANN's board of directors, Esther Dyson, many board members were chosen by their national governments and instructed closely as to which positions to take (private communication with Dyson, January 1, 2001). For a historical overview of ICANN and its policy and political implications, see Milton Mueller, *Ruling the Root: Internet Governance and the Taming of Cyberspace* (Cambridge, Mass.: MIT Press, 2002) and Daniel J. Paré, *Internet Governance in Transition: Who Is the Master of This Domain?* (Lanham, Md.: Rowman & Littlefield, 2003).

8. Christopher R. Drahozal, "Commercial Norms, Commercial Codes, and International Commercial Arbitration," *Vanderbilt Journal of Transnational Law* 33 (2000): 79–146. On the International Chamber of Commerce, see also Karsten Ronit and Volker Schneider, "Global Governance through Private Organizations," *Governance: An International Journal of Policy and Administration* 12 (1999): 243–266.

9. John Peterson, "Get Away from Me Closer, You're Near Me Too Far: Europe and America after the Uruguay Round," in *Transatlantic Governance in the Global*

Economy, ed. Mark A. Pollack and Gregory C. Shaffer (Lanham, Md.: Rowman & Littlefield, 2001): 45–72; Sol Picciotto, "Networks in International Economic Integration: Fragmented States and the Dilemmas of Neo-Liberalism," *Northwestern Journal of International Law & Business* 17 (1996/1997): 1014–1056; and Stephen J. Toope, "Emerging Patterns of Governance and International Law," in *The Role of Law in International Politics*, ed. Michael Byers (New York: Oxford University Press, 2000), 91–108.

10. Amitai Etzioni, *Political Unification Revisited: On Building Supranational Communities* (Lanham, Md.: Lexington Books, 2001).

11. Amitai Etzioni, *Political Unification: A Comparative Study of Leaders and Forces* (New York: Holt, Rinehart, and Winston, 1965).

12. Alexander Wendt, "Collective Identity Formation and the International State," *American Political Science Review* 88, no. 2 (1994): 384.

13. Ernst B. Haas, *The Uniting of Europe: Political, Social, and Economics Forces, 1950–1957* (Stanford, Calif.: Stanford University Press, 1968).

14. Others whose supported this line of analysis include Leon N. Lindberg, *The Political Dynamics of European Economic Integration* (Stanford, Calif.: Stanford University Press, 1963) and Stephen George, *Politics and Policy in the European Community* (New York: Oxford University Press, 1985).

15. Andrew Moravcsik does not see any prospects for supranationality in the European Union, which he equates with federation and the end of national autonomy by the members (personal communication, July 3, 2003). A detailed theorizing of Moravcsik's ideas about the European Union can be found in Andrew Moravcsik, *The Choice for Europe: Social Purpose and State Power from Messina to Maastricht* (Ithaca, N.Y.: Cornell University Press, 1998). Early criticisms of Haas and other neofunctionalists can be found in Roger D. Hansen, "Regional Integration: Reflections on a Decade of Theoretical Efforts," *World Politics* 21, no. 2 (1969): 242–271 and Stanley Hoffman, "European Process at Atlantic Crosspurposes," *Journal of Common Market Studies* 3 (1965): 85–101. A more recent criticism is Çinar Özen, "Neo-Functionalism and the Change in the Dynamics of Turkey-EU Relations," *Perspectives: Journal of International Affairs* 3, no. 3 (1998). Available at: http://www.mfa.gov.tr/grupa/percept/lll-3/ozen.htm. Accessed 8/29/03.

16. Etzioni, *Political Unification* [1965].

17. For more analysis on the evolution of the European Union today, see Loukas Tsoukalis, *What Kind of Europe?* (Oxford: Oxford University Press, 2003).

18. Note, though, that neither Germany nor Italy was a nation in the full sense of the term and that in all cases force was used in bringing about the merger or sustaining it.

19. Thomas Jansen, *The European People's Party: Origins and Development*, trans. Barbara Steen (New York: St. Martin's Press, 1998), 19.

20. Christopher Lord, introduction to *Transnational Parties in the European Union*, ed. David S. Bell and Christopher Lord (Aldershot, U.K.: Ashgate, 1998), 5; Julie Smith, "How European Are European Elections?" in *Political Parties and the European Union*, ed. John Gaffney (London: Routledge, 1996), 275–290.

21. Ulrich Beck, "Understanding the Real Europe," *Dissent* 50, no. 3 (2003): 32–38; and Keith B. Richburg, "A Generation on the Move in Europe: For Continent's Young, Borders Are No Longer an Obstacle," *Washington Post*, July 22, 2003, A1.

22. "How Football Unites Europe," *Economist*, May 31, 2003, 55.

23. Charles Taylor, "No Community, No Democracy, Part I," *Responsive Community* 13, no. 4 (2003): 17–27.

24. Joshua A. Fishman, "The New Linguistic Order," *Foreign Policy* 113 (1998–1999): 26.

25. See Morton H. Halperin, *Bureaucratic Politics and Foreign Policy* (Washington, D.C.: Brookings, 1974).

26. Scott Morrison, "The Tobacco Moguls and Canada's Dollars 1 Billion Charge of Smuggling," *Financial Times* (London), January 6, 2000, 14.

27. "Responsible Regionalism," *Economist*, December 22, 2000, 19.

28. In October 2003, ASEAN members signed the Bali Concord II, which is intended to turn into a "European-style economic community in less than two decades." See "S.E. Asian Leaders Sign Landmark Accord," *Associated Press*, October 7, 2003, Lexis/Nexis.

29. International Bank for Reconstruction and Development, International Finance Corporation, International Development Association, "Executive Directors and Alternates," February 1, 2003. Available at: http://siteresources.worldbank.org/EXTABOUTUS/Resources/b-eds.pdf. Accessed 3/20/03.

CHAPTER 13

1. Benedict R. O. G. Anderson, *Imagined Communities: Reflections on the Origin and Spread of Nationalism* (London: Verso, 1983); For a cosmopolitan examination of the emerging global political community, see Andrew Linklater, *The Transformation of the Political Community* (Cambridge: Polity Press, 1998).

2. Richard N. Haass, *The Reluctant Sheriff: The United States After the Cold War* (New York: Council on Foreign Relations Press, 1997).

3. Fred Kaplan, "JFK's First Strike Plan," *Atlantic Monthly*, October 2001, 81.

4. Walter Pincus, "'67 Study Discouraged Use of Nuclear Weapons in Vietnam War," *Washington Post*, March 9, 2003, A26; and James A. Nathan, "The Heyday of the New Strategy," in *The Cuban Missile Crisis Revisited*, ed. Nathan (New York: St. Martin's Press, 1992), 9.

5. Benny Morris, *Righteous Victims* (New York: Alfred A. Knopf, 1999), 404.

6. See, among others, William Alonso, "Citizenship, Nationality, and Other Identities," *Journal of International Affairs* 48 (1995): 585–599; Rainer Baubock, *Transnational Citizenship: Membership and Rights in International Migration* (Brookfield, Vt.: Edward Elgar, 1995); Richard Munch, *Nation and Citizenship in the Global Age: From National to Transnational Ties and Identities* (New York: Palgrave, 2001); Daniel M. Weinstock, "Prospects for Transnational Citizenship and Democracy," *Ethics & International Affairs* 15, no. 2 (2001): 53–66. See also the website of the World Service Authority, which issues passports and other documents for "world citizens": http://www.worldgovernment.org.

7. Martha Finnemore, "Norms, Culture, and World Politics: Insights from Sociology's Institutionalism," *International Organization* 50 (1996): 325–348; Volker Rittberger, ed., *Regime Theory and International Relations* (Oxford: Clarendon Press, 1993); Peter J. Katzenstein, ed., *The Culture of National Security: Norms and Identity in World Politics* (New York: Columbia University Press, 1996).

8. Lawrence Lessig, *Code, and Other Laws of Cyberspace* (New York: Basic Books, 1999), 226.

9. Francis Fukuyama, "Has History Restarted Since September 11?" John Bonython Lecture, Melbourne, Australia, August 8, 2002). Available at: http://www.cis.org.au/Events/JBL/JBL02.htm. Accessed 9/16/02.

10. See Richard Falk and Andrew Strauss, "On the Creation of a Global Peoples Assembly: Legitimacy and the Power of Popular Sovereignty," *Stanford Journal of International Law* 36 (2000): 191–220, who envision civil society coming together to write the treaty or begin the meetings for the Global People's Assembly.

11. Eugene Webster, *A Modern History of Europe* (New York: W. W. Norton & Company, 1971), 4–5.

12. Shepard B. Clough, *A History of the Western World* (Boston: D.C. Heath and Company, 1964), 234.

13. Alexander Nicoll, "Gay Activists Welcome Forces' Code of Conduct," *Financial Times*, January 13, 2000, 2.

14. Mark Gibney, "The Evolving Architecture of International Law: On the Need for an International Civil Court," *Fletcher Forum of World Affairs Journal* 26 (2002): 47–56.

15. See the essays in Lawrence C. Dodd and Bruce I. Oppenheimer, eds. *Congress Reconsidered*, 5th ed. (Washington, D.C.: CQ Press, 1993), and Elizabeth Drew, *Politics and Money: The New Road to Corruption* (New York: Collier, 1983).

16. According to former Secretary General Javier Pérez de Cuéllar, it was the role of the Secretariat, and not the Security Council, to uphold the principles set forth in the UN Charter and therefore "speak for the wider international interest, an interest greater than the sum of the interests of member states." Quoted in Bruce Cronin, "The Two Faces of the United Nations: The Tension Between Intergovernmentalism and Transnationalism," *Global Governance* 8 (2002): 53–71.

17. Louis Fisher, "The Korean War: On What Legal Basis Did Truman Act?" *American Journal of International Law* 89 (1995): 33.

18. Stephen Zunes, "United Nations Security Council Resolutions Currently Being Violated by Countries Other than Iraq," *Foreign Policy in Focus*, October 2, 2002. Available at: http://www.fpif.org/pdf/gac/0210unres.pdf. Accessed 2/11/03.

19. Ibid.

20. Commission on Global Governance, *Our Global Neighborhood* (New York: Oxford University Press, 1995), 242.

21. Joseph P. Bialke, "United Nations Peace Operations: Applicable Norms and the Application of the Law in Armed Conflict," *Air Force Law Review* 50 (2001): 15.

22. Richard Butler, "Improving Nonproliferation Enforcement," *Washington Quarterly* 26, no. 4 (2003): 142.

23. David Usborne, "Diplomatic Defeat for Britain and US, But Squabbling Continues," *Independent* (London), March 18, 2003, 5.

24. See, among many others, Commission on Global Governance, *Our Global Neighborhood*, and The Independent Working Group on the Future of the United Nations, "The United Nations in its Second Half-Century." Available at: http://www.library.yale.edu/un/un1e.htm. Accessed 8/15/03.

25. See, for example, Thomas G. Weiss, "The Illusion of UN Security Council Reform," *Washington Quarterly* 26, no. 4 (2003): 147–161.

26. Erskine Childers and Brian Urquhart; Yale Report on the Future of the United Nations; UN Research Institute for Social Development; and the World Commission on Culture and Development quoted in Campaign for a More Democratic United Nations, "High-Level Support For Citizens' Representation in the

UN." Available at http://www.camdun-online.gn.apc.org/support.html. Accessed 7/7/03.

27. Charles Taylor, "Democratic Exclusion (and Its Remedies?)," in *Citizenship, Diversity, and Pluralism: Canadian and Comparative Perspectives*, ed. Alan C. Cairns et al. (Ithaca, N.Y.: McGill-Queen's University Press, 1999): 271. See also Sunil Khilnani, "Democracy and Modern Political Community: Limits and Possibilities," *Economy and Society* 20, no. 2 (1991): 196–204. For additional discussion, see James G. Marsh and Johan P. Olsen, *Democratic Governance* (New York: Free Press, 1995).

28. Amitai Etzoni, *The New Golden Rule: Community and Morality in a Democratic Society* (New York: Basic Books, 1996).

29. See the Commission on Global Governance, which argues that "The General Assembly was, from the outset, only a deliberative form; it had power to discuss and recommend, to debate and pass resolutions, but no real authority, certainly no power to take decisions binding on member states." Commission on Global Governance, *Our Global Neighborhood*, 242.

30. I am fully aware that consensus and moral legitimacy do not amount to the same thing. Reference here is to political consensus. For additional discussion see Etzioni, *New Golden Rule*, 217–257.

31. Commission on Global Governance, *Our Global Neighborhood*, 219–221.

In Conclusion

1. For my views on communitarian thinking, see Amitai Etzioni, *The New Golden Rule: Community and Morality in a Democratic Society* (New York: Basic Books, 1996). For the text of the communitarian platform, those who endorse it, and information about the Communitarian Network, see http://www.communitarian-network.org. Articles from a communitarian perspective can be found in *The Responsive Community*, the only journal of communitarian thought. For other major communitarian texts by sociologists see especially Philip Selznick, *The Communitarian Persuasion* (Washington, D.C.: Woodrow Wilson Center Press, 2002) and *The Moral Commonwealth: Social Theory and the Promise of Community* (Berkeley: University of California Press, 1992); Robert N. Bellah, Richard Madsen, William M. Sullivan, Ann Swidler, and Steven M. Tipton, *Habits of the Heart: Individualism and Commitment in American Life* (Berkeley: University of California Press, 1985); as well as previous works by Martin Buber, Emile Durkheim, Robert Nisbet, and Ferdinand Tönnies. Political theorists writing about communitarianism include Michael Sandel, Charles Taylor, and Michael Walzer. A particularly well-written and well-documented book is Alan Ehrenhalt's *The Lost City: Discovering the Forgotten Virtues of Community in the Chicago of the 1950s* (New York: Basic Books, 1995). Other good books include Daniel A. Bell, *Communitarianism and Its Critics* (Oxford: Clarendon Press, 1993); and Henry Tam, *Communitarianism: A New Agenda for Politics & Citizenship* (New York: New York University Press, 1998). Responsive (or new) communitarianism should not be confused with authoritarian communitarianism.

2. Robert Kagan, *Of Paradise and Power: America and Europe in the New World Order* (New York: Knopf, 2003).

INDEX

ACKNOWLEDGMENTS

I AM INDEBTED TO ANNE HARDENBERGH FOR STAYING with this book from beginning to end, guiding the research, and making numerous contributions of her own. I am also indebted to Emily Pryor for numerous editorial suggestions as well as to Jared Bloom. Deirdre Mead assisted with research and editing in the early phases of this project. Comments on previous drafts from John Ikenberry, Hans Joas, Lawrence Korb, Katherine Marshall, and Andrew Volmert are appreciated. I am especially indebted to James B. Steinberg for his detailed and very telling comments on a previous draft.